TERRY DURACK

NEW HOLLAND

Published in 1998 by
New Holland Publishers Pty Ltd
Sydney • London • Cape Town • Singapore

First published 1996 by William Heinemann Australia
a part of Reed Books Australia

Produced and published in Australia by
New Holland Publishers Pty Ltd
3/2 Aquatic Drive, Frenchs Forest
NSW 2086 Australia

24 Nutford Place
London W1H 6DQ
United Kingdom

80 McKenzie Street
Cape Town 8001
South Africa

Copyright text © Terry Durack 1996
Copyright photographs © Louise Lister 1996

All rights reserved. No part of this publication may be reproduced, stored in a retrieval system or transmitted, in any form or by any means, electronic, mechanical, photo-copying, recording or otherwise, without the prior written permission of the publishers and copyright holders.

ISBN 1 86436 351 7

National Library of Australia
  Cataloguing-in-Publication data:

Durack, Terry.
   Yum: a voyage around my stomach.

   1. Cookery – Anecdotes. 2. Gastronomy – Anecdotes.
641.013

Designed by Mary Callahan
Printed in Australia by 'Kyodo Printing Co in Singapore'

contents

My life as a flavour raider 1
Six recipes that changed my life 4
Moules à la marinière 5
Fegato alla Veneziana 6
Thai chicken and basil 7
Spaghetti alla carbonara 9
Cheese soufflé 10
The miraculous flourless chocolate cake 11

The meaning of soup 12
Vaguely Hungarian chicken soup 16
Blonde roots soup 17
Stracciatella 19
Vichyssoise 20
Celtic revival lamb and barley soup 21

Coming in from the cold 23
Vareneki 26
Ukrainian bortsch 28
Holubtsy 29

The death of the foodie 30
Omelette with fresh morels 35

It's my oesophagus and I'll cry if I want to 36
The ultimate mashed potato 41

Like a bull in China 43
Scallop and pork kidney 48
San choy bau 50
White cut chicken 51
Spring onion and ginger dip 51
Fried hor fun rice noodles with beef 53
Eight treasure duck 54
Lion's head meat balls 55

Yum! Something smells terrible 56
Aioli 61
Spaghetti aglio e olio con peperoncino 62
Italian potatoes with garlic and rosemary 62

Fashion plates 64

Eat my words 70
Sichuan hot and sour soup 75
Pho ga 78
Tom yam goong 79

The best things in life aren't free 81
Cassoulet 84

Pleasures of the flesh 87
La soupe au pistou 90
Gado gado 92
Chilli and peanut sauce 92
Rigatoni with broccoli and pine nuts 93

Crabs I have known 94
Crab and sweet corn soup 99
Singapore chilli crab with coconut rice 100
Sand crab pasta 101

Inner beauty 103
Andouillettes 106

Playing with fire 108
Cha gio with nuoc cham 113
Moroccan chicken with tomato, olives and preserved lemon 114
Harissa 114
Fish cutlet with Thai sweet chilli sauce 116
Penne all'arrabbiata 117
Char kueh teow 118
Curry puffs 119
Curry laksa 120

Cashing out 122
Bollito misto with salsa verde 127
Carciofi alla Giudea 128
Polenta con funghi 130
Swordfish with lemon and herb sauce 131

Survival of the fattest 133
Sticky toffee pudding 137

A load of tripe 138
Trippa alla Fiorentina 142
Tripe à la mode de Caen 143
Callos a la Madrilena 144

Cold comfort 147
Pea and ham soup 151
Old-fashioned oxtail stew 152
Sticky chocolate pudding 153

Marriages made in the kitchen 154
Insalata Caprese 158
Tagliatelle with tomato and basil 160
Napoletana pizza with tomato and basil 161

The big chill 163
Hot chocolate sauce for icecream 166
Lemon and sugar crêpes 167

The invisible man 168
Malaysian fish head curry 172

The missing link 175
Cotechino with lentils 178
Risotto with red wine and sausages 179

Japan to a tea 181
Dashi 186
Chawan mushi 187
Vinegared carrot and daikon salad 188
Agedashi dofu 189

Le grand buffet 191
The antipasto table 196
Roast capsicum salad 197
Mushrooms in oil and vinegar 197
Mussel salad 198
Suppli 199
Crostini di fegatini 199

Turn over a new leaf 200
Black pudding and glazed apple salad 205
Salade Niçoise 206
Greek salad 207

Blue jackets, grey pants and white truffles 209
Osso buco Milanese 213
Risotto alla Milanese 214
Mascapone with strawberries 215

The accidental gourmet 217
Wor tip 221
Caesar Salad 222
Tarte tatin 223

An ode to udon 224
Tsukumi udon 228

Mum's the word 230
Pock-marked grandmother's beancurd 234
Son-in-law eggs 235

It mixes! It stirs! It blends! 236
How to make pasta 240
Pumpkin ravioli with mustard fruits 242
Tagliolini with lemon and caviar 243
Pappardelle with chicken livers 244
Fettuccine with Gorgonzola 245

Clang, clang, clang went the trolley 247
Rice congee with white fish 251
Siu mai 252
Har gau prawn dumplings 253

Feet first 255
Grilled pig's trotters 259

Cafe society: the long and the short of it 260
Tirami su 265
Roast lamb with coffee 266
Gelato affogato 267

To die for 268
Michel Guerard 272
Georges Blanc 273
Claude Terrail 274
Andre Daguin 276
   Le pastis Gascon 'estirat' 277
Arrigo Cipriani 278
   Torta di cioccolato from Harry's Bar 280
Fred Ferretti 282
Bruno Loubet 283
Raymond Blanc 284
Margrit and Robert Mondavi 286
Michel Roux 287
Pierre Koffman 288
Marc Meneau 289
Pierre Wynants 290
   Les truffes comme je les aime 291
Roger Vergé 292

Thanks 295

Bibliography 296

Index 299

My life as a

flavour raider

It was the slippery, silky, mother's nightie feel of it that got me at first; a reassuring and arousing smoothness of impossibly luxurious proportions.

Then, as my innocent tongue squeezed it curiously against the roof of my mouth, the first of the taste sensations enveloped everything. It was a soft sweetness that oozed like the creamy filling of a rich chocolate truffle. Suddenly, out of nowhere came a salty tidal wave, washing away all other sensations as if they were so many grains of sand. Once it had crashed upon my consciousness, it too fell away leaving something in my mouth that tasted the way a barbecue smells, all sweet and spirity and smokey.

I was six years old, and I had just tasted my first smoked oyster. My life as a flavour raider had begun.

Just as some people are powered through life by a full-throttle sex drive, and others are catapulted through it by an unquenchable thirst for knowledge, I have tended to lead with my stomach.

Food, after all, is the last great adventure left in the world.

The highest mountains have already been climbed, and are now littered with diet soft-drink cans. The great rivers have all been charted, the lost tribes have all been found, and the great wild animals have all either been herded into parks and zoos, or simply driven off the face of the earth.

But new, delicious, wonderful flavours are everywhere, just waiting to titillate any one of the several thousand tastebuds that populate the upper surface of the human tongue.

Every one of these extremely small food-loving critters is made up of tiny sensory cells, which in turn contain around fifty nerve fibres that transmit electrical impulses via the nerves to the brain.

Children, of course, have many more tastebuds than adults. Our supply of taste buds tends to drop off dramatically around middle age.

I couldn't have known this way back then, yet somehow I was gripped by a feeling of urgency and a sense of panic. There were so many flavours, and so little time.

Shortly after my culinary epiphany came the singularly most shocking flavour I have ever encountered in my entire life. My first black olive. Nothing in my experience had prepared me for it. After all, it looked just like a dark, ripe cherry, all sweetness and innocence. Then kapow! Like a machete-wielding guerrilla, it slashed and burned its way through my mouth, raping and pillaging the trusting tastebuds with an almost obscene force. When the acrid, acidic after-burn wore off, a wondrous thing happened.

I wanted another one.

And so it went. My first soused mussel was a vinegary slippery dip; my first prawn was a head-spinning roller coaster of sweetness and salt; my first mango was a fluid, lush merry go round; and my first bite of crumbed brains an entire adventure playground of taste thrills.

Who needs virtual reality? I had tastebuds instead.

As the years passed, the flavours got more complex, and even more rewarding.

Life-changing revelations came with my first Haagen Daaz icecream (a creamy snowflake), my first fresh dank and earthy white Alba truffle (like breathing in cobwebs), my first porcini mushroom (freshly turned grave), and my first taste of Chateau d'Y Quem (honey with a kick).

Well into my twenties, I tasted fresh

Beluga caviar for the first time, and immediately came to the conclusion that all my flavour raiding up to that point had been but a dress rehearsal.

I once saw a map of the tongue which dramatically showed the areas that are most sensitive to various taste sensations. The tip of the tongue is most sensitive to sweetness, while just behind that is the salt-sensitive region. A heightened ability to register sourness stretches down both sides of the tongue, and the recognition of bitterness encompasses a broad band at the back of the tongue.

Caviar is the only thing I know that can trigger off every single one of those taste sensations, plus quite a few others that aren't even on the map.

This love of flavour has dictated many things in my life. Jobs, marriages, homes and holidays have all been taste-driven. It's the reason I'm a restaurant critic. It's the reason I love wine. I have a taste memory that kills my memory for faces, places and names. I may not remember who the hell you are twenty years after we dined together, but I will still be able to taste the 1971 Veuve Cliquot we had, and recall with pleasure how it played with the salmon sushi.

In my search, I have been tossed out of restaurants, reviled by the politically correct and abused by vegetarians and moon-followers. But today's intelligent flavour raider draws the line when it comes to eating rare species of animal, vegetable or mineral. It's not political correctness. It's a sense of decency.

Every now and then I punish my little tastebuds with something nasty, either by accident or by design. Bad flavours are just as important to the learning curve of a conscientious tastebud as good flavours. They warn us of poison, of 'offness' and of danger, picking up what our nose has omitted to tell us.

Then there are flavours I crave. Sometimes I want flavours to sting, like salt in a wound. I want to be woken up by flavour, I want to be hit in the head with it, I want it to make me feel alive. Sometimes I want it to flow over me, like a slow wave.

But even as I sit here, I can hear the gentle popping as my tastebuds disappear into thin air, minute by minute. No! You can't go yet! I haven't eaten that Mexican hangover stew of menudo yet. Or raw Japanese fugu. There are still several varieties of American oyster I have yet to try, and a couple of rare Welsh farmhouse cheeses. And I still haven't tasted Gary Rhodes' faggots, or anything cooked by Alain Ducasse of Monte Carlo.

Oh thank heavens. It's just the bubbles in my champagne.

Six recipes that changed my life

Every now and then, a dish comes along that totally changes the way you look at food. It doesn't have to be particularly fancy, or complicated, but in its own way, it can provide you with a fascinating insight into the marvellous alchemy that is cooking.

These six dishes have taught me more about flavours than any cooking teacher.

Moules à la marinière

Once upon a time, I could never cook seafood — no matter how hard I tried — without it ending up overcooked. Then I stopped treating all seafood as if it were one being, and started treating each shell, each little prawn, and each baby fish as an individual.

This dish, apart from teaching me about timing, is why mussels were created, making the most of their luscious texture and their wake-up, sea-fresh flavour. The essence of this dish is to catch the mussels just as they spring open, otherwise the flesh will become overcooked and boring. I take this task so personally, I virtually name each mussel as it comes out of the pot.

- 2 kilograms (4 pounds) mussels
- 2 tablespoons butter
- 6 shallots or one onion, finely chopped
- 250 ml (8 fluid ounces) dry white wine
- 2 garlic cloves , bruised
- 10 black peppercorns
- handful of parsley stems
- bay leaf
- a few celery leaves, chopped
- 2 tablespoons chopped parsley

Soak the mussels in several changes of cold water for several hours to reduce saltiness. Drain, scrub clean under cold running water, and yank the little beards from the shells.

Heat the butter in a large frypan, and cook the shallots until they become translucent. Add the white wine, garlic, peppercorns, parsley stems, bay leaf and celery leaves, and boil over a high heat for one minute. Keeping the heat high, add the mussels, and cover with a tight-fitting lid.

Shake the pan with all your might after a minute or two, and remove any mussels that have opened. Keep them in a warm place. Cover the pan and return to the heat for another minute, then shake, and check for more opened mussels.

Repeat process, discarding any mussels that don't open.

Strain the stock through muslin and return to the heat, simmering it until it is reduced by a quarter. If the stock is too salty, add a little chicken stock to soften the flavour.

Sometimes, I add a little cream to the juices at the end, and just heat it through.

Distribute the mussels among six soup bowls, pouring a few spoonfuls of the liquid over them. Sprinkle with chopped parsley and serve.

Serves 6.

Fegato alla Veneziana

What is it about liver and onions? Apart, they are two respectable, if unexciting ingredients. Together, they let off fireworks. Flavours mesh and meld; juices run; sweetness flows. To get the best out of this dish, cook the liver as little as possible and the onions as long as possible. This dish taught me how to use onions.

1 kilogram (2 pounds) calves' liver
4 tablespoons butter
1 kilogram (2 pounds) onions, finely sliced
2 cups (500 ml or 16 fluid ounces) dry white wine
½ cup (125 ml or 4 fluid ounces) chicken stock or water
salt and freshly ground black pepper
1 tablespoon light olive oil
4 sprigs of sage

Skin the liver, remove veins and slice thinly. Place three tablespoons of the butter and the onions in a heavy-based pan and cook gently, tossing occasionally, until onions are soft and translucent. Add the wine and cook over a high heat for a minute or two to lose a little of the alcohol, then reduce the heat and cook gently for 30 to 40 minutes, until the onion is almost melting.

Add a little chicken stock or water if needed, to keep it moist and creamy. (If it is too moist, remove the cover and cook over a high heat for a minute or two.) Add salt and pepper at this stage.

Heat the rest of the butter and the oil in a second heavy-based pan and add half the sage leaves, to flavour the oil. Cook liver over a high heat, very quickly. It should almost be crusty on the outside, and pink inside.

Divide onion sauce between the plates, and top with liver, piled high. Add a sprig or two of fresh sage and serve.

Serves 6.

Thai chicken and basil

This could lay claim to being The Easiest Dish In The World. But in spite of how preposterously simple it is to make, the flavours are deliciously complex, compatible and complete. It taught me that you could toss things in the wok while half-drunk and without a care in the world, and still be able to feed people without killing them.

   1 small chicken
   3 to 4 red or green chillies
   2 tablespoons flat leaf parsley
   bunch of fresh basil leaves
   4 tablespoons vegetable oil
   3 tablespoons fish sauce (nam pla)

Remove the meat from the breasts, the thighs and legs of the chicken, and slice into strips. Slice the chillies into thin slivers and finely chop the parsley. Pluck the basil leaves from the stems and reserve.
   Heat the oil in a wok and cook the chicken over a moderate heat for three or four minutes, then add the chillies, most of the basil, and the chopped parsley.
   Cook, stirring as you go, for another three or four minutes. Splash in the fish sauce and stir through. Add remaining basil, and serve with plenty of jasmine rice.
   Serves 4.

Spaghetti alla carbonara

If your idea of carbonara is a tight little concoction of nowhere spaghetti dotted with ugly little crumbs of eggy omelette, prepare for a life-changing revelation. This recipe taught me the value of not overcooking.

>   4 egg yolks
>   2 tablespoons cream
>   2 tablespoons grated Parmigiano
>   salt and freshly ground black pepper
>   500 grams (1 pound) spaghetti
>   4 thin slices of bacon, diced

Beat the egg yolks in a bowl, then beat in the cream, cheese, salt, lots of black pepper, and set aside.
    Cook the pasta in plenty of boiling, salted water until al dente, tender but firm to the bite. Fry the bacon in a non-stick pan until it is crisp. Drain the pasta and toss immediately with the bacon, then combine with the egg mixture. Toss quickly to allow the heat of the spaghetti to cook the egg into a creamy cheese sauce.
    Serve immediately on warm plates.
    Serves 4.

Cheese soufflé

Worry not. Soufflés are nowhere near the delicate, complex, unpredictable creatures we think they are. No, you don't have to walk around like church mice while they are cooking. Just go about your business normally, and your soufflé will do the same. This taught me that there's really very little to be scared of in the kitchen.

150 grams (5 ounces) grated cheese (Gruyère or mixture of Gruyère and Parmigiano)
75 grams (2½ ounces) butter
50 grams (1½ ounces) flour, sifted
350 ml (11 fluid ounces) milk, heated to boiling
salt and pepper
grated nutmeg
4 large egg yolks
5 egg whites

Heat the oven to 200°C (400°F).

Butter a 20-cm (8-in) soufflé dish and tie a collar of greaseproof paper roughly 10 cm (4 in) high around the outside, securing it with string.

Melt 50 grams (1½ ounces) of the butter in a heavy-bottomed pan and stir in the flour. When smooth, gradually pour in boiling milk and stir for about ten minutes over a medium heat until thick. Add salt, pepper and nutmeg to taste.

Let the mixture cool for a minute or two, then stir in the remaining butter, and the egg yolks, one at a time. Add the cheese and stir through.

Beat the egg whites until they form stiff peaks. Stir a spoonful of beaten egg white into the mixture to lighten it, then pour the mixture into the egg whites, folding it in with a slow, gentle motion.

Pour into the soufflé dish and cook in the oven for 30 minutes. Don't open the oven door during this time.

Remove the string and paper, and serve immediately.

Serves 4.

The miraculous flourless chocolate cake

This is the mother of all chocolate cakes. No flour. No anxious pacing up and down. You just bung everything in, and enjoy its small imperfections. Don't worry if it cracks on top. It's amazing what a little strategically placed icing sugar can do. I borrowed this from Jill Dupleix, who borrowed it from Elizabeth David, who borrowed it from the French. It taught me the value of borrowing recipes.

220 grams (7 ounces) dark, bitter chocolate
1 tablespoon rum or brandy
1 tablespoon strong black coffee
150 grams (5 ounces) castor sugar
150 grams (5 ounces) butter
100 grams (3½ ounces) ground almonds
5 eggs, separated
icing sugar

Heat the oven to 180°C (350°F).

Melt the chocolate, rum, coffee, sugar and butter in a bowl sitting in a pot of simmering water.

Remove from heat, stir thoroughly to combine. Mix in the ground almonds, then beat in the egg yolks one by one.

Beat the egg whites until they form stiff peaks, and stir a couple of spoonfuls into the chocolate mixture to lighten it, before gently folding in the rest.

Turn into a buttered and floured 20-cm (8-in) round or square cake tin, and bake for 40 to 50 minutes.

Leave to cool before removing from tin. Dust with icing sugar.

Serves 6.

The meaning of soup

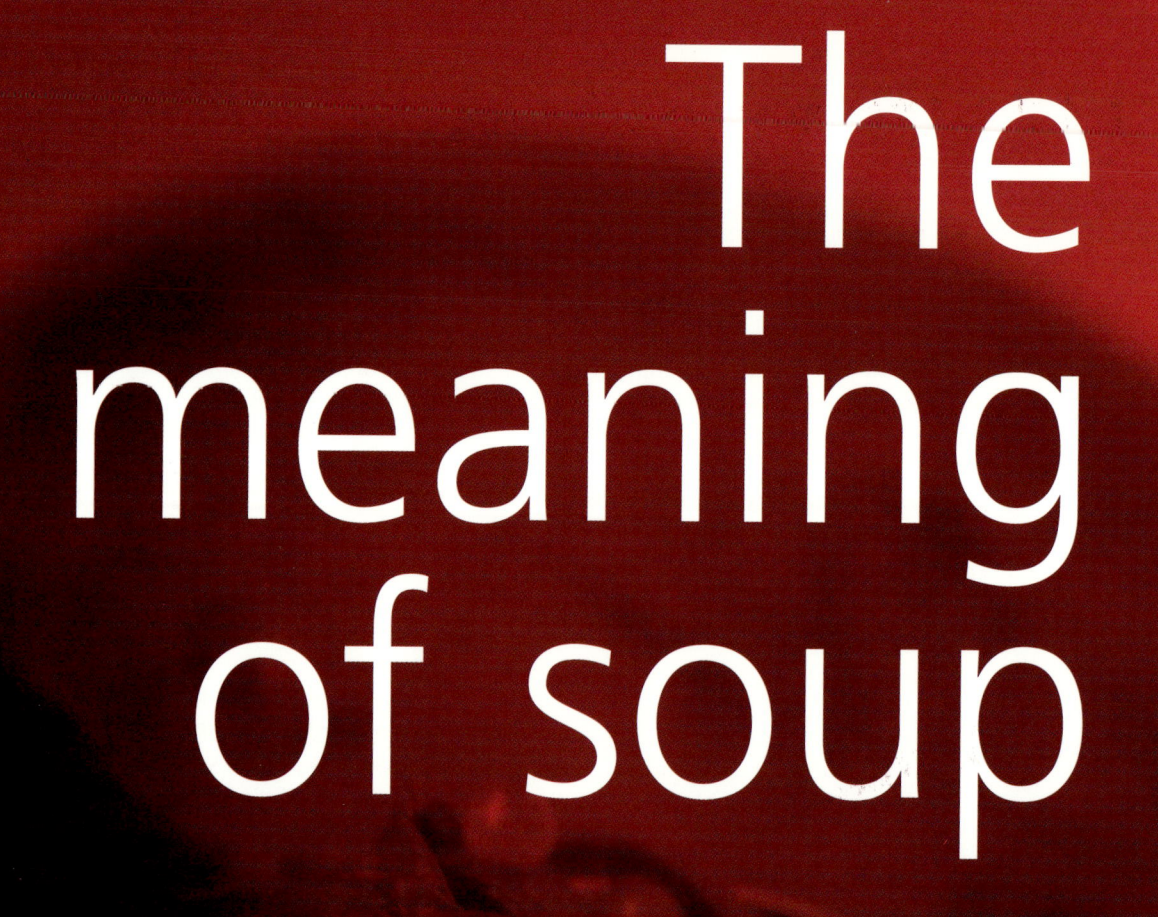

The true meaning of soup became as clear as consommé to me at a relatively early age. I was eighteen at the time, and my foot was planted firmly on the first rung of what promised to be a glorious advertising copywriting career, just as soon as I got out of the dispatch department.

My head, on the other hand was busily trying to work out how I could stretch a meagre salary to cover the basic necessities of life (rent and cigarettes), and still have something left over for little luxuries, like food.

I lived in a boarding house that had been a brothel in a former life, but had been transformed, ironically, into a home for single men. I would see my fellow boarders only at dinner time in the large, bare, communal kitchen, with its four green enamel Kooka stoves, and long scrubbed wooden dining table covered in a sensible, plasticised green and white tablecloth.

Not that a lot of actual cooking took place in that kitchen. Charlie the baker mainly made sandwiches, Kevin the apprentice plumber was constantly thawing out frozen pies, and Nick the mysterious travelling salesman used the battered Kelvinator fridge merely as a receptacle for beer and ice. I, too, needed minimum shelf space, having become a master at making a single can of Tom Piper sausages and vegetables last three meals, aided and abetted by copious quantities of very cheap rice.

The only dedicated cook among us was the landlord, a lean, lanky Hungarian in his mid-seventies with bottle-brush eyebrows, a permanent stoop, and a gentle, gentlemanly manner that permeated everything he did.

Kevin told me that the old man had owned his own café in Hungary. It was a real lesson to watch him at work, fastidiously chopping, tasting and seasoning, as if he still had a dining room full of hungry diners waiting for him.

Every Friday he would make the same thing, a simple soup of chicken giblets and egg noodles. He would begin by painstakingly cleaning the giblets under running water, removing every trace of fat and gristle, then slicing them into thin, truffle-like slices, which were then placed into a saucepan of cold water along with a handful of diced carrots, a couple of sliced onions, a little salt and pepper, and a bay leaf.

Within half an hour, the kitchen would be full of the most delicious aromas. After cooking a small amount of egg noodles in a separate saucepan, the old man would sit down at the end of the table with a glass of water, and slowly eat his soup, blowing cautiously on each spoonful, then sipping with an appreciative, loud slurp. He never once took his eyes off the dish as he ate.

Until one Friday night, when he was leaning against the stove, watching me scrape the last few potato squares out of the Tom Piper can. Out of the blue, he asked me if I would care to join him for dinner.

'Yes, *please*', I said, the aroma of carrots and chicken stock wafting around my brain.

He immediately set two places opposite each other at the table, cut two thick slices from a Vienna loaf, and put the noodle pan on the stove.

With a rare spring in his step he ran off down to his room, where he changed out of his grey cardigan into a tweedy well-cut jacket and emerged clutching a hip flask of Hennessy Brandy and two Vegemite glasses.

Ceremoniously, he poured a couple of

fingers into each glass, then set down two steaming bowls of soup.

We toasted life and each other in good gulps of brandy, then set about attacking the soup with bread in left hand and spoon in right.

I was instantly bowled over by the purity of the flavour, the bouncy little slices of giblet and the comforting, familiar feel of the noodles, as accommodating and as relaxed as old friends in a bar.

Although we had barely said more than a few words to each other in the six months I had been living in the house, here we were, suddenly exchanging intimate details of our lives.

I asked him about café life in Budapest, and he asked me about the songs he could hear me play on my guitar in my room.

I told him that most of them were written by a young man from the mid west of America by the name of Robert Zimmerman. He commented that Mr Zimmerman wrote directly from the heart, and we drank a toast to Mr Zimmerman's passion and sensitivity.

After a second bowl of soup and a third glass of brandy, I felt a sense of belonging and well-being and warmth that enveloped me like a shawl. I was at once oriented, anchored, fortified and restored.

To this day, whenever I am alone, or low, I run down to the shops for some giblets, carrots and a packet of egg noodles.

Only soup can do that. We could never have crossed the boundaries of age, race, and culture with a lamb chop, a sandwich, or a can of Tom Piper.

Vaguely Hungarian chicken soup

My landlord's simple soup has grown somewhat, as I learnt the pleasures of making my own chicken stock, and eventually earned enough money to buy a big pot. But it is still a simple chicken broth strewn with giblets and egg noodles, that tastes of love, smells of friendship, and settles a gnawing, uneasy, restless, feeling somewhere deep down inside.

- 1 kilogram (2 pounds) chicken giblets
- 1 kilogram (2 pounds) chicken bones
- 3 carrots, peeled and roughly chopped
- 3 onions, peeled and quartered
- 1 celery stalk, roughly chopped
- 10 parsley stems, a sprig of thyme and 2 bay leaves, all tied together with string
- 5 litres (8 pints) water
- salt and pepper to taste
- 100 grams (3½ ounces) thin egg noodles
- 1 tablespoon chopped parsley

Clean the giblets under running water, removing any fat, sinew, or tough, green skin.

Place giblets in a large saucepan along with chicken bones, carrots, onions, celery, herbs and water. Bring to the boil and simmer for around an hour and a half. Season to taste, then allow to cool down on top of the stove. Remove bones, celery and herbs. Slice giblets into slivers, then return to the soup and re-heat.

In another saucepan, cook the egg noodles in plenty of boiling salted water for a few minutes until tender.

Drain the noodles and divide between six soup bowls. Ladle the soup over the noodles and sprinkle with fresh parsley.

Serve with a small glass of brandy if feeling lonely.

Serves 6.

Blonde roots soup

I invented this soup one day when the only things I had in my life were a bunch of parsnips, half a nobbly bulb of celeriac and a tub of chicken stock.

2 large parsnips
1 large onion
1 potato
½ celeriac bulb, peeled
1 bay leaf
1.5 litres (2½ pints) chicken stock
a little grated nutmeg
½ cup (125 ml or 4 fluid ounces) milk
1 tablespoon cream
salt and pepper to taste
a little parsley, finely chopped

Peel and dice the vegetables coarsely. Toss vegetables and bay leaf into the chicken stock and bring to the boil. Skim off any scum that forms on the surface, then lower the heat and simmer, partly covered, for about half an hour or until the vegetables are soft. Remove the bay leaf and whizz soup in a food processor until smooth.
   Bring back to the boil, adding nutmeg, milk, cream and seasoning. Serve with parsley and a little pan-fried ham and cheese sandwich.
   Serves 6.

Stracciatella

Italians regard this soup in much the same way as I regard my vaguely Hungarian chicken soup. It's the eggy thing that does it.

   3 eggs
   1 tablespoon cold water
   1.5 litres (2½ pints) really good chicken stock
   2 tablespoons parsley, finely chopped
   ¼ nutmeg, grated
   50 grams (1½ ounces) Parmigiano, grated

Beat the eggs and the water together with a fork.
   Bring the stock to a medium boil, and skim off anything that rises to the surface. Pour in the egg mixture over the back of the fork, so that it falls in fine strands, then quickly mix the egg through the hot stock so that it forms fine, scattery threads. Sprinkle with parsley, nutmeg and Parmigiano, and serve.
   Serves 4.

Vichyssoise

A lot of people like to serve Vichyssoise chilled. That is missing the point entirely. This soup needs warmth to come alive. But doesn't everyone?

4 leeks, white part only
4 large onions
4 tablespoons butter
6 pink-skinned potatoes
1.5 litres (2½ pints) chicken stock
salt and pepper to taste
freshly ground nutmeg to taste
250 ml (8 fluid ounces) thick cream
2 tablespoons finely chopped chives

Wash the leeks carefully, and cut into thin slices. Slice the onions to about the same thickness and sauté with the leeks in the butter over a gentle heat. They should soften and go transparent, but do not let them turn golden.
　Peel and slice the potatoes, and add to the leek and onion mixture. Then pour in chicken stock and simmer gently until the vegetables are soft, about an hour. Add salt, pepper and nutmeg and sieve through a food mill or blend until smooth in a food processor.
　Serve hot with chives and cream. Or if you want to go trad, serve cold.
　Serves 4.

Celtic revival lamb and barley soup

This is a sort of Irish and Welsh cum Polish broth that I make to get through winter. I'm still alive, so it has worked so far.

1 cup (220 grams or 7 ounces) pearl barley
2 litres (3½ pints) water
3 scrag ends of lamb neck
2 lamb shanks
2 carrots, peeled and sliced
2 celery stalks, sliced
2 onions or 3 leeks, chopped
2 bay leaves
2 parsnips, peeled and sliced
2 turnips, peeled and sliced
heart of a small cabbage
2 potatoes, peeled and finely chopped
salt and freshly ground pepper
2 tablespoons freshly chopped parsley

Cover barley with cold water, bring to boil, then strain.
   Trim the lamb of excess fat, and arrange in a heavy-based soup pot with the water, barley, carrots, celery, onions and bay leaves. Bring to the boil and skim, then reduce heat and simmer for an hour and a half.
   If you like, leave the soup to cool overnight, and remove any fat that forms on the surface. Remove meat from the liquid and shred into small pieces. Return the meat to the stock with the parsnip, turnip, cabbage and potato. Cook for a further 30 minutes until the vegetables are tender. Season to taste, and serve with a sprinkle of freshly chopped parsley.
   Serves 6.

Coming in from the cold

As love lives go, mine was going nowhere fast. At the tender age of nineteen, I had learned the hard way that not only did love not conquer all, but I was yet to be convinced that it conquered any.

My problem was that there were simply too many things that I wasn't.

For a start, I wasn't Jewish, which was an insurmountable obstacle for Mr and Mrs Kaplan who gently suggested it might be better if I didn't see their daughter again.

I wasn't Roman Catholic either, which was a cross I was just going to have to bear, according to Mr and Mrs Angelucci, both of whom could say the words 'Sorry, Maria isn't home at the moment' and make it sound like 'Burn in hell, you atheist scum'.

Whatever I wasn't, at least I knew what I was. I was an outsider, a misfit, an interloper, and an alien. It was like being invited to a really exciting function, then turning up and finding that your name isn't on the list.

All I needed now was to meet a Greek Orthodox, and it would be three strikes and I'm out of here.

I came close.

Anna's father was Russian Orthodox, and while I didn't exactly know what a Russian Orthodox did, apart from paint some pretty mean patterns on eggs at Easter time, it didn't seem to matter.

He was from Kiev in the Ukraine, and his wife was Polish, and both were inordinately civil to me. Except, of course, when Anna first introduced me, and they nearly spat out their vodka. Apparently, my surname sounds uncannily like the Russian word for stupid.

While even the vaguest possibility of their daughter one day becoming Mrs Stupid probably didn't thrill them, they nevertheless managed to take me in their stride.

I couldn't believe it. No dark, meaningful glances. No relentless grilling about my parents and my background, and my...um, beliefs.

After about five weeks, came the ultimate compliment.

They asked me to come and have dinner with them.

In the course of picking Anna up, I had witnessed a few dinners in the house, and I'm here to tell you that they were miraculous affairs, comprising much toasting with cherry vodka and enough food to keep the whole of Kiev going for weeks.

I remembered pots of plump cabbage rolls, known in the Ukraine as holubtsy, piping hot and slathered in sour cream. Then there were large, smug boiled dumplings known as vareneki, overflowing bowls of deeply purple bortsch, huge puffy deep-fried, meat-filled doughnut affairs known as piroshki, and gargantuan tureens of stews that you could get lost in for days at a time.

But it wasn't the food that got me, it was the gesture.

It meant that, at long last, I belonged.

For the course of the meal at least, I would be one of them, and the idea of it made me feel warm and grounded.

So when the big night came and I took my place at the kitchen table surrounded by the inevitable casseroles, tureens, pots and bowls, I was in a totally euphoric state, my head spinning from the delicious aromas and the cherry vodka, as I pondered a particularly vexing question: whether to start with cabbage roll or vareneki.

But before I had made my final decision, Anna's mother was standing over me, holding yet another plate, the contents of which I could not quite see.

A little pickled herring perhaps? Or maybe some golden little blinis, filled with cheese and wrapped up like a folded bed sheet?

But no, as the plate descended in front of me like a slow motion sequence from a B-grade movie, I saw what lay on it, and my smile became a lip-stretching grimace.

It contained a large T-bone steak, a few chips and a fried egg.

Somewhere, a long way away, I heard a door slam shut, and the sound of heavy iron bolts being drawn.

I can see now that she didn't mean to hurt my feelings. Maybe previous boyfriends of her daughter had said 'I'm not eating that muck', and she didn't want to risk being hurt again. Maybe she genuinely thought she was doing me a favour, that her homely food wasn't good enough for me.

Nah.

I got to know the family pretty well over the next ten years (I married Anna). I even lived with them for several years. Eventually, my mother-in-law had to feed me as if I were a part of the family. And every time I bit into a holubtsy, or a vareneki, I told her how much I enjoyed it. I don't think she ever really believed me.

Vareneki

Similar to the Polish pierogi and the northern Russian pelmeni, vareneki is like an instant Ukranian homesick kit, all wrapped up in white shiny dumpling skin.

    Ask five different Ukrainians to describe vareneki and you will probably get five different answers. Some swear by them stuffed with cherries, while others fill them with a fine dice of mushrooms. There are those who know them only stuffed with sugar and cottage cheese, while still others prefer buckwheat and sauerkraut. The first vareneki I ever tasted were made by my inaugural mother-in-law, Mary Bandurka. They were filled simply with mashed potato and onion, which to me will always be the one, the true vareneki. This, with enormous gratitude, is her recipe, which until this time has never been written down.

2 cups (250 grams or 8 ounces) plain flour, sifted
pinch of salt
2 egg yolks (Mary made it without egg, but I prefer it with)
4–5 tablespoons tepid water
350 grams (11 ounces) potato, peeled and quartered
1 large onion, chopped
4 tablespoons butter
salt and pepper
1 egg white, beaten
melted butter for serving
sour cream for serving

Place the flour and salt in a large bowl and make a well in the centre. Gradually add egg yolks and water. Using your finger tips, work the dough until it is fairly stiff, adding more water if it becomes dry and crumbly. Knead the dough on a lightly floured surface until it can be gathered into a smooth, compact ball. Wrap in cling wrap or cover with a tea towel and leave to stand for an hour.

In the meantime, boil the potatoes in plenty of salted water until soft. Cook onion in butter until soft and brown. Drain and mash the potato, adding the butter, onions and salt and pepper, and keep covered.

Roll out the dough until very thin, then cut into 8-cm (3-in) rounds. While still warm, place ½ tablespoon of mashed potato into the middle of each circle. Brush a little egg white around the edge of the dough, then fold it over, making a half-moon shape. Pinch the edges together with your fingers or crimp with a fork.

Bring a large pot of salted water to the boil, and drop in six of the vareneki. Simmer, uncovered, for about ten minutes, until they float to the surface. Remove with a slotted spoon and keep in a covered casserole while you cook the rest.

Moisten with melted and slightly burnt butter and serve with sour cream. Cold vareneki can be reheated by frying in yet more butter.

Makes 15–20 dumplings.

Ukrainian bortsch

Forget your well-mannered restaurant bortsch with its delicate chicken stock, fine, transparent ruby good looks, and token beetroot cubes. The real thing isn't supposed to tide you over until main course, it's supposed to tide you over until spring.

This is how Mary Bandurka made it, although I have added meat for extra flavour.

- 2 tablespoons butter
- 1 onion, diced
- 2 garlic cloves, peeled and chopped.
- 3 tablespoons tomato paste
- ½ white cabbage, cored and shredded
- 1 carrot, peeled and cut into matchsticks
- 3 medium beetroot, peeled and cut into matchsticks
- 1.5 litres (2½ pints) beef stock
- 1 bay leaf
- 1½ tablespoons red wine vinegar
- ½ teaspoon sugar
- salt and pepper
- 250 grams (8 ounces) boiled brisket or boiled ham, cut into chunks
- 3 medium potatoes, peeled and diced
- ¼ cup (55 grams or 1½ ounces) white beans, soaked overnight and cooked until tender
- sour cream for serving
- chopped parsley for garnish

In a large saucepan, melt the butter and fry the onion until lightly browned, adding garlic towards the end of this time. Add the tomato paste and cook for one minute. Add the cabbage, carrot, beetroot, stock, bay leaf, vinegar, sugar and salt and pepper. Bring to the boil, then cover and simmer for 15 minutes.

Add the diced meat, potatoes and beans and cook for a further 15 minutes.

Serve with sour cream and parsley, accompanied with fresh dark rye bread.

Serves 6 normal people, or 4 Ukrainians.

Holubtsy

When I first ate these with Mary's husband, Makar, he told me, quite definitely, and with much pointing, that the name meant little pigeon in Ukrainian. When I asked him why, he laughed, and scratched his head, and said 'They look like pigeons?' We both stared at them, hard. I don't think either of us could see the resemblance.

>   large head of white cabbage
>   I large onion, chopped
>   2 tablespoons butter
>   500 grams (1 pound) minced beef
>   1 cup (155 grams or 5 ounces) rice
>   salt and pepper
>   1 egg, beaten

Remove the core from the cabbage and blanch it in a large pot of simmering, salted water for about ten minutes. Drain, and carefully remove the leaves, spreading them on tea towels to dry slightly. When the leaves become hard to detach, return to the water for a couple of minutes and continue to remove remaining leaves.

Fry the onion in butter until golden, then add minced meat and cook till well coloured.

In the cabbage water, boil the rice for about 12 minutes. Drain and combine with meat and onion mixture. Add salt and pepper to taste. Allow to cool, then mix in the egg with your hands.

Cut away some of the thick rib from the larger leaves

Place a good, large dollop of stuffing onto each the leaf, and roll up like a parcel, tucking in the ends as you go.

Place the rolls in layers in a saucepan, salting each layer. Cover with water and simmer gently until cooked, about 30 minutes.

Serve with sour cream.

Note: In some parts of Russia, instead of being simmered in water, the rolls are baked in a casserole with a sauce of sour cream flavoured with tomato paste, which is also similar to the Hungarian way of doing things.

Makes about a dozen rolls.

The death

of the foodie

Nobody knows exactly when he died.

Most people agree that it was some time towards the end of the Eighties. Some say it was the very same day the great Alain Chapel passed away.

Others swear blind that it was on Escoffier's birthday. Another popular theory has it that he died on the last day of the truffle season in Perigord, and that he breathed his last breath as the last, precious dark jewel changed hands in a nearly deserted market square.

Nobody even knows who he was.

All we know is that he was the last of the great foodies, and with him died a lifestyle and an appetite the likes of which we may never see again.

Yet he died unheralded and unsung. There were no reports of his death in the newspapers, no blow-by-blow television coverage, and no long-winded eulogies in *Time* magazine. Nobody moved to erect a tomb to the unknown foodie. Nobody suggested we pause for three and a half minutes' silence (the time of the perfect boiled egg) each year so that we might reflect silently on his achievements. We simply preferred not to be reminded of his excesses.

His death, after all, was not unexpected.

Even by the mid Eighties, the foodie was as endangered a species as many of the animals and plants he insisted on eating.

Everything was conspiring against him: the economy, the environment and the new age of enlightenment. Overindulgence had suddenly become as unfashionable as spats, flares, and hating the Russians.

People had ceased to worship food, and were content merely to eat it. No longer did they travel through Europe flitting from one three-star restaurant to the next with open mouths and open cheque books, clutching souvenired menus like a fresh crop of scalps. They became sightseers instead, taking photographs of churches, cathedrals, city skylines and country landscapes instead of plates of bouillabaisse, chocolate marquise, and foie gras.

The distinctive red Michelin food guides were replaced by the green touring variety. They stayed in pensiones and Holiday Inns, and paid advance excursion fares to fly economy. The memory of days when the choice of airline depended heavily on what brand of champagne it served in First Class seemed somehow irrelevant, incongruous, and somewhat shameful.

Oh, there were a few die-hard survivors. People who proudly and defiantly claimed that the microwave was only good for cooking vegetables, who still called Sauvignon Blanc 'cat's piss', who still read cookbooks in bed, and who boasted loudly that the only things they kept in their freezers were chicken stock, ice cubes and vodka.

Most foodies had gone underground, buying caviar in brown paper bags from 'mates' in the business, and trading truffles in small airless rooms with the lamps low and the blinds drawn. Luxuries like lobster were relegated to special occasions only, like Christmas Day and Paul Bocuse's birthday. Some, like the heroes of Ray Bradbury's novel *Fahrenheit 451*, dedicated themselves to memorising nouvelle cuisine cookbooks page by page so their contents would never be totally lost to mankind.

But they should have realised that they didn't have a chance.

The foodies have been replaced by the foodists, a new breed full of sensitive new age consumer knowledge (S.N.A.C.K.) who can tell at the merest flick of their food-value calculator the vitamin, mineral and kilojoule content of every morsel they place in their mouths They buy bran in bulk, eat breakfast every day, and confine drinking to the evening meal. They eat so many pulses and grains they are rarely far from a public convenience. Worse, they are slim, clear-skinned, and ruddy-cheeked, and talk about things other than food while they eat.

Every year on the first day of autumn, that finest of foodie seasons with its treasury of mushrooms and game, I visit a small, unmarked grave in a quiet little cemetery on the outskirts of town, and silently pay my respects.

Once again, that day has arrived.

When I awake, it is still dark, and I am filled with that peaceful contentment only devout believers will ever know.

I slip into my Savoy Hotel monogrammed white towelling robe and prepare Michel Guerard's oeufs poule aux caviar, and Raymond Blanc's moussette de saumon fumé.

For toast, I cut off two thick slices of dusty, nutty pain Poilane, smuggled in by a friend fresh from Paris.

Such a repast demands a 1980 Krug Clos de Mesnil champagne sipped from the finest Lalique cherubim glasses, followed by freshly roasted Blue Mountain coffee from Jamaica prepared in my trusty canary yellow Baby Gaggia espresso machine.

It is a breakfast fit for a foodie, and I eat it slowly, reflecting upon the passionless, obsessionless modern world. Are we really better off, without excess? Have we lost the art of stretching the boundaries of our lives, having the courage to take a craving all the way, risking life and limb in search of new experiences, or recapturing precious old ones?

There is a special creativity in searching for flavours, in making the most of what one has, in seeking the essence of things. It is the life of the artist, the criminal, the explorer, the slightly insane, to devote one's life to the pleasures of eating. It's *romantic*, for god's sake.

Where is the passion in muesli?

I realise I haven't felt that inner peace, that vital sense of aliveness I used to feel after a great meal, for years. Since I was a foodie. My inner child hasn't been fed, hugged and spoilt rotten. I've been a boring, responsible adult, a ghost of children past trapped in a grown-up body.

Food is not the enemy. Cold logic and reason are. We need to be happy on the inside, before we can be happy on the outside. The words echo inside me like bells in a graveyard church. 'Better to be hated for who you are, than loved for who you are not.' Then I sigh, and change into my suitably chocolate brown suit, complemented by my Yves Saint Laurent teacup tie, and drive to the cemetery.

I pull up near the grave just as dawn is breaking. A sad teary mist hangs heavily over the graveyard. The air is heavy with a silence as thick as oatmeal.

Even the birds are strangely quiet, as if respectfully observing the solemnity of the occasion. With a deep sigh, and a heavy heart, I gather up a large, colourful herb posy from the back of the car and walk up a grassy hill towards the grave, thinking about the way breaking bread together makes friends of strangers, how good food can heal all wounds, and turn war into peace, and how good wine can turn a dull clod into a poet.

I find myself repeating the same word over and over, like a mantra. Butter, butter, butter, butter, butter...

Slowly I place the posy at the foot of the grave. That's when I see it.

It sits on a silver platter that winks and shimmers with the first of the day's sun. It is a flawless roulade, a vegetable terrine: pretty rows of haricots verts, petits pois, artichokes, baby carrots set in a farce of ham lined with vine leaves. I haven't seen a Terrine de legumes Olympe since Jean and Michel Troisgros proudly plated it in 1984.

Next to it is another platter bearing a magnificent whole fish en croute, in the style of Bocuse's legendary dish. As I look around, I notice more offerings, vintage wines, jars of preserved truffles, perfectly poached pears.

Over there is Girardet's tart Vaudoise à la crème. Chapel's terrine de foie gras d'oie dans sa graisse sits right next to Maximin's praline Negresco.

With hope welling in my breast, I turn and walk back to the car, my emotions as mixed as mesclun. I don't feel alone any more. They are out there, in silence, behind closed pantry doors, just waiting for this politically correct, nutritionally balanced and economically challenged era to be over.

I look down. I notice a mushroom growing in the grass. I pick it up and examine it. It couldn't be...but it is.

It is a large, perfect morel. More than that, it is a sign.

I very carefully place it in my jacket pocket and get in the car.

Omelette with fresh morels

Fresh eggs fragrant with garlic, chives and the magnificent, earthy flavour of morels: a meal in minutes, that can make foodie memories last for hours.

>   handful of fresh morels
>   2 tablespoons butter
>   1 garlic clove, crushed
>   5 free-range eggs
>   salt and freshly ground black pepper
>   1 tablespoon snipped chives

Check morels for grit, and wipe clean. Do not wash or they will go soggy. Melt one tablespoon of butter in a frypan. When foaming, add garlic, swirl and add morels. Sauté, stirring for a few minutes until they soften. Set aside and keep warm.

Beat eggs with salt and pepper. Heat the second tablespoon of butter in non-stick frypan. When foaming, pour in the eggs. Cook over a gentle heat, tipping the pan occasionally to allow the egg to run towards the sides and set.

Spoon the warm morels onto one side of the omelette, sprinkle with chives, and carefully fold the other half on top. Slide out of the omelette pan onto a warm plate, add a little dob of butter on top and serve immediately.

Serves 2.

It's my oesophagus and I'll cry if I want to

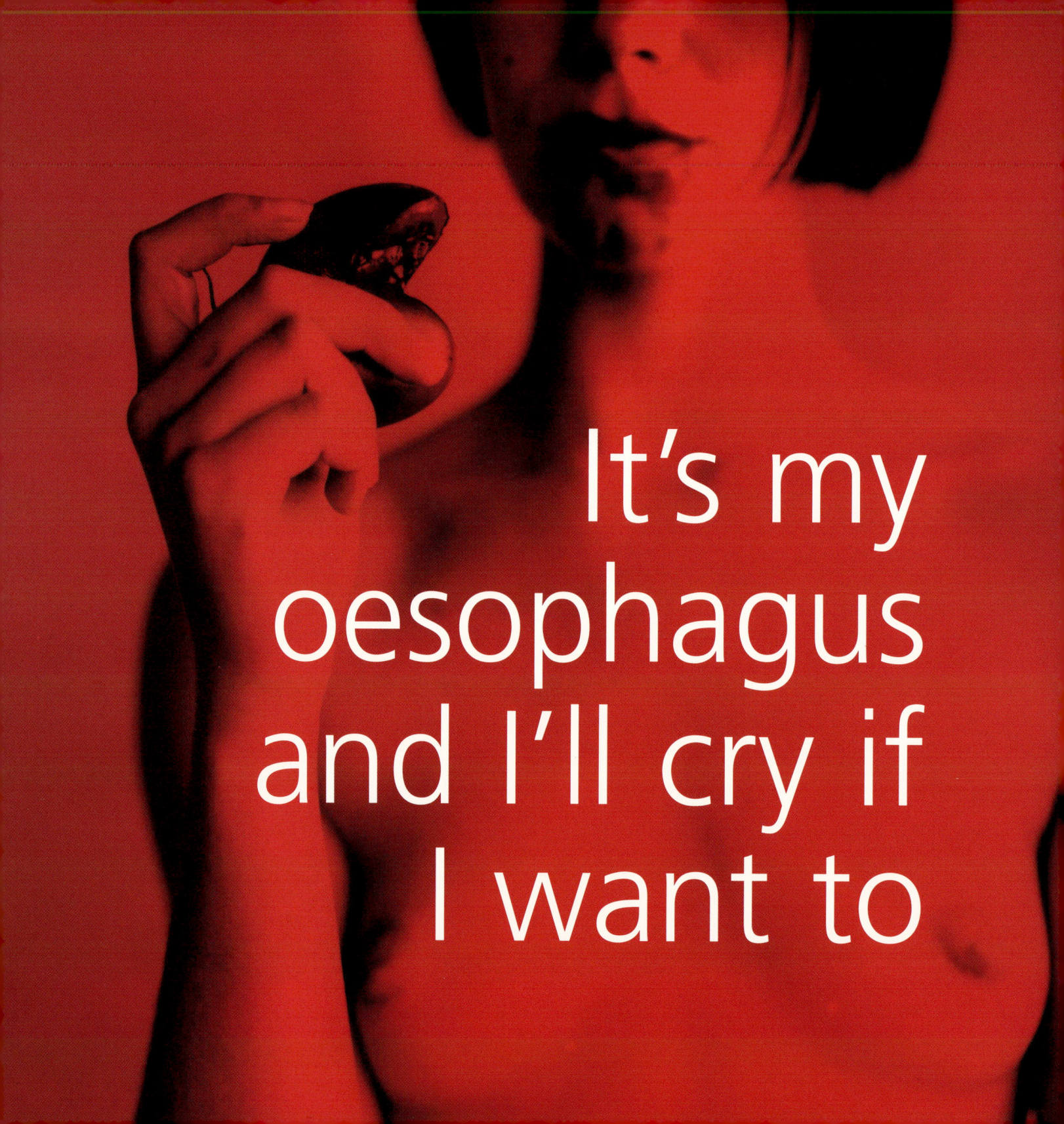

Very Strange Phenomenon Number One.

I can't swallow. At first, I thought it was God's way of punishing me for eating airline food. I should have known better than to eat the grey beef in matching gravy but give me a break.

I had skipped breakfast and looked like missing anything edible for lunch, so I placed my tastebuds on hold, and put the first piece of beef into my mouth. It was also my last.

I tried to swallow, but it stopped somewhere between my tonsils and my appendix.

It wasn't even a particularly large piece of meat, yet it wouldn't budge.

I felt like the boa constrictor in Antoine de Saint-Exupery's *The Little Prince*, who consumed an entire elephant in one go. It remained clearly outlined within the boa's skin. So, it felt, did this.

No problem, I thought. Everything that goes down, must go down. (Not exactly a desirable thought to have in an aeroplane.) I picked up my glass of water and took a good long gulp.

Very Strange Phenomenon Number Two. I felt my throat fill up like a chemistry laboratory beaker. As it reached my tonsils, the air supply shut down. I was literally drowning in a glass of water.

Panic set in. Somehow I had to get to the toilet, but I was trapped in the middle of three seats with a complete stranger between me and the aisle. As he lifted a piece of grey meat to his mouth, I vigorously tapped his arm.

He must have caught the terror in my eyes, because he didn't argue. Just quickly picked up his tray, lifted his tray table, and leapt up.

So did I. When I expelled the water into the toilet bowl, air came rushing into me like the first blast from the rather fierce air conditioner in my car.

But the meat was still there. I could neither eat nor drink anything until that evening, when suddenly, for no apparent reason at all, it decided to complete its downward journey to my stomach.

Later that night, my wife, Jill, and I gave each other lessons in the Heimlich manoeuvre, a life-saving sub-diaphragmatic thrust developed by a certain Doctor Henry Heimlich in 1974.

She tried to take my mind off things, as she read the instructions.

'Over 3,000 Americans a year die by choking', she said.

'Thank you, my darling', I replied.

'A recent survey found that 55 out of 56 restaurant deaths were caused by choking, with only one being a heart attack', she added.

'It was nice knowing you', I said, grabbing the instructions. 'Now, make a fist, and place it on my stomach.' She did.

'Take your fist with your other hand and thrust it sharply into the abdomen as if...'

I collapsed breathlessly to the floor. The 55 out of 56 deaths were obviously caused by an overly conscientious application of the Heimlich manoeuvre. As was, no doubt, the heart attack.

In the ensuing weeks, she had plenty of opportunities to hone her technique, as my little problem occurred at increasingly frequent intervals. It wasn't just airline food. It was breakfast, lunch and dinner food.

The Heimlich manoeuvre had no effect whatsoever, and, invariably, the offending object would glide away into oblivion at a later stage. This went on for about four or five months, before I willed myself to do something about it.

More than anything, I was embarrassed. A full time, practising restaurant critic who can't swallow is about as useful as a film critic who can't see.

After asking for a list of suitable restaurants for an upcoming birthday dinner, my doctor sent me to a throat specialist who put me in a hospital, ran a camera down my gullet and concluded that I didn't have a problem.

After requesting a suitable restaurant for an impending wedding anniversary, he sent me on my way.

It was nice to know there was nothing wrong, and I used this thought to comfort me every time something stuck in my throat, which was now happening roughly once a day.

It wasn't just big, bad things like a piece of steak any more, either. A prawn could do it, and so could a piece of bread. Once I even got a lettuce leaf stuck.

A lettuce leaf! I would have been scared, had I thought there was anything wrong with me.

As the years passed, I discovered that if I chewed lots and drank copious amounts of water after every mouthful of food, I could keep things moving reasonably well.

Apart from the slight sloshing sound I made when I walked, I was able to lead a relatively normal life.

Scary, but. Like the time I was trapped in a four-hour tea ceremony in Japan, eating twenty-nine different courses with only a small flat saucerful of sake to drink.

To leave even a scrap of food on one's plate was regarded as the vilest of insults, so I pressed on regardless. Being seen as rude seemed far more daunting than being seen as dead.

In spite of all my water guzzling, the problem steadily worsened. Jill grew to dislike my habit of throwing down cutlery and rushing off to inspect the porcelain at every restaurant, bar and café in town. She covered for me with friends and business colleagues as I spent more and more time in bathrooms and toilets, hiding her anxiety but not always her annoyance.

Not a few chefs wondered desperately what was wrong with their succulent roast duck as it came back from my table only slightly nibbled at.

Once, while eating a bowl of noodle soup in a neighbourhood Vietnamese restaurant, I heard my name whispered at a table for eight next to me. It's always nice to know that I'm not the only one who reads my reviews.

I soon forgot all about it when disaster struck yet again, and I rushed to the toilet, my personal laboratory beaker full, and gratefully expelled the liquid, without even pausing to close the cubicle door.

Out the corner of my eye I noticed one of the young men from the next table walk in. He stopped, frozen in his tracks, as he saw me leaning over the toilet bowl. He either figured I was bulimic — unlikely, with my figure — or that it was Something I Ate.

Either way, he was out of there in a flash. By the time I returned to the dining room, the table for eight was deserted, and Jill was hiding her anxiety under her usual veil of annoyance.

Before I emptied out half the restaurants in town and lost custody of the family wok, I figured it was time to take action.

Another doctor, another specialist, another tracheoscopy, another restaurant recommendation.

Still, the specialist was happy to report that nothing appeared to be wrong. Another year went by, looking at ham sandwiches and wondering if I was going to end up like Mama Cass.

Then came my Waterloo, as if I hadn't seen enough of both water and loos. The Battle of Pai Gwat. A morsel from this usually tender yum cha dish of deeply steamed pork spare ribs stopped somewhere near my heart. Four hours later, nothing.

By dinner, there was still no movement.

For thirty-six hours I could not eat or drink a single thing.

Was this it? Something from the 'X Files' had taken over my body? Oh, hell. Not cancer.

I had just moved into a new neighbourhood, with a doctor's surgery at the end of the street. I ran.

'I have something caught in my throat', I said.

'I think not', said the gently spoken Malaysian-born doctor, having pushed and prodded his way through a lengthy examination.

Within hours, I was sitting in the office of one of our finest gastroenterologists. He explained, as if to a child, how the release of excess acid from the stomach can cause a stricture of the lower part of the oesophagus, which can dramatically narrow the opening.

'We'll know more after the marshmallow test.'

The marshmallow test?

The following day, I am lying down on a radiologist's mammoth X ray machine eating a large marshmallow while watching its progress on a television screen. Sure enough, when it hits the lower part of my oesophagus, it stops, only to dissolve very gradually, and eventually pass through, like sheep having to reduce to single file to get through a narrow gateway.

'Bingo!' says the radiologist, which is hard to say with one's mouth full of marshmallows. He walks out of the room, his hand diving into the rest of the packet.

'Got any more of those marshmallows?' asks the patient, but he is ignored, as patients are.

Three days later, I am on the operating table with a wire threaded through my insides. A small tapering device is threaded onto the wire and sent down the oesophagus where it gently stretches open the restricted section. I feel like a cyberspy being programmed with vital data. I also feel like a marshmallow.

'The wire could kink, you know', said the specialist.

Don't you hate those people who like to tell you everything about what you're going through?

I don't particularly care about dying, by this stage. I am in the middle of a strange, anaesthetised dream in which Mama Cass has a bit part.

And that's it. Six days of mashed potato, risotto, soup and pasta later, and I am ready for anything. Six weeks later, and I burst into my specialist's office with a copy of my latest cover story, a comparative study of six of the city's best steak houses.

He nods gravely. And asks me if I know a good seafood restaurant.

The ultimate mashed potato

Mashed potato became a good and trusted friend during my deep-throat days. In fact, I had plenty of time to perfect it, on a mission to recreate Joel Robuchon's famed purée de pommes de terre. This is as close as I got. It's not the same, but hey, it saved my life.

> 1 kilogram (2 pounds) pink-skinned potatoes, such as Desiree or Pontiac
> ½ cup (125 grams or 4 ounces) unsalted butter, cut into pieces
> ½ cup (125 ml or 4 fluid ounces) hot milk

Peel and cut the potatoes into thick slices and simmer in salted water for around 20 minutes or until tender. Drain off the water and return the pot to the heat momentarily to allow any moisture to evaporate.
   Put the potato through a food mill if you have one, or mash thoroughly with a good, old-fashioned potato masher.
   Gradually add the butter, stirring strongly with a wooden spoon
   Once the butter is incorporated, add boiling milk slowly, beating as you go. Keep the pot warm over a gentle heat as you beat. If it feels heavy, add extra cold butter and hot milk, beating all the time. Add salt to taste, and serve.
   Serves 4 to 6.

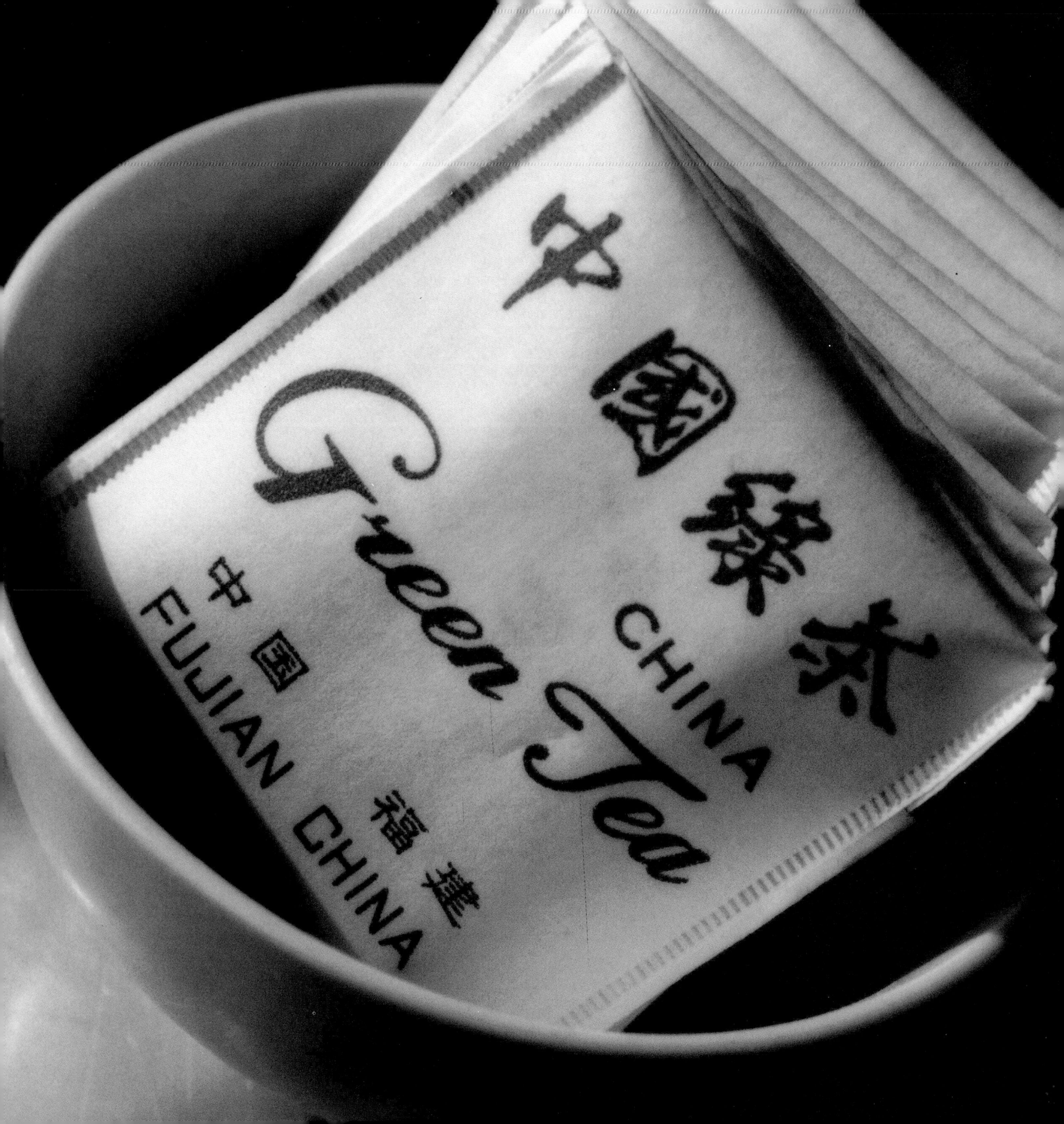
中國綠茶
CHINA
Green Tea
中国福建
FUJIAN CHINA

Like a bull in China

'I'm not going. I'm simply not going.' The voice cut through my dreams of misty, mystical lotus-clad lakes like a foghorn. I kept my eyes closed, but I knew she was sitting bolt upright in bed, clutching her book.

Any normal human being planning a trip to China would read Fodor or the Lonely Planet guide. But Jill is not normal.

She has to read Paul Theroux, the man described as the great grump of travel writing.

'Of course you're going', I grunted, clinging to my dream. 'It's the trip of a lifetime, travelling through China with thirty Chinese restaurateurs, meeting chefs and gourmet associations, attending demonstration classes, and generally eating everything in China except the table. Besides, I've sent the cheque.'

She looked unconvinced. I played my last card. 'Think of the Great Wall, the Entombed Warriors, the limestone cliffs of Guilin. And finally, after all these years of eating my version of Grandma's beancurd, we can have it at the original Ma Po beancurd restaurant in Chengdu.' The ma po usually did the trick, but not this time. Her features assumed that expression normally reserved for warning me I had cauliflower soup clinging to my top lip.

'Ah yes. The Ma Po beancurd restaurant', she said, and began reading aloud from Theroux. Something about satisfied eaters blowing their noses in their fingers, hoicking loudly, then spitting on the floor, and ending with: 'Was I a silly, ethno-centric, old fussbudget for finding a brimming spittoon unwelcome in a restaurant?' She closed the book, her face forlorn. 'I can't go', she cried. 'The spitting. The toilets. Bad hotels. Hepatitis. MSG. The Chardonnay.' The last was a sort of a whimper from under her continental pillow. 'But they won't have Chardonnay', I said, confused.

'I know!' she wailed, thumping the bed. It was time for decisive action, something I rarely pull off with any style.

'You're worrying unnecessarily', I said firmly, my mind swimming with brimming spittoons.

'You're right', she said.

'I am?'

'Yes. The plane is going to crash anyway.'

As it turned out, the plane didn't crash, and we arrived at Guangzhou (Canton) airport without incident. Unless of course, you call being assigned two seats that didn't exist an incident. Instead of 32 D and 32 E, there was a toilet block.

On the connecting flight to Beijing, we received our first, honest-to-goodness Chinese meal. It came in a large cardboard box covered in bright blue and red fairytale illustrations, and inside was a cross between kindergarten rations and your worst nightmare. A sticky red bean lolly lay next to a packet of sesame seed nibblies and a pack of preserved mandarin peel. Next, there was a miniature apple pie that tasted like yellow plasticine, more sweet pastries, and a pale, bready frankfurt in a squishy bread roll. Separate little sachets contained salt, pepper and MSG. I could feel myself being glared at by someone dear to me, but I pretended to be asleep.

From Beijing airport, a bus carried us through the night to the five-star Tian Lun Dynasty Hotel near Tiananmen Square, passing several kerbside mountains of ripe, round watermelons. Sleeping boys stood guard. In an all-night noodle shop, a man deftly pulled noodles apart, while long lines of mules and carts headed wearily to market.

Our allotted guide, the snappily dressed William, entertained us with an impromptu recital of traditional Chinese music played on his nose. Jill smiled tightly. It was clear that this would be no ordinary tour.

She was placated somewhat by our allotted room being allotted to us and to nobody else, by the presence of running water, air conditioning, and by a hotel bar that served large glasses of Tsing Tao Riesling. From the next day on, we diligently worked our way through seven provinces, six China Airlines lunch packs, and twenty-eight full-scale banquets, comprising a grand total of seven hundred individual courses.

The people of China welcomed us with open arms and open doors. They could not have been nicer had we been made of red bean paste. Out in the provinces, the locals stopped and gaped in awe, giggling at our silly height, and our, ah, size. 'Sumo, sumo', chanted one crowd happily as they caught sight of a pleasantly rotund member of our party.

The sightseers soon became the sightseen. After trying to take a few inconspicuous shots of the thousands of local Chinese trudging along the Great Wall, I turned around to discover that my floppy yellow shorts, ice-blue T-shirt, red baseball cap and I were the centre of attention, and will no doubt be giggled about on a hundred different Chinese slide nights for years to come.

In Xian, the whole town turned out to see us when we lunched at the Tong Sheng Xing restaurant. I was wearing a sedate cinnamon and rust that day, so I could only blame the fact that we were a highly important food group who it had become something of a political exercise to honour. The restaurant itself was swathed in banners and flowers. Brass bands, local dignitaries and groups of school children all gathered to greet us, clapping and cheering. Going to the lavatory was a more hazardous affair than usual here, as the brass band would start up again, the minute anyone emerged from the dining room.

One particularly hot and steamy night in Chengdu as we dipped and swooped over hot pots laced with whole chillies at the China Gourmet World restaurant, families gathered outside, as if at a zoo. Mothers holding young children in pyjamas, waited patiently in the hope of getting a glimpse of us. The more beer we drank, the more snake we ate and the more we dripped with chilli-induced perspiration, the more fascinating we became to them. Flattered by the attention, we took to the streets and turned the night into a carnival of picture-taking, hand-shaking and baby-kissing.

Everywhere we went, we were swanned, ducked, pigged and chickened. We systematically demolished the artistically arranged plates of cold cuts. We fought chopstick duels to the death over the last crisp slice of suckling pig, the remaining slippery baby eel, the final finger of luscious, deep-fried soya bean cream. We sipped glasses of snake bile and snake blood mixed with pungent mao tai, tried seventeen different kinds of local beers, and drank all the tea in China.

Every town had its own special allure, like an animal and its scent. Beijing was big, bustling and businesslike with billboards advocating one family/one baby and street meetings publicising the government-sponsored 'respect women' campaign. Xian was as well-worn as its Entombed Warriors. Guangzhou was steamy and crowded while Shanghai was a cross-between Gotham City and the set from *Blade Runner*. Then there was Chengdu, with its laid-back lazy feel, and craggy, scraggy Guilin, a giant, living, breathing picture postcard.

But the most beautiful city of all was Hangzhou. With the impossibly poetic Westlake as its centrepiece, Hangzhou was full of sycamore trees, winding streets, and silk-strewn windows that summoned up images of the old, romantic China we all have locked away in our minds.

We visited places with hopelessly romantic names like 'Listening To Orioles Singing In The Willows' and 'Three Ponds Mirroring The Moon'. Jill was moved to write poetry, and I was moved to enjoy several glasses of Italian–Chinese joint venture wine called Vinitalia in the cocktail bar of the Hangzhou Shangri-La.

Most of our sightseeing was done around a dining table. There was a Peking Duck banquet in Beijing where we ate every part of the duck except the quack, and a twenty-course dumpling banquet in Xian, where we rolled out of the restaurant, proving beyond a doubt that you really are what you eat.

Then there was a remarkable twenty-four-course beancurd banquet at the Yulan Hotel in Xian, which included sunflower beancurd, lotus seed beancurd, red-boxed beancurd, chilli donkey with beancurd, grilled banjo beancurd, fish-fragrant beancurd, and three fairies beancurd soup.

We ate lizards, snakes, frogs, turtles, shark fin and jumping prawns.

But the banquet I will never forget took place in Beijing's venerable Long Hua Yao Shan herbal restaurant where everything we ate was good for something or other. I don't know what the first course of deep-fried scorpions complete with raised stingers was good for, but it certainly wasn't my heart. Eventually I got over the shock and managed to swallow the crunchy little critters. Now I figured, I could handle anything. Even overflowing spittoons.

Instead, all I had to handle was black ants clinging to sweet walnut paste balls, deer penis garnished with dried seahorses, bull testicles, pig stomach and snow fungus. Indiana Jones, eat your heart out. By the time dessert came, I was getting jumpy. 'Look!' I shrieked. 'It's all pink and fleshy, with yucky black things in it!'

'Relax', said my colleagues. 'It's watermelon.'

China was one continuous banquet, an endless succession of new tastes and textures, full of sweet surprises and savoury shocks.

So much has been lost or destroyed, yet so much remains. There are now ten colleges teaching a new generation of chefs old Imperial tricks and techniques once thought to have been lost forever.

But today, they have new emperors to please: the foreign tourist, the overseas Chinese, the Taiwanese and Hong Kong business communities.

'Well?' I said on our last night in China, as I packed her five new purple sand-clay tea pots in among the dozens of polished silk shirts and shorts she had found in Beijing. 'Now what do you think about China?' She looked up from the book she was reading and stretched out on the bed.

'The aeroplane didn't crash', she admitted.

'And the food?'

'Sensational', she said peeling a lychee, Mae West fashion, from a branch I had bought for her in the streets of Guangzhou.

'The hotels were terrible, I suppose?'

She smiled a dreamy smile. 'When I die, I want my body to be checked into a corner suite of the Shangri-La in Hangzhou.'

'And the toilets?'

'I'll hold on that one.'

'Well, it's time we left for the airport', I said, zipping up the suitcase, my head already filled with cravings for espresso coffee, farmhouse cheddar, fresh oysters and my own bed.

'I'm not going', she said, and popped another lychee into her mouth. 'I'm simply not going.'

Scallop and pork kidney

The Chinese are terribly annoying. Think of a dish, any dish, and they will have thought of it first, from noodles and toffee apples to the seemingly contemporary combination of surf and turf.

While this combination might sound like the Walter Matthau and Jack Lemmon of the food world, the coupling of these two lush ingredients is anything but odd.

    4 fresh pork kidneys
    500 grams (1 pound) scallops, white part only
    2 tablespoons peanut oil
    2 or 3 slices of fresh ginger
    2 garlic cloves, peeled and bruised
    ½ teaspoon sesame oil
    3 teaspoons soya sauce
    1 teaspoon sugar
    salt, to season
    I tablespoon Shao hsing Chinese rice wine
    ¼ cup (60 ml or 2 fluid ounces) chicken stock
    1 teaspoon cornflour
    1 tablespoon cold water
    2 spring onions, including stems, finely sliced

Skin the kidneys and split them in half lengthways. Cut around the core of white fat in each half, pulling it down carefully to remove completely. Score the curved surface of each kidney with light criss-cross cuts (don't cut right through the kidney), then cut the kidneys into strips, roughly measuring 2 cm (1 in) by 5 cm (2 in).

Wash the scallops and cut in half horizontally if they are on the large side.

Heat wok until hot, then add two tablespoons of the peanut oil, and reduce heat to moderate. Add ginger and garlic. Cook until golden, then remove. Add scallops and stirfry lightly for about a minute, just until they begin to change colour. Remove scallops and keep covered.

Add the remaining spoonful of peanut oil, plus the sesame oil, and stir-fry the kidneys for about two minutes. Add the soya sauce, sugar, salt, Shao hsing wine and stock, and return the scallops, with any juices, to the wok.

Mix the cornflour and cold water, and add to the mixture, and stir through briefly, just until the juices go glossy. Sprinkle with spring onions and serve immediately.

Serves 4.

yum.

San choy bau

What the spring roll was to the Chinese restaurants of the Seventies and Eighties, so this lettuce bun is to the Nineties. Well made, it is still nevertheless a gem of the Cantonese repertoire. For a special treat, use the more traditional pigeon instead of quail.

- 1 iceberg lettuce
- 2 tablespoons peanut oil
- 8 quail breasts, finely chopped
- 1 lup cheong sausage, steamed then chopped
- 4 dried Chinese mushrooms, soaked for 30 minutes, then chopped
- 8 water chestnuts, finely chopped
- 1 cup (125 grams or 4 ounces) bamboo shoots, finely chopped
- 2 spring onions, finely chopped
- salt and freshly ground black pepper
- 1 tablespoon Chinese rice wine or dry sherry
- 1 teaspoon light soya sauce
- 1 teaspoon oyster sauce
- 1 teaspoon cornflour
- 1 tablespoon cold water

Gently peel the leaves from the lettuce. Choose four cup-shaped ones, wash, dry, trim the edges with a pair of scissors and chill.

Heat the peanut oil in the wok until it is just smoking. Add the quail and stirfry vigorously for two minutes. Add the sausage, chopped mushrooms, water chestnuts, bamboo shoots, and spring onions and stirfry for another minute over a high heat. Add the salt, pepper, rice wine, soya sauce and oyster sauce, and stir through.

Mix the cornflour with the water and stir into the mixture. Raise the heat until the sauce thickens. Serve in a bowl so that everyone can spoon some quail mixture into their lettuce leaf, roll it up and eat it with their fingers.

Serves 4.

White cut chicken

I know of no other way of cooking a chicken as thoroughly satisfying as this. It is blindingly simple, yet, because the chicken steeps rather than simmers, the method somehow manages to extract the very essence of the bird. With a brilliant recipe like this, a nation has no need for feed-em-fast, take-away chicken chains.

- 1 chicken, about 1.5 kilograms (3 pounds)
- 2 spring onions, sliced
- 2 slices fresh ginger
- 1 tablespoon salt
- ¼ cup (60 ml or 2 fluid ounces) peanut oil, warmed in a pot and then cooled

Place the chicken in a pot just large enough to hold it snugly, and cover with cold water. Add spring onions, ginger and salt and bring to the boil. Simmer for five minutes, then turn chicken over and cook for a further five minutes. Cover the pot with a tight-fitting lid, and switch off the heat.

Allow the chicken to steep for about 40 minutes, without lifting the lid to see how it is going.

Lift out the chicken, rinse and dry with paper towels. Brush all over with peanut oil.

When cool, cut chicken into bite-sized pieces and arrange on a platter with a couple of little bowls of spring onion and ginger dip.

Serves 4.

Spring onion and ginger dip

- green stems from 1 bunch of spring onions
- 8 tablespoons peanut oil
- 2 tablespoons grated ginger
- 1 teaspoon of salt

Finely chop the green stems of spring onions. Gently warm the oil with ginger and salt, stirring, until the salt dissolves. Add spring onions and stir for a moment until they wilt and soften, then remove from the heat.

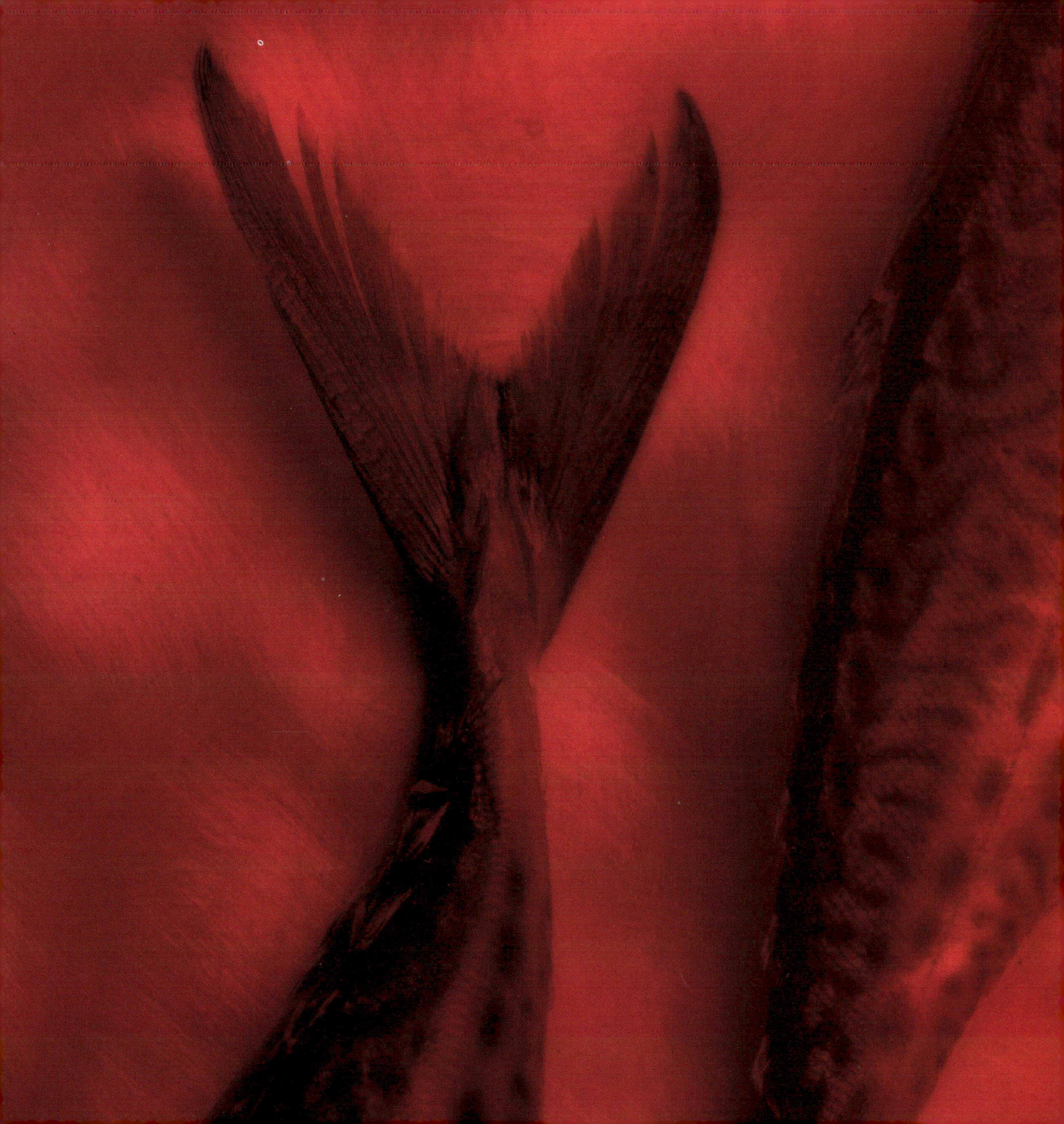

Fried hor fun rice noodles with beef

This is home-in-a-bowl for Cantonese families. You'll find packets of slippery, fresh, white, hor fun rice noodles in the refrigerator section of Asian food stores.

    500 grams (1 pound) rice sheet noodles
    200 grams (6½ ounces) lean beef, thinly sliced
    1 cup (125 grams or 4 ounces) bean shoots, rinsed
    2 slices of ginger, shredded
    2 spring onions, finely chopped
    5 tablespoons peanut or vegetable oil
    4 teaspoons light soya sauce
    1 teaspoon cornflour mixed with 1 tablespoon cold water
    1 teaspoon sugar
    2 tablespoons dark soya sauce

Cut the rice sheets into 1-cm (½-in) strips, like tagliatelle, if not already cut. Place in a heatproof bowl and pour boiling water on top until they are covered, shaking the strips apart with a pair of chopsticks. Drain immediately, cool under cold running water and set aside.

Heat the peanut oil in a wok, cook for two minutes, then cool. Mix two tablespoons of the oil with the beef, two tablespoons of light soya sauce and cornflour mixture and marinate for 30 minutes.

Mix sugar, dark soya sauce and remaining light soya sauce and set aside. Heat wok, add the remaining peanut oil. When hot, add the ginger and spring onion and cook for one minute before removing. Add the beef mixture and fry, stirring until it changes colour, about one minute. Add the bean shoots to the wok and fry for a further minute. Lift out and set aside.

Quickly add drained noodles, with a little more oil if needed, and stirfry for two minutes. Add sugar and soya sauces, and stir well. Return beef to the wok and stir, mixing thoroughly.
Serves 4.

Eight treasure duck

And you thought the galantine was a French invention. While this dish takes a fair amount of work, you are rewarded many times over with the sheer amazement in the eyes of your dinner guests as you blithely cut right through the 'whole' duck, effortlessly dividing it into nice, thick slices.

- 1 cup (185 grams or 6 ounces) glutinous or short-grain rice, soaked in cold water for 2 hours, then drained
- 6 dried Chinese mushrooms
- 30 grams (1 ounce) dried Chinese shrimps
- 1 duck, approximately 1.5 kilograms (3 pounds), boned
- salt to taste
- 2 tablespoons peanut oil
- 220 grams (7 ounces) minced pork
- 1 tablespoon Shao hsing rice wine or dry sherry
- 2 tablespoons soya sauce
- 2 tablespoons water chestnuts, coarsely chopped
- 2 tablespoons Chinese roast pork (char sieu), finely diced
- 60 grams (2 ounces) gingko nuts or white nuts
- 1 x 440-gram (14-ounce) can of whole water chestnuts in water

Heat the oven to 220°C (425°F).

Transfer the rice to a steamer lined with greaseproof paper and steam for 30 to 40 minutes.

Soak the mushrooms and shrimps in hot water for an hour, then drain. Discard the stems from the mushrooms and slice into thin strips.

Rub the inside of the duck with salt and leave for 30 minutes, as you prepare the filling.

Heat the wok until hot, and add the oil. Stirfry the minced pork for a few minutes, until it colours. Add the wine and soya sauce, stirring, then the mushrooms, water chestnuts, rice, roast pork, gingko nuts and drained shrimps. Toss to mix thoroughly, cooking for a few minutes more.

Now carefully spoon in the chestnuts and a little of their water, and cool. Prepare the trussing needle and string. Sew up the neck opening, stuff the duck loosely moulding it into the shape of a whole duck, then sew up the tail opening.

Place it breast-side up, on a lightly oiled rack set over a roasting tin half-filled with water. Roast for 30 minutes, then reduce heat to 180°C (350°F) for one hour.

Carve at the table, cutting directly across the 'whole' duck shape for extra dramatic effect.

Serves 6.

Lion's head meat balls

This is Shanghai's answer to the hamburger: subtle, soft, silky pork dumplings bathed in stock, and cloaked with a 'mane' of cabbage.

100 grams (3½ ounces) bean-thread (transparent) vermicelli noodles
6 dried Chinese mushrooms
600 grams (1¼ pounds) minced pork
50 grams (2 ounces) water chestnuts
1 egg white
3 spring onions, chopped
2 slices ginger, finely chopped
1 tablespoon cornflour
1 tablespoon Shao hsing rice wine or dry sherry
salt
2 tablespoons peanut oil
6 small bok choi cabbages
1 dessertspoon soya sauce
3 cups (750 ml or 24 fluid ounces) chicken stock, heated

Pour boiling water over the noodles and leave for one minute to soften. Drain, cover with plastic wrap and reserve. Soak the mushrooms in hot water for one hour, remove the stems and slice each cap in half.

Place the pork, water chestnuts, egg white, spring onions, ginger, cornflour, wine and salt in the food processor and blend until smooth.

Shape the mixture by hand into large meat balls, then roll in a little extra cornflour. Heat the oil and fry the meat balls until well browned.

Clean the cabbages and cut into quarters lengthwise.

Add half the cabbage, mushrooms, noodles, soya sauce and chicken stock to the meat balls in a clay pot or covered flame-proof casserole, and bring to boil. Cover, reduce the heat and cook gently for 45 minutes. Add the remaining cabbage and cook for another ten minutes. Serve the meat balls with the cabbage forming the 'manes'.

Serves 4.

Yum! Something

smells terrible

'What on earth is that smell?' The woman at the newsagent cash register was wrinkling her nose like a squashed tissue. The man beside me sniffed the air with a serious, puzzled expression.

Then he sniffed the magazine he was holding. Finally, he checked the soles of both shoes. I couldn't smell a thing, but I checked the soles of my own shoes. It seemed to be the thing to do.

I left them concluding that the mysterious, vile smell must have either come from the workmen in the street hitting a rotten gas pipeline, or a free inserted perfume sample in one of those power-broking women's magazines.

I had neither the time nor the energy for detective work. I was tired, I was hungry, and as Leonard Cohen so succinctly put it, my body was aching in all the places I used to play. I had just put in a twelve-hour non-stop, back-breaking day working in the kitchens of a large city restaurant. It was one of the few times in my life I wanted to go home for dinner, rather than out to a restaurant.

Just as my key slipped in the lock, Jill opened the door with a strange grimace on her face.

'What on earth is that smell?'

'I think it's coming from the newsagent', I replied.

She looked at me curiously, then her expression changed to something that could only be called aghast.

'It's you!'

'Tis not.'

'What have you been doing today?'

'Oh not much. Washed 600 plates. De-bearded 55 kilos of mussels. Opened 100 dozen oysters. Peeled 420 garlic cloves...'

'Garlic!' she hissed, drawing herself up to her full Amazonian height. Her body fell naturally into a Joan of Arc stance as she pointed to the bathroom.

'Go. And do not use the good towels.'

Within minutes, the bath was transformed into a giant, aromatic tub of bagna cauda. I went straight to bed after that, feeling like an outcast from society.

The next morning, I was informed that being in bed with me was like sleeping with a large slice of Tuscan bruschetta, and that she had dreamt of garlic-scented chicken all night. I couldn't see a problem in any of that, but knew enough to keep my mouth shut.

I also knew enough to drop off the laundry, even though it was her turn. I deposited a few garlic-scented clothes and garlic-scented towels into the laundry bag, along with the garlic-scented sheets and pillowslips. Then I replaced the garlic-scented soap in the shower, and wondered vaguely whether there was anything one could do about a garlic-scented hairbrush.

'What on earth is that smell?'

I suppose I should have expected it. Joan, the all-powerful keeper of the laundry, had her nose in the wind like a red setter.

Okay, I admit it. Garlic has a delicate, lingering quality that lasts long after lesser vegetables have faded away.

In fact, one merely needs to rub the soles of one's feet with it in order to make one's breath reek, so powerful are its suffusive qualities.

Yet garlic has survived a long history of being reviled and abhorred. Hindus banned the stuff, while the Roman poet Horace blamed garlic for his illness after a particularly heavy meal, pronouncing it worse than hemlock. The Spanish Queen, Isabella the Catholic, not only detested garlic, but refused to eat parsley because it grew too close to the garlic patch. Fellow Spanish alliaphobe, King Alfonso XI, founded a knightly order in 1330 that forbade its members to eat the odious bulb.

In ancient Greece, certain temples were made out of bounds to anybody smelling of garlic, something that would be difficult to police in modern Greece.

But when it came to despising garlic, nobody came near the English, as witnessed by this letter written by Percy Bysshe Shelley to a close friend:

'There are two Italies', he wrote. 'The one is the most sublime and lovely contemplation of man; the other is the most degraded, disgusting and odious. What do you think? Young women of rank actually eat — you will never guess what — garlick! Our poor friend Lord Byron is quite corrupted by living amongst these people.'

A survey in the *San Francisco Chronicle* showed that America's most hated odour was garlic, followed by lard and frying oil. And it wasn't that long ago that the statute books in Gary, Indiana, carried a law that forbade anyone from taking a street car or going to the theatre within four hours of eating the accused.

What has garlic ever done, to deserve such bitter enmity and fear? With its innocent fragrance and subtle flavour, it should be our best, most intimate kitchen friend, not treated like a silent-but-deadly smelling stranger.

Not that this member of the allium family has any shortage of allies. Don't bother picking up an Elizabeth David cookbook without first having a head on the chopping block.

The late James Beard admitted that he could never have enough of garlic's honest flavour, while Eleanor Roosevelt attributed her super memory and energy to exercise, vitamins, and the three chocolate-coated garlic tablets she took every day.

Writer and gastronome Marcel Boulestin claimed that peace and happiness began wherever garlic is used in cooking. Louis Diat, the creator of crème Vichyssoise, went even further. 'Garlic is the fifth element, as important to our existence as earth, air, fire and water', he wrote. 'Without garlic, I would simply not care to live.'

In ancient Egypt, the workers on the pyramids were so fond of their garlic, that when rations were cut, they staged the world's first-recorded strike.

Another big stink was created when a group of New York residents tried to have a local restaurant closed because they found the smell of garlic wafting from it to be offensive. The judge threw the case out of court, ruling that the odour was beneficial to civilisation. Justice may be blind, but at least it has a keen sense of smell.

In fact, *Allium sativum* is as close to a miracle food as we will ever get, with a rich history of curing practically everything that has ever ailed mankind.

Those garlic-mad ancient Egyptians invented the first home pregnancy test, by inserting a garlic clove in the woman's womb. If her breath smelt of garlic in the morning, she was pregnant. Modern medical science should probably get onto this one, although I'm not sure how many takers there would be.

In the Middle East, a clove of garlic

worn in the lapel of a bride groom ensured a happy wedding night.

Spanish bullfighters carried garlic to prevent the bull from charging them, and Mediterranean sailors believed it could avert shipwrecks. Many civilisations still hang garlic in windows to guard against evil forces, and place it under the pillows of new-born children as protection, while no self-respecting Transylvanian vampire slayer would ever be seen dead without a good-sized bulb of garlic.

Old wives' tales are now backed by modern medicine and science. The sulphur compounds that are responsible for garlic's distinctive aroma also possess the ability to reduce bacteria and fungi. Contemporary research is also investigating the use of garlic for lowering blood cholesterol, dilating the arteries, and treating intestinal disorders.

Chinese research suggests that garlic may play an important role in lowering the incidence of bowel cancer, while Yoshio Kato's Oyama garlic clinic in Amagasaki in Japan is continually testing garlic remedies for just about everything from hepatitis to frostbite.

From my own personal research, I can quite positively attest to the fact that garlic can stimulate the appetite, relieve boredom, and fire the imagination.

Take a freshly grilled slice of country-style bread, brush it with olive oil and rub it with a garlic clove, and you have humble perfection.

Make a rich aioli of garlic, eggs and olive oil, and you have an elixir as powerful as any pharmaceutical concoction, capable of transforming a humble fish soup into a meal fit for the gods.

Seal a corn-fed chicken and forty unpeeled garlic cloves in a terracotta baking dish with a few herbs and vegetables and a splash of wine, and you have a magnificent, aromatic Provençal dish that sustains and inspires at the same time.

For me however, the top of the garlic pops is without a doubt spaghetti aglio e olio con peperoncino. Here, garlic is not just a foreign accent, but the body, heart and soul of the dish, infusing the oil, mingling with the heat of the chilli, and penetrating into the very core of the pasta. I cook it often for myself, but am a little shy of foisting it upon strangers.

The eating of garlic with others demands a certain intimacy and understanding. It is a bonding kind of thing, as intensely personal as sharing a bathroom. If you do not know the other well, it is an investment in the future of the relationship that carries risk as well as reward.

Knowing all this, I still chose to cook it for some new friends recently. I set out the finest olive oil, the most artisan-produced durum wheat pasta, the fieriest chillies, the freshest, plumpest heads of garlic. I chilled wine, picked my most prized green leaves from the garden, and turned out sweet little apple tarts for dessert.

Then, that night, as I could hear my guests coming down the corridor to the dining room, I surveyed the scene and judged it appropriately simple, sophisticated and stylish.

That's when the first guest walked into the room and kissed me on both cheeks.

Drawing back a little, a tiny crease formed between two delicately arched eyebrows.

'What on earth is that smell?'

Aioli

Forget lavender. Aioli is the true breath of Provence. A gorgeously garlicky mayonnaise it is simply waiting for a bouillabaisse, a plate of freshly cooked asparagus, or a bowl of just boiled potatoes to come along.

    4 garlic cloves, peeled and crushed
    2 egg yolks
    salt to taste
    2 tablespoons lemon juice to taste
    1 cup (250 ml or 8 fluid ounces) olive oil

Blend the garlic, egg yolks and salt together in blender until smooth. Add half of the lemon juice and mix in. With the motor running, add olive oil very slowly, teaspoonful by teaspoonful. Once you have incorporated half the olive oil, add some more of the lemon juice. Continue adding olive oil by the tablespoon. Taste for lemon juice and salt. If too thick, just add a little warm water.

Spaghetti aglio e olio con peperoncino

Welcome to spaghetti heaven, tossed with garlic, oil and chilli. This is both a great dish to get drunk with and a great hangover cure.

> 100 grams (3½ ounces) spaghetti per person
> salt
> 3 tablespoons extra virgin olive oil
> 2 garlic cloves, peeled
> 1 red chilli, chopped
> 1 tablespoon chopped parsley

Cook the spaghetti in plenty of boiling, salted water until al dente, so it is tender but still firm to the bite. Meanwhile, heat the oil in a heavy pan, add the garlic and chilli and warm gently, allowing them to infuse the oil.

Drain the spaghetti thoroughly and pile into a warmed serving dish. Pour the garlic and chilli oil over the spaghetti. Add parsley, toss quickly and serve.

Serves 4.

Italian potatoes with garlic and rosemary

A fantastic accompaniment to a simple roast chicken, although they taste so fabulous, I have been known to forget the chicken.

> 4 red-skinned potatoes, peeled
> 6 garlic cloves, left unpeeled
> 3 stalks of fresh rosemary
> 1 tbsp extra virgin olive oil
> sea salt

Heat the oven to 180°C (350°F). Chop the potatoes into cubes about the size of a thumbnail. Pour the olive oil into a roasting pan, add potatoes, garlic and salt. Strip the rosemary stalks of their leaves and toss with potatoes until well-coated. Bake for 40 minutes, shaking pan occasionally, until potatoes are golden brown and garlic is soft.

Serve with sprigs of fresh rosemary.
Serves 4.

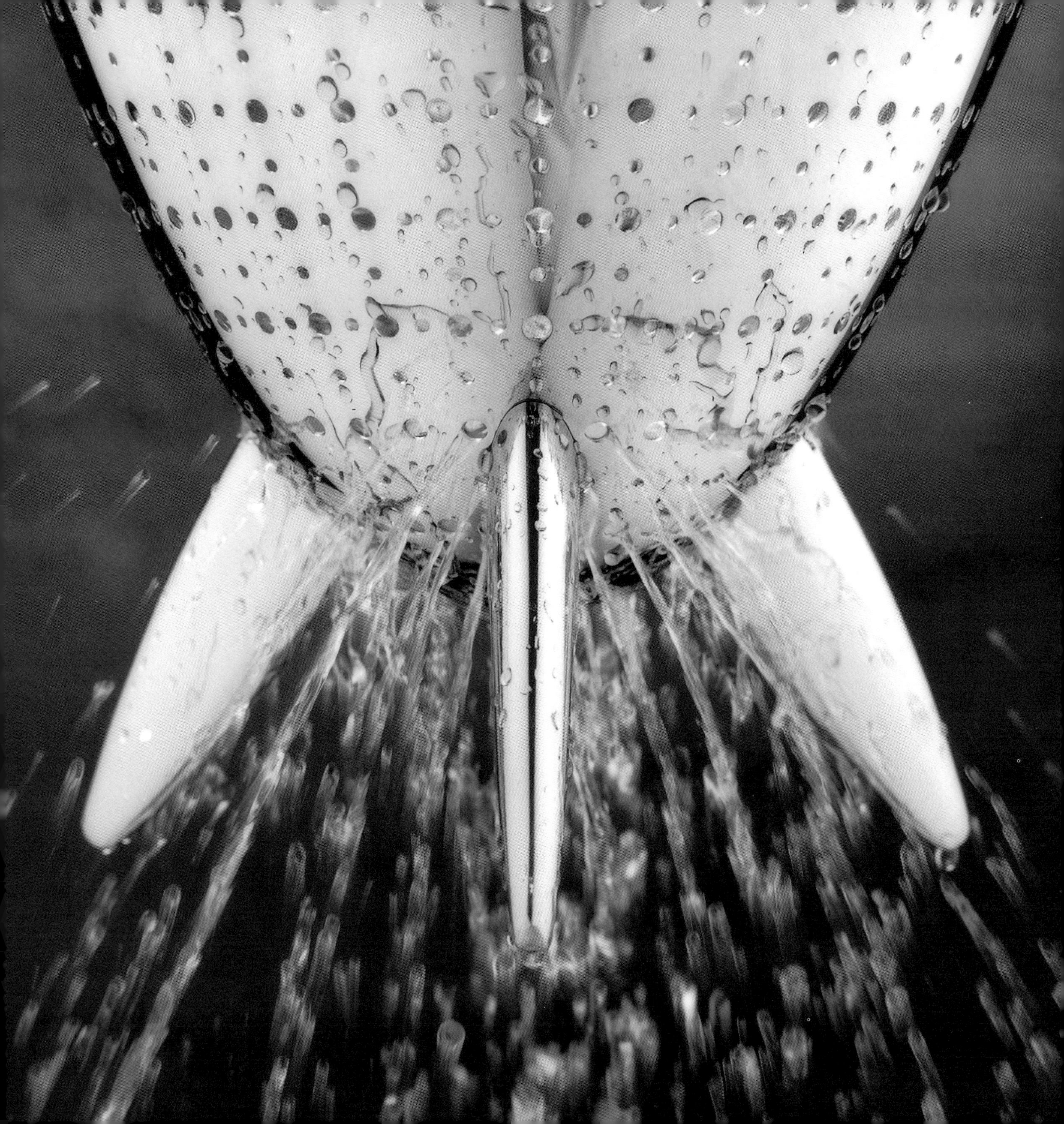

Fashion plates

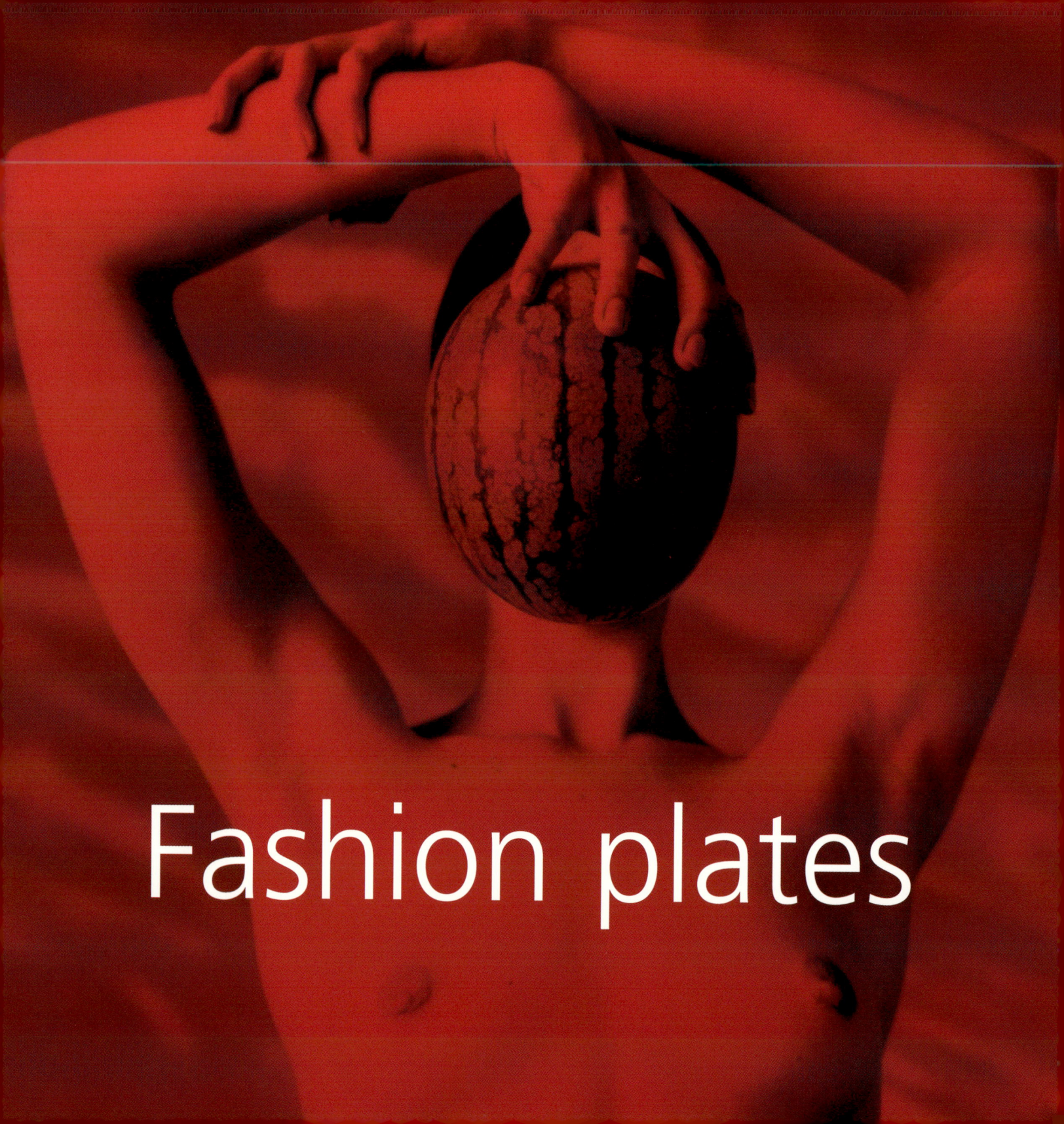

We're talking loose and floaty.

We're talking earthy colours.

We're talking free and easy.

We're talking spiritual.

We're talking romantic.

We're talking real.

We're talking now.

We're talking *lunch*.

The days of eating something simply because you were hungry are long gone. Food is now fashion, and the restaurants, the cookbooks, the magazines, the food writers and the designer chefs aren't going to let us forget it for a minute.

Our food now defines us, sustaining our image first, and our body second. If you are so un-now as to be seen in public tucking into deep-fried camembert and tournedos Rossini, it's as plain as a white tee that you have nothing of value to contribute to today's society.

Food, like fashion, regenerates itself season by season in a process that inspires the spirit, the mind and the soul, touching our lives with beauty and wit and fulfilling our fundamental human need for change.

Just when we've had it up to here with asparagus, along comes broccoli to relieve the boredom. Colours come in and out of favour, as last year's black squid ink pasta and black Sambuca cleave unto this year's olive, mushroom and chestnut.

When Thai food was hot, we lauded our hosts on their ever-so-clever tom yam soups until our mouths blistered. Women who two months earlier couldn't stand even their coffees hot were suddenly packing a little stash of white-hot nam prik chillies in their Prada carry-alls in case of emergencies. Then we became obsessed with finger food. First came antipasto, then Greek mezes, then Spanish tapas. These were the days you could pick up whole cutlery sets for a song.

Cajun came next, dragged out of the bayou into smart, uptown eateries. Suddenly we could have any fish we liked, as long it was blackened.

Then there was Cal-Ital-Pac-Rim, and Mod-Med-Tex-Mex, East-Meets-West, North-Meets-South, and Afro-Cuban-Meets-Ethnic-Metro.

It has always been so. Catherine de Medici caused a veritable fashion furore by introducing the concept of icecream into France in the sixteenth century. No French restaurant today, be it in Antibes or Africa would open its doors without a sorbet or glacé on the menu. Anna, Duchess of Bedford, did the same thing for tea at a house party in 1840 when she came up with the novel idea of accompanying the newly fashionable beverage from China with little cakes and sandwiches.

The latest trend, of course, is retro.

We've had the oysters kilpatrick of the Fifties, the chicken paprika of the Sixties, and the steak Diane of the Seventies, and now we're having them again.

One savvy chef reports that his sour cream paprika is putting more bums on seats than his guinea fowl with pea purée and seared sweetbreads.

So the pattern has been set. We gobble up food trends by the large, white Ginori plateful, only to be left waiting hungrily for the next season, the next prediction, and the next gastronomic wave.

We have our classics, of course. The pizza base is our white tee shirt. Pasta is the denim jean of the kitchen, to dress up or down as you wish. Salmon is our silk, lamb is our linen, and caviar is our cashmere.

With food, as with other, flightier worlds, God is in the accessories.

Sun-dried tomatoes, baby Ligurian olives, char-grilled artichokes, pesto and verdant green olive oil, are our shoes, hats and handbags.

If dedicated fashion watchers want to know what's next, they need only go to lunch and look at their plates. We had the peasant look, with hearty cassoulets and daubes, long before Lacroix played with dirndl. East met West in the kitchen long before Miyaki, Yamamoto and Commes des Garçons fused them on the catwalk. And foodies went through their waif stage in the early Eighties, only then it was called Cuisine Minceur.

Now, in much the same way that the American push of Karan, Lauren and The Gap took haute couture by the scruff of its pin-tucked, silk-lined neck and made it wearable, usable and affordable, the young chefs of today are leaving Escoffier behind, tossing out the elaborate edifices and rich cream sauces, picking up the olive oil bottle and throwing everything on the grill. Their food is eatable, usable and affordable.

There are good trends, like the current ones towards bistro simplicity and our almost puritan need for essential, edited flavours; and there are bad trends, like taking a perfectly good local pub and turning it into a pink-neon rock'n'roll pasta deli.

The increased fragility of our environment has led us to seek out and pay extra for free-range eggs, range-fed beef, and organically fed ducks, but has also sanctioned the environmentally correct diner, who can't have the tuna because of driftnet fishing, the chicken because of battery-rearing, the bunya nuts because of imperialist attitudes towards Aboriginal land rights, or the beef because of the effect of hard hooves on the topsoil and its subsequent contribution to the earth salinity problem.

There is, sadly, another group whose unhappy lives reveal the intimacy of the bond between food and fashion; those who make themselves desperately ill in their efforts to be slim, and therefore, they believe, attractive.

Haute couture and prêt-a-porter have always been mirrored by haute cuisine and ready-to-eat, the equivalents being just as elitist and inaccessible, or just as popular and directional.

The very smart now invest in one or two fine pieces each season, supplementing them from the more accessible racks. In the same way, we dine out in restaurants as special occasions, and the new, casual breed of café and bistro more often. Our butchers sell marinated meats, fish shops plait fish and greengrocers toss salads to make their food more attractive, more usable, more *wearable*.

The thing to remember is that fashions are just that: fashions. Some of them are slowly shaping and directing the way we eat, while others will be digested momentarily and just as quickly expelled. Just as there are still a lot of shoulder-pads, distressed jeans, boob tubes, and bolero jackets out there, Mum, Dad, Jason and Kylie aren't starting with jellied cocktails and going on to noisettes of lamb in a jus scented with olive tapenade. They're starting with a slice of bread and butter and going on to grilled lamb chops, mashed potatoes and peas.

The other worrisome trend is that some very valuable information is being demeaned by being labelled as a trend, dooming it to a short and sharp life span instead of a long and healthy one. Will we have time, for instance, to absorb and inwardly digest the real health benefits of the traditional Mediterranean diet before everyone groans about how 'Medded-out' they are? How do we ensure it becomes a part of our lives, like the legacy of Coco Chanel, rather than the puffball skirt of Lacroix?

   I mean, we're talking healthy, here.
   We're talking down home country.
   We're talking Rockwellian.
   We're talking pagan, if not feral.
   We're talking real food for real people, at real prices.
   We're talking now.

Recipe

There was going to be a recipe on this page, but by the time the book got to the printers, it was already out of fashion.

Eat my words

'Thursday was good.'

'Really?'

'Very good. Not many bookings, but then people just kept showing up all night.'

'Well, that's good.'

'In fact, it was good from Thursday through to Saturday. Packed solid. Two sittings on Friday night.'

'Two sittings? That's great.'

'Makes up for Monday. Not a whisker.'

'Oh well, maybe it's got something to do with the weather.'

'Then Tuesday you couldn't move.'

'Well, maybe it's got something to do with the economy.'

'But Thursday…boy, that was a real surprise packet.'

'Funny how things happen. Um, do you think we could have a look at the menu?'

If you ever need to know the most intimate details of restaurant traffic and its myriad of influences from school holidays to road works, I'm your man.

I can tell you the inner workings of a dishwasher, the price of an industrial-strength slicer, the vagaries of town councils, the wholesale cost of orange roughy, and the difficulty of finding good staff. Not because I'm a restaurateur, but because I'm a restaurant critic.

Restaurateurs tell me things they wouldn't dream of telling their mothers, partners, accountants — especially not their accountants — and town planning officers.

Half the time I don't know whether to tell them to do three hail Marys and an act of penance — like seeing twelve wine reps in one morning — or just nod politely, and hope my companion isn't ravenous enough to be too rude to them.

Restaurant critics do for a living what normal people do for fun. And I've never once stopped having fun.

Over the last ten years alone, I reckon I have eaten out 3,640 times. That's 3,640 times looking for a car spot; 3,640 times being told that the soup of the day is pumpkin and the fish is blue-eye cod; 3,640 times waiting for the bill; and 3,640 times trying to work out what ten per cent of the total comes to while the brain is still savouring the last honeyed tones of a particularly fine botrytis.

And no, I never get bored with it, or dread going out, even though I eat very well at home. Occasionally, things have been known to get me down, like the seventh ordinary meal in a row, or being threatened within an inch of my life by an irate restaurateur, but it's never been enough to make me lose my appetite.

The restaurant critic has a far more important role to play than just advising as to where one may avoid contracting food poisoning. A good critic can enthuse, inform and inspire diners, making them not only want to look for something better, but giving them the necessary powers to recognise it when they finally get it.

The country that has an informed, aware and critical dining public is a country with great restaurants. The more people know, the more they care. The more they care, the more they dictate the quality they want, and the standards they expect. Competition gets tougher, and the eating establishments have to lift their game. In this environment, chefs, restaurateurs and even whole cities can develop their own style. Everyone wins.

So in the interests of making my already enlightened readers even finer diners, I want to share a few of my thoughts and prejudices, best summed up in the line 'and She Who Must Be Obeyed pronounced the dish very tasty'.

These words are the deep-fried camembert and oysters mornay of food criticism. Over the years we have been subjected to a plague of so-called critics who insist on referring to their dining partners in coy terms or by pet names, the more twee and sexist the better. Said dining companions never speak, comment, opine or suggest, but always, inevitably, pronounce.

In the same way, food is rarely delicious, scrummy, rich, tart, bitter, sweet, delicate, spicy, luscious, juicy, succulent, piquant, tangy, pungent, creamy, or over-salted, but always tasty.

Sorry, but the only time the word tasty should ever be used is when one is talking about the opposite sex.

Anyone wishing to be a restaurant critic should be able to distinguish couscous from bulgur, beef from pork, Chardonnay from Semillon, and fawning obeisances from attentive and efficient service. They should have an open mind, an open mouth, an open cheque book — it pays to be financially independent to keep up your own food education and knowledge — a vast knowledge of cooking, an invincible palate memory, boundless curiosity for and a healthy awareness of different cuisines and cultures, and the one thing money can't buy: an absolutely fabulous digestive system.

In an age where more and more people are eating Asian food when they go out, it also helps to be on good eating terms with Vietnamese pho soup, Thai tom yam goong and Chinese hot and sour, as well as French onion and minestrone.

Though critical, I see the role of the restaurant critic as being very positive. It's like your best friend telling you that you have bad breath, or putting you onto the one dandruff shampoo that works. Who else is going to tell you?

My personal charter as a critic includes banning the mouth-numbing sorbet as a between-course palate cleanser, making illegal the reheating of bread rolls until they shatter into shell grit, and encouraging local Chinese restaurants to produce authentic regional Chinese dishes instead of homeless hybrids. I also hate butter that has gone rancid (one in four tables), my wineglass being filled to the brim by waiters hovering like blowflies at my shoulder, and pre-grated Parmigiano cheese.

It has always been a great job, and even used to be a cushy one, until these new twisted timber, three-legged slippery-dip chairs came into vogue. Now, my chiropractor can eat out on my monthly payments.

Okay, okay, you get to ask the questions now. I know you have some. They are the same as I always get asked on my morning jog, or when I whizz into the men's loo for ten seconds.

Yes, I always book under an assumed

name. Even if I am recognised at the door as I turn up, it means I have still undergone the same telephone treatment and table allocation as any Mr Armstrong or McGregor.

Armstrong and McGregor are the names of streets in my suburb, as are Fraser and Langridge. I use them constantly, although I have been known to forget under which one I have booked. Then there is that time halfway through the evening, when someone slides up to the table and murmurs 'is everything all right, Mr Armstrong', at which point I usually get kicked from the other side of the table, and I finally realise I am Mr Armstrong, with a sore shin.

Yes, I disguise myself when I dine out, like Gael Greene of *New York* magazine, who always wears large hats to avoid being photographed, and former *New York Times* reviewer Bryan Miller, who refused to be photographed at all, and who paid for his meals with a credit card in his wife's maiden name, to avoid being sprung.

I tend to dine out as an extremely tall man with unruly hair and a fierce set of eyebrows, a disguise which has served me well in some of the finest establishments in the country.

Yes, I am aware that when I am known, I am often given preferential treatment, larger entrées, and better wine service. I can easily tell this when my entrée of ten bouncing fresh prawns carefully arranged in neatly concentric circles and spiked with a feathery dash of dill, is ordered by the next table, where it arrives as three scrawny prawns dropped onto the plate from a great height. Naturally, I try to review the plate at the next table.

No, I don't like to write about bad restaurants. I assume my readers would rather find out where to go, than where not to go. On occasion, however, I do write about appalling meals, where I have felt the diner is in danger of being put off dining by what was going on in the kitchen.

And yes, it is better than working for a living.

And no, you can't have my job.

Just as good diners begat better restaurants, good readers beget better restaurant critics. Be as tough and as fair on your critics as they are on restaurants. Monitor their consistency, and the quality of the information they communicate, which is far more important than their actual judgement. Find a critic you can stand, and you will be able to dine out vicariously together for years.

I recently received a letter from an elderly woman who has been on the pension for many years. In it, she explained that she rarely went out, because of lack of funds, but thanks to my reviews, she felt as if she had dined like royalty in some of the best restaurants in town.

It made my day. But then, Thursdays are always good. Fridays are generally better, except for last week. And have I mentioned Monday?

Sichuan hot and sour soup

I have never eaten anything in Sichuan that didn't have a lot of chilli and a lot of Sichuan pepper. I should also add that I have never eaten anything in Sichuan that wasn't totally delicious. The secret of this peppery soup is the addictive Sichuan pepper, which you can find in Asian food stores. Or buy some under the counter at any good Sichuan restaurant.

- 1.5 litres (2½ pints) stock
- 100 grams (3½ ounces) lean, boneless pork, cut into matchstick strips
- 3 tablespoons bamboo shoots, cut into fine matchsticks
- 1 slice fresh ginger, cut into fine matchsticks
- 1 teaspoon salt
- 1 tablespoon soya sauce
- 4 dried Chinese mushrooms, soaked and cut into thin strips
- 2 squares fresh beancurd, cut into shreds
- ¼ teaspoon white pepper
- 1 teaspoon sugar
- 2 tablespoons white vinegar
- 1½ tablespoons cornflour, mixed with a little water
- 2 eggs, beaten
- 1 teaspoon sesame oil
- 1 teaspoon freshly ground Sichuan pepper
- 1 tablespoon chopped coriander

Bring the stock to the boil, then add the pork, bamboo shoots, ginger, salt, soya sauce and mushrooms. Reduce the heat and simmer for about three minutes. Add the beancurd, pepper, sugar and vinegar, and bring to the boil again. Stir the cornflour mixture well, then slowly add to the soup, stirring well. Pour in the beaten egg in a thin steady stream, again stirring as you go.

Pour soup in a serving bowl, adding sesame oil, ground Sichuan pepper to taste, and coriander.

Serves 4.

yum

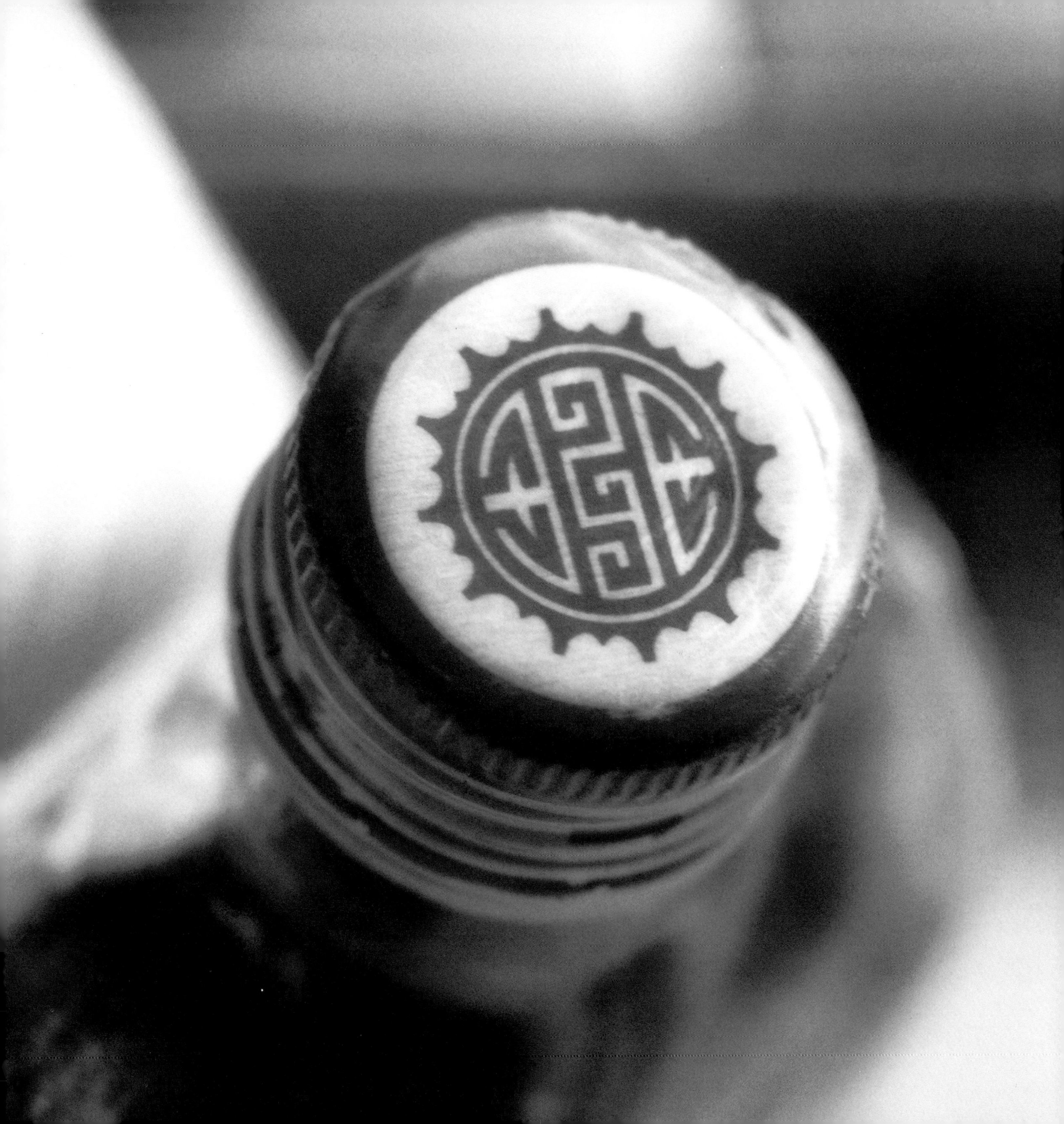

Pho ga

This is soup as life, and life as soup. In Vietnam, this steaming bowl of life-enhancing noodles and broth, with its barrage of fresh herbs and trusty sidekick of pungent chilli and fish sauce can serve either as breakfast, lunch, a tide-me-over, or a social lubricant as effective and as bonding as any alcohol. If soup is fuel, then this is super, not standard.

The classic version is beef broth (pho bo), but I love pho ga, layered with tender chicken breast, golden fried shallots, and curls of spring onion. Fresh rice noodles are easily available in Asian food stores, variously called pho, kuay teow, or hor fun.

3 litres (5 pints) water
1 teaspoon salt
1 whole chicken, preferably with head and feet
1 kilogram (2 pounds) chicken bones
2 white onions, finely sliced
5-cm (2-in) knob of fresh ginger, peeled and sliced
1 cinnamon stick
1 star anise
2 teaspoons white sugar
2 tablespoons fried shallots
3 tablespoons fish sauce
400 grams fresh rice noodles
extra fried shallots for garnish
4 spring onions, finely sliced

Combine water, salt, whole chicken, bones, one of the sliced onions, ginger and spices in a large pot and bring to the boil. Skim off any froth that rises to the surface, then lower heat and cook for 45 minutes. Remove chicken and allow to cool slightly. Carve off the breasts and legs and return chicken carcass to the soup. Add sugar and cook gently for one and a half hours, skimming occasionally. Add fried shallots and fish sauce and cook for an extra half an hour. Strain stock through a fine sieve.

Cut the chicken leg and breast meat into fine slices. Cut the rice noodles (if not pre-cut) into 1-cm (½-in) strips like tagliatelle. Place in a heatproof bowl, cover with boiling water, separate with a fork, and drain.

To assemble the soup, divide the rice noodles among four deep soup bowls. Layer chicken meat neatly on top, and spoon hot soup into each bowl. Sprinkle with fried shallots and spring onions. Serve with an accompanying platter of bean shoots, quartered lemons or limes, chopped fresh red chilli, sweet Asian basil and coriander, for each person to add according to their taste.

Serves 6.

Tom yam goong

With the universal popularity of Thai food, this soup has probably been ruined by more cooks in more countries than any other dish you'd care to name. Treated with respect it is a wonderful thing, all lightness and depth and good-time smells. It works just as well with scampi, and is a dream with lobster or crab.

> 500 grams (1 pound) fresh prawns peeled, with shells and heads reserved
> 1½ tablespoons peanut oil
> 2 litres (3½ pints) chicken stock
> 1 teaspoon kaffir lime peel, shredded
> 2 stalks lemongrass, white part only, finely sliced
> 3 kaffir lime leaves
> 3 fresh red chillies, sliced
> 12 straw mushrooms
> 12 abalone mushrooms
> 2 tablespoons fish sauce
> 3 tablespoons lime juice
> 3 tablespoons coriander leaves, coarsely chopped

Sauté the prawn heads and tails in the oil in a large saucepan for about four minutes, tossing all the time. Pour in the stock, lime peel, lemongrass, lime leaves and two of the chilllies and simmer for 15 minutes. Strain. Add remaining chilli, straw mushrooms, abalone mushrooms and fish sauce and simmer for two or three minutes. Add prawns and cook just until they change colour, about a minute. Remove from heat, add lime juice and coriander leaves.
    Serves 4 to 6.

CASPIAN CAVIAR
ASTRAKHAN
BALYK CORPORATION

The best things in life aren't free

The grey-gold grains of oscietra caviar gleam in the sunlight as the golden Petrossian paddle lifts them gently out of the ice sculpture and onto her hot blini.

The soft tinkle of the Krug bottle as it returns to the icy comfort of the Baccarat crystal champagne bucket creates a musical backdrop to what is clearly a perfect afternoon.

Yet I am uneasy. The task that lies ahead of me is not a pleasant one, but it has to be done. I had been reading a book that strongly advised spending less money on food and wine, and more on paying off the mortgage. It was our bank book.

I take a bracing sip of Krug and catch her slender wrist as the next blini-load is being lifted to her lips.

'Oh, to be a peasant', I cry.

Her eyes, ready to be amused, meet mine, then narrow in disbelief as I upturn my glass, tipping my Krug onto the Italian tiles.

'To stop work at midday and take a well-earned rest under the shade of a noble tree. To dip a crust of bread into your wine, and carve off a hunk of hard, honest cheese, instead of toying with noisettes of corn-fed lamb in burgundy-infused jus with shredded mignonette and crushed hazelnut salad dressed in sherry vinegar and a dialogue of vegetable purées.'

I push my caviar plate away from me. 'And at night! Ah, the night! Coming home to the big pot of soup that has been bubbling away all day!'

There is something about noble peasantry that makes me want to talk in exclamation marks. There is also something about it that makes her drain her glass and go off in search of headache tablets.

I know she'll come round to the idea eventually. After all, she has eaten humble peasant food once or twice over the years. There was that boudin noir, for instance, at the three-starred Côtes Saint Jacques in Burgundy, that came after the foie gras and before the salmon. And there was the mashed potato she had at Joel Robuchon, the liver and onions at Harry's Bar in Venice, and the veal kidneys at Taillevent in Paris.

But I have her measure. I shall create the ultimate peasant dinner at home. It will be the epitome of all that is good and honourable and satisfying about real, old-fashioned food. It will show her the error of her profligate ways, and convince her to tighten her Nicole Farhi belt.

I rack my brains for the right dish. Brains? No. Minestrone? Perhaps. Risotto? No. She would only cover it with shaved truffles. At last, I have it. I decide upon that most peasant of peasant dishes: the cassoulet.

While deep down, it might just be a bean stew, this wonderful feast of a dish is loved and revered in every corner of France, particularly in the south-west. Given good ingredients, and slow, careful cooking, cassoulet rewards its makers with a meal unequalled anywhere in the world for heartiness, honesty and good old-fashioned flavour.

One of the dish's greatest advocates was Prosper Montagne, who told the story of a little shoemaker's shop in his home town of Castelnaudary. One day, Montagne went to the shop and found the shutters and doors locked. Fearing a death in the family, he took a closer look, and noticed a piece of paper on the door. It read: 'Closed for cassoulet'.

I gather together the works of Jane Grigson, Elizabeth David, Waverly Root and Anne Willan, and plan my attack. We all agree that cassoulet isn't cassoulet without a confit of salted goose or duck, cooked slowly in goose fat. I manage to find a fresh, plump Muscovy duck, and after salting it, and leaving it overnight, I spend a good part of the next day simmering it in clear goose fat.

By the end of the day, there is a thin film of goose fat over the kitchen walls, the stove, and parts of my anatomy. But no matter. I store my precious confit in a stone jar and leave it in the bottom of the fridge for six weeks so it can gain its full flavour. When the big day finally comes, I combine white haricot beans, carrots, onions, pork fat, fresh pork rind, a piece of lamb shoulder, some pork spare rib, tomatoes, good beef stock, garlic, some saucisson Lyonnaise, and of course, the duck confit. I create a masterpiece.

The hours of back-breaking work melt into nothingness as I gently lift the casserole out of the oven. I peer into the pot and can't help but marvel at the glorious golden breadcrumb crust that has formed over the still bubbling stew beneath.

The kitchen is now full of the most delicious smells as I triumphantly carry my cassoulet to the table. Jill tries to look unmoved by it all, but I can tell she is impressed. I pour her a glass of good honest red wine (a bargain, on special at the local supermarket), and then anxiously watch as she takes her first forkful of cassoulet.

'Mmmm', she says. 'It's very good.'

Ah, how delicious those words sound. There is no nectar that can match the sweet taste of victory.

'Tell me', she says matter-of-factly. 'How much did the duck cost?'

'Oh I don't know', I reply, confused. 'About $25. Why?'

'And the cans of goose fat?'

'About eight or nine dollars a can.'

'And how many cans did you use?'

'Six.'

'And I suppose the salt you used was my Maldon sea salt?'

'Er, yes.'

'And how much would you have spent on all the other ingredients?'

I am squirming uncomfortably.

'Oh I suppose somewhere in the vicinity of $85.'

Her eyes were now glowing like hot, evil coals. 'So this simple, honest dish has set us back a good $170.'

I cough nervously. 'A bit more, actually. I had to buy a special pot to cook it in.'

'Darling', she purrs, her golden bracelets jingling like coins. 'About this living like a peasant business.'

'What about it?'

'Are you really sure we can afford it?'

Cassoulet

I once cooked this simplified cassoulet at a charity night for two hundred chefs and food industry personalities who were expecting something with a wisp of pastry and smoked salmon.

    You can get away with doing your confit just a day or two ahead, but it is far better to make it three or four weeks ahead, and store it in the cooled goose fat in the least cold part of your refrigerator until you need it.

The confit

8 duck legs
50 grams (1½ ounces) coarse salt
5 or 6 sprigs of thyme
2 bay leaves
1 garlic clove
enough goose fat to cover
    (three cans)

Rub each duck leg with coarse salt and place in a casserole, along with the thyme. Refrigerate overnight.

    When ready to cook, rinse the salt from the duck and pat dry. Heat one to two tablespoons of goose fat in a large casserole and slowly brown the legs, skin-side only, in a frypan over a low heat for about 15 minutes until the fat runs and the skin browns lightly. Add the bay leaves, more thyme, garlic and enough goose fat to cover the duck legs. Cover and cook in a warm oven (150°C or 300°F) for two hours until duck is very tender and juices from the thigh run clear. The oven must not be too hot or it will toughen the duck, so keep an eye on it and act accordingly.

    Cool, and refrigerate, making sure all duck legs are well covered by fat.

The cassoulet

- 3 garlic cloves
- 4 onions
- 2 carrots
- 2 tablespoons goose fat
- 500 grams (1 pound) kaiserfleisch, or bacon or salt pork
- 500 grams tomatoes (1 pound), peeled and chopped
- 1 tablespoon tomato paste
- 1 bouquet garni
- 1.5 litres (2½ pints) veal stock
- ½ cup (125 ml) white wine
- 1 large boiling sausage (such as Swiss saucisson or saucisson Lyonnaise)
- 4 pieces duck confit
- 500 grams (1 pound) dried haricot or cannellini beans, soaked overnight
- 2 onions, studded with 2 cloves each
- 250 grams bacon bones
- 5 tablespoons fine dry bread crumbs

Peel garlic and squash it with the side of a knife to flatten.

Pile garlic, onion, carrot and goose fat into a big casserole, and gently cook for a few minutes. Slice kaiserfleisch and add to the pan with tomatoes, tomato paste, bouquet garni, veal stock, and wine and simmer for half an hour. Add the saucisson, sliced on the diagonal; with the skin split to prevent curling. Simmer for a further 30 minutes, then add confit and cook for another 20 minutes. Meanwhile, drain beans, then cover with cold water, adding onions spiked with cloves, and bacon bones. Bring to boil and simmer for around 40 minutes, skimming. Discard bones and onion.

Combine beans with the meats and discard the bouquet garni.

Sprinkle generously with the breadcrumbs, then bake uncovered for 30 minutes in a hot oven (200°C or 400°F), until a golden brown crust has formed. Serve with a fresh green salad.

Serves 4.

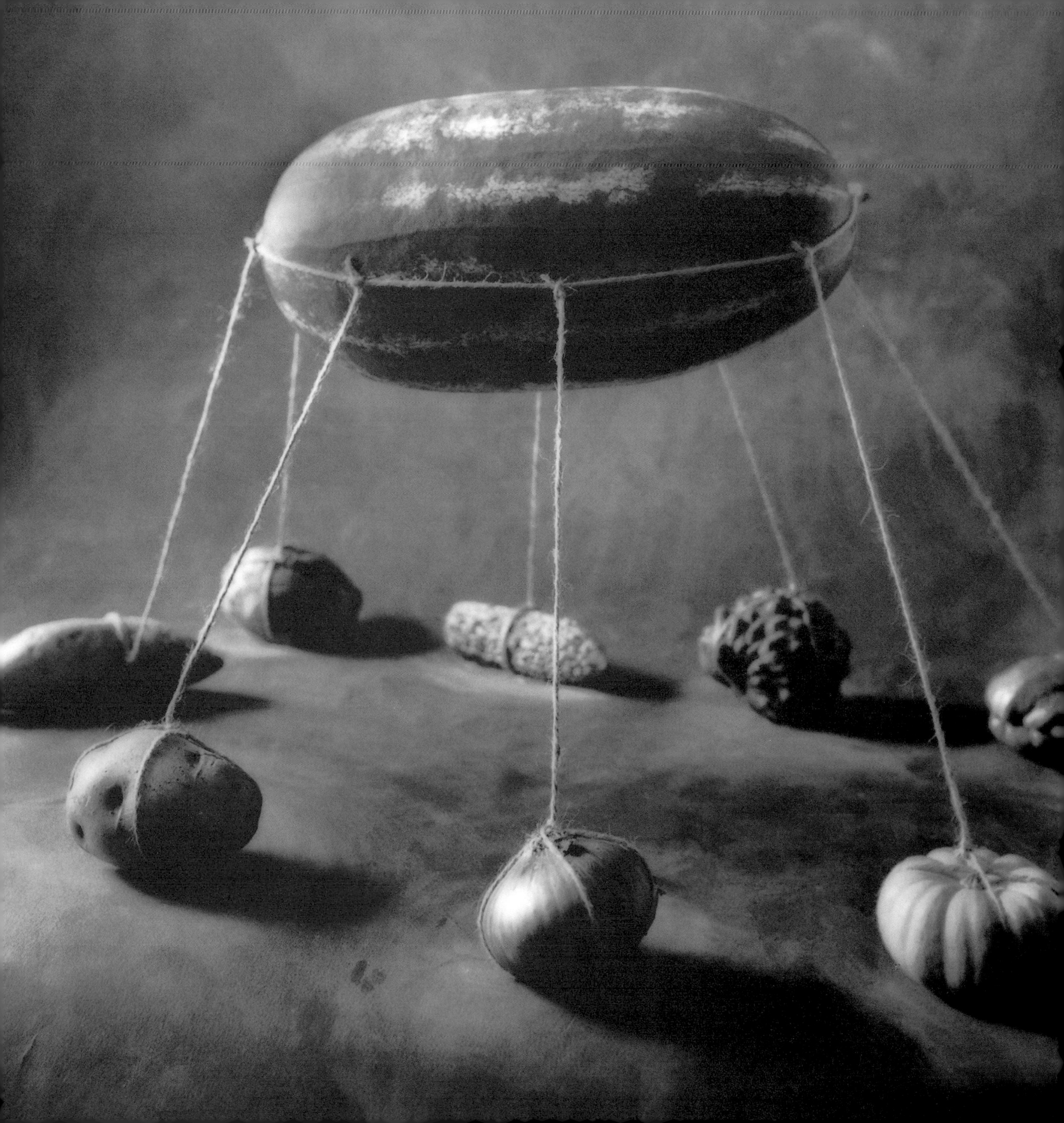

Pleasures of the flesh

I've become a vegetarian. Scoff all you like. I'm used to it. Thus do committed, socially aware, politically correct, sensitive, new-age trail-blazers grow accustomed to the mocking jibes of the disbelievers.

It's the first thing you discover, long before you start soaking your lentils and planting your tomatoes. You learn that you are a figure of fun, a misfit, an eccentric, selfish, difficult person who is no fun to invite to dinner any more.

You know you're going against mainstream public opinion when you get put down in the Bible. God wasn't too thrilled when Cain brought Him an offering of the fruits of the earth. Very nice, Cain, put it over there, will you? But when Abel came along and sacrificed the first born lamb from his flock, God was beside Himself with heavenly rapture.

Making fun of vegetarians goes back a long way. In the sixth century BC, the followers of Pythagoras, a rigid vegetarian, were stock characters in the comedies of the day and were portrayed as pathetic creatures of ridicule, always good for a quick laugh.

But frankly, my dear, I give a damn. And because I give a damn, I suffer no more spasms of guilt about the slaughtering of animals and the deforestation of the earth. I've swapped red meat for green vegetables, chicken for chickpeas, fish for farfalle, bacon for barley, and a bad conscience for good karma.

Why did I do it? Because I was feeling somewhat icky about the state of the world. Because I had just been to a seminar and heard scientists like Cornell University's T. Colin Campbell urging us to swap foods of animal origin for foods of plant origin, for our own health, and for the world's health.

Because the earth now supports eleven billion meat-supplying animals who between them manage to rustle up a staggering eight million tonnes of methane gases a year, which is burping and begging-your-pardon an enormous hole in the ozone layer.

Because I wanted to tread more lightly on the earth, and make some belated apology for eating anything that moved for the last thirty years.

Because Leonardo da Vinci, George Bernard Shaw, Percy Bysshe Shelley, Benjamin Franklin, Leo Tolstoy, Voltaire, Mahatma Gandhi, and Richard Wagner all had a lot more time to do what they wanted to do instead of hovering over cassoulets of confit duck and smoky ham or charring chops on the barbie.

Because I could save an awful lot of money by not being addicted to crisp-skinned Cantonese roast duck and French foie gras.

And because it couldn't be any harder than giving up smoking.

Having made the decision, however, I suddenly had more decisions to make. What sort of vegetarian was I going to be?

It was like waking up one morning, believing in God, but not sure which God.

I considered gentle, sensible Buddhism, but the robes put me off. Saffron makes my cheeks look quite ruddy.

Similarly, I couldn't see myself as a Hindu, Parsee, Quaker, or Seventh Day Adventist.

I could just do my own thing and become a vegan, the radical celibate of vegetarianism, and not eat any animal produce at all, including milk, eggs or honey ('stolen food'), nor use wool for my clothing or leather for my shoes. And I would have, too, but for several convincing and unassailable reasons known only as caffe latte, fried eggs, crumpets, Ermenigildo Zegna, and Ferragamo.

Or I could go all the way, and become a fruitarian, living on avocadoes and self-righteousness.

No, I am happy to become your normal common or garden, small 'v' vegetarian, willing to stretch my scruples far enough to fit in a little dairy produce, and the odd egg.

And you know what? It's fantastic. While this has all been relatively recent, I suddenly feel energised, fit, and healthy. I'm something else, too, which I only just realised: I'm chic. Vegetarianism is almost as chic as lesbianism.

For someone brought up believing that vegetables were something you had to eat before you were given any dessert, the transition, surprisingly enough, has been a piece of cake.

Take this morning. A luscious Swiss bircher muesli, a fresh, ripe mango, a slice of crusty casalinga bread topped with my own fabulous four-fruit marmalade, and I was revving to go.

Lunch was a high-energy fuel stop of a deep bowl of vegetable pistou soup and orecchiette pasta tossed with cauliflower. Magnificent!

As for dinner, I'm considering a Thai red curry of bean curd, or a golden couscous piled high with chickpeas, carrots, zucchini, raisins and pine nuts. Or zucchini flowers stuffed with truffles, with Parmigiano fritters and grilled radicchio. Or a rich, meaty spaghetti Bolognese. Or a giant slab of corned beef and onion sauce. Or prosciutto wrapped around figs. Or soup made from boiling fresh chicken bones for four hours, flavoured with carrots and onions and served with egg noodles. Or just some char-grilled road-kill.

Oh dear. I gave up smoking, no problem. I've really cut down on going to the football, and I'm getting my habit of watching quiz shows under control, but it looks like I've failed vegetarianism.

Why do things have to be so black and white? Even when I was a meat-eater, I would often find that I had gone for days without eating meat. What if I just build more grains and pulses and fruits and vegetables into my diet, and cut down on animal fats, and refuse to be obsessed with everything I put in my mouth?

I'll be the world's first foodarian.

Look, I don't regret my time as a vegetarian. It was a very positive thing to do. I tried. You can't ask more than that. Anyway, they always say that the first day is the hardest.

La soupe au pistou

Non-vegetarians can make this with chicken stock quite happily, but there is one big difference. Made with chicken stock, it will taste of chicken stock. Made with good, old-fashioned water, it will taste of fresh vegetables and basil.

    2 cups (440 grams or 14 ounces) dried white beans, soaked overnight
    2 cups (250 grams or 8 ounces) green beans, sliced
    2 zucchini, sliced
    2 medium carrots, sliced
    2 potatoes, diced
    2 leeks, sliced
    2 litres (3½ pints) boiling water
salt and freshly ground black pepper
shavings of Parmigiano

Pistou sauce

    4 garlic cloves
    bunch of fresh basil
    125 ml (4 fluid ounces) olive oil
    2 tablespoons grated Parmigiano

Drain the soaked beans and add to a large pot with the sliced green beans, zucchini, carrots, potatoes, leeks and boiling water. Season to taste with salt and pepper and cook at a high simmer until vegetables are cooked.

    Make the pistou sauce by crushing the garlic and blending it in food processor or mortar and pestle, with fresh basil. Add a few tablespoons of olive oil, little by little, and blend thoroughly, then add grated Parmigiano and mix to a paste.

    Add pistou sauce to the soup and cook gently for another five minutes. Serve with shavings of Parmigiano.
    Serves 6.

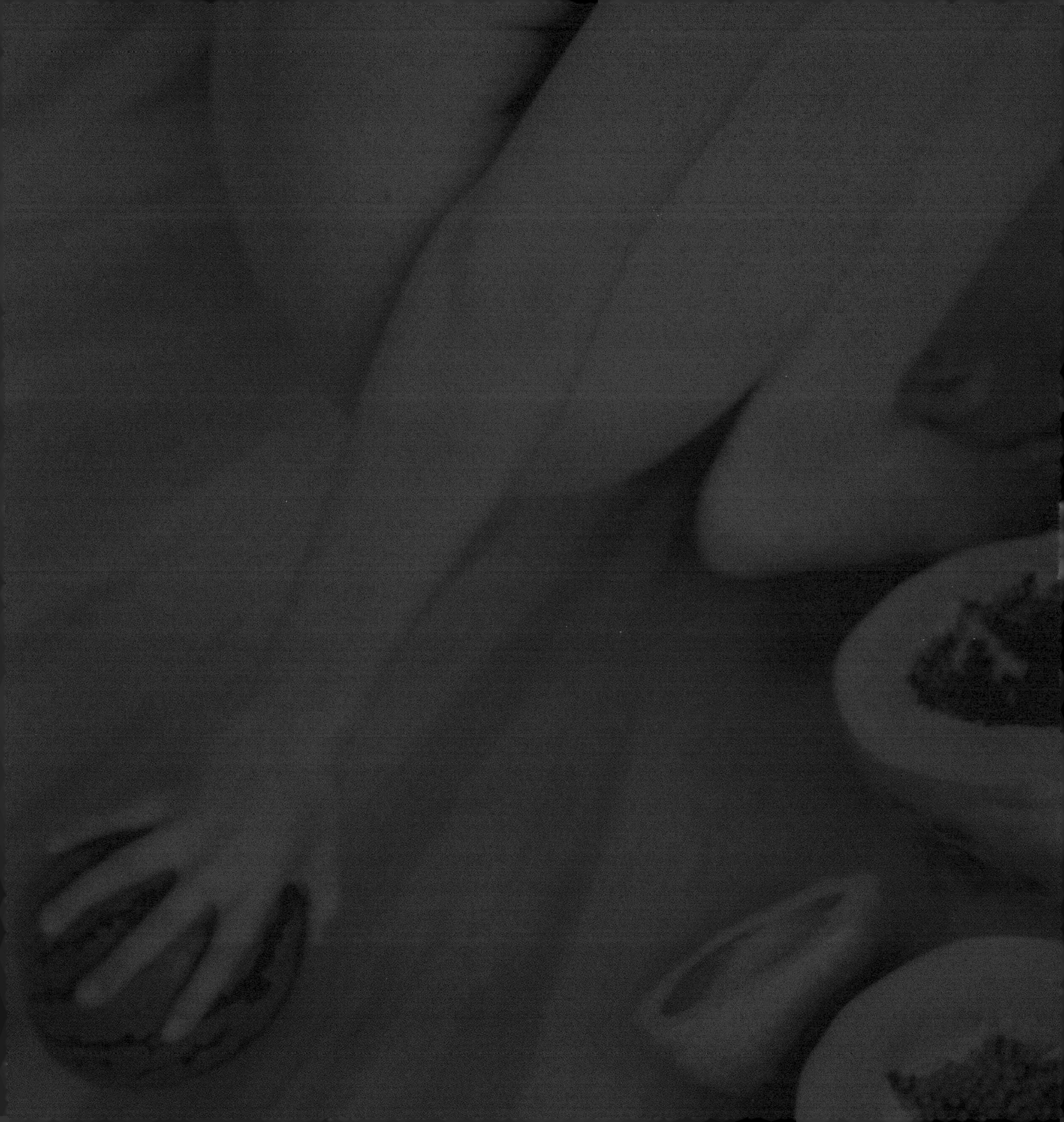

Gado gado

Now you know why nobody complains about being vegetarian in Indonesia.

cos lettuce leaves
2 cups (250 grams or 8 ounces) bean shoots
2 tablespoons vegetable oil
4 squares fresh beancurd, cut into strips
1 cup (100 grams or 3½ ounces) cabbage, roughly chopped
1 bunch spinach
1 cup (125 grams or 4 ounces) cauliflower, broken into florets
1 large carrot, cut into matchsticks
1 cup (125 grams or 4 ounces) green beans
1 cucumber, cut into matchsticks
2 tomatoes, thickly sliced
2 hard-boiled eggs
1 cup (250 ml or 8 fluid ounces) chilli and peanut sauce (see recipe)

Line a large platter with lettuce leaves. Pour boiling water over the bean shoots, drain and rinse, and arrange on platter.
　Heat oil and fry beancurd quickly. Drain on paper towel. Steam the cabbage, spinach, cauliflower, carrot and beans until lightly cooked, drain, cool, and pile on top of the bean shoots. Add the cucumber, tomato and beancurd. Slice the egg and arrange slices over top. Pour peanut sauce over the vegetables or use as a dipping sauce.
　Serves 4.

Chilli and peanut sauce

This is also a great sauce for the backyard barbecue.

1 teaspoon tamarind
2 tablespoons peanut oil
1 garlic clove, crushed
1 onion, finely chopped
1 teaspoon grated ginger
3 red chillies
½ cup (50 grams or 1½ ounces) peanuts, ground
2 tablespoons palm sugar or brown sugar
1 tablespoon lemongrass, finely chopped
1 teaspoon blachan or shrimp paste, diluted in a little water
1 tablespoon soya sauce
1 tablespoon tomato paste
salt to taste
1 cup (250 ml or 8 fluid ounces) coconut milk

Soak the tamarind in a tablespoon of hot water and leave for five minutes. Strain and reserve tamarind water.
　Heat the oil in a frypan and fry the garlic, onion and ginger. Add chillies, tamarind water, ground peanuts, sugar, lemongrass, blachan, soya sauce, tomato paste and salt.
　Stirfry for five minutes, then purée in a blender or push through a sieve. Return to the pan, add the coconut milk, turn heat to low, and stir on a gentle simmer until sauce is thick and smooth. Cool.

Rigatoni with broccoli and pine nuts

This dish works really well with a couple of anchovies thrown in, but you don't really, truly absolutely need them. Honest you don't.

- 90 grams (3 ounces) sultanas (seedless white raisins)
- 2 tablespoons pine nuts
- 1 whole broccoli
- 3 tablespoons olive oil
- 1 onion, finely sliced
- 500 grams (1 pound) ripe or canned tomatoes
- salt and freshly ground black pepper
- 2 tablespoons small Ligurian olives
- 500 grams (1 pound) rigatoni, penne or maccheroni
- 2 tablespoons grated Pecorino

Soak sultanas in warm water for 30 minutes. Toast the pine nuts in a warm oven for two minutes. Cut broccoli into florets and cook in a little salted, boiling water for three minutes. Drain and keep warm.

Heat two tablespoons of the olive oil in a frypan, add the onion and cook until soft but still pale. Add the tomatoes, salt and pepper and simmer for a few minutes. Add the broccoli, cover, and cook very gently.

Heat the remaining olive oil in a small frypan. Add the olives, tomato sauce, pepper, sultanas and pine nuts amd stir gently.

Cook the pasta in plenty of boiling, salted water until al dente, tender but firm to the bite.

Drain well, tip into a warmed serving bowl and mix with sauce. Sprinkle with grated cheese and serve.

Serves 4.

yum

Crabs I have known

Being a crab is not all it's cracked up to be.

One can only assume that Mother Nature had given the production budget a bit of battering by the time she got around to crustaceans, and was forced to go to some second-rate back-alley design consultant.

Housing one of the most delicious food sources known to man is a pretty poor package. Nothing works: crabs don't stack properly, there is no easy-open attachment, and there are fiddly little bits of thin, brittle shell everywhere you look. And why would you go to all the trouble of giving something ten legs, if you're not going to put meat in half of them?

In spite of all the problems, I have to admit to a bit of a soft spot for the odd decapod crustacean of the brachyura persuasion. In fact I can honestly say that I have yet to meet a crab I didn't like, from the tiny peacrabs that live inside mussel shells to the monstrous Alaskan King Crab, weighing in at around 10 kilograms (20 pounds), with its majestic claws that can grow to more than 40 cm (16 in).

Australia does very well, crabologically speaking, from the fleshy Queensland and Northern Territory mud crabs and the succulent Giant Tasmanian King Crab, right down to the red spot crab, the velvet crab, the spider crab, the coral crab, and the curiously named spanner crab.

Serious contender for the title of World's Most Delicious Crab is the Dungeness crab from the west coast of America. Every year, a priest still blesses the crab fleet as it sets off from the magical San Francisco harbour in search of these green-shelled beauties, although if the truth be told, he should be at the airport blessing the jumbo jets that fly in most of the crabs from Alaska.

One of the great champions of the Dungeness crab was the American foodie, James Beard who once said: 'I will match a good Dungeness against the best lobster in America and against the best langouste in Europe'.

My own first encounter with this sensational sweet meat took place one fine spring day at the legendary Swan Oyster Depot on Polk Street, San Francisco.

The Swan has been dispensing freshly shucked oysters, cracked crab, good humour and crash-bang, Italo-American panache since 1945. The legacy of thousands of satisfied customers has been etched into the ancient marble counter, worn into an undulating, wave-like pattern by more than forty years of crab-cracking elbows.

Even today, the five members of the family are a constant blur of action as they crack jokes, open oysters, fill glass jars with tomato ketchup and prescribe huge mugs of local Anchorsteam beer.

After a dozen bluepoint oysters were thrown onto the counter in front of me, and I had waded through a bathtub bowl of great, golden, silky clam chowder, I moved on to a huge cracked Dungeness crab served with a swish little paper cup of sauce Louis, a glossy combination of mayonnaise, cream and sweet chilli sauce.

Not even James Beard had prepared me for this. I may have been sitting on a rickety stool in a downtown fishmonger's shop, but the flavour belonged to the finest three-star restaurant.

'This is fantastic', I said, breathless.

'You bet', replied one of the owners, scuttling sideways around his brothers as they attempted to feed the three-deep crowd. According to him, the Swan Oyster Depot's crabs come from nearby Half Moon Bay, where they get to eat their fill of oysters. 'Other crabs just eat kelp', he said with a pitying shake of his head, 'and you can taste it in the flesh'.

He may have been pulling my leg, but I was too busy pulling ten legs of my own to care.

Next stop is Hong Kong, as long as it's October. Every year around this time, strange, luridly coloured posters, depicting a particularly menacing, alien-like creature begin appearing in shop fronts and restaurants all over town. They look like ads for a bad Japanese sci-fi movie called something like 'They Crawl by Night', but the only thing lethal about these particular aliens is the price on their heads.

The Shanghai hairy crab is one of Hong Kong's big taste thrills, and the posters mean that they are now showing at your local Shanghainese restaurant.

These small, square-bodied freshwater crabs are brought from the north-east of China every year to a wave of publicity that could rival an American presidential election.

The name comes from a small clump of thick black hair on each claw. The reputation comes from the sublime, pure sweet flavour, particularly of the female, which carries the extra bonus of a mustardy, golden roe tasting for all the world like freshly scrambled eggs. The roe is also supposed to do wonders for the complexion.

At Hong Kong's irresistibly Shanghainese Snow Garden restaurant in Causeway Bay, hairy crab is accompanied by warm ginger wine, and followed by a cleansing, refreshing cup of ginger tea. Of course, such pleasures do not come cheaply. A good meal of hairy crabs can wind up costing hundreds of dollars.

If this is a little rich for your blood head straight for the hawker market at Singapore's Newton Circus, where half the fun is picking out your crab from a basket of lively specimens, usually a local mangrove crab or dark-shelled Sri Lankan variety, then haggling about the price with the old lady who runs the stall. The longer you are prepared to haggle, the further the price will fall, although even the first price quoted is a shop-over bargain.

Nobody does chilli crab quite like the Singaporeans, with its lashings of chilli, ginger and good old tomato ketchup. Gastrobods on return journeys to Singapore promote their tastebuds to the more refined pleasures of black pepper crab, a fiery, fragrant stirfry that makes even the chilli crab look like a processed seafood stick.

Rarely do crabs reach such heights as they do in the easy-going tropical paradise of Vanuatu, home to the world's only tree climbing crab.

The coconut crab, reared commercially in nearby coconut plantations, features on the local currency and on just about every menu in Vila. Its delicate, succulent flesh, imbued with the faint aroma and flavour of the fresh coconuts it gathers from the top of swaying palm trees is absolutely ruined by most local restaurants, who stirfry it with onions, garlic and ginger and serve it with a creamy tomato sauce.

It is at its best steamed and served at beach temperature, with a bottle of chilled champagne. I know, I know. Simple is hard to do.

The coconut crab is particularly ugly, looking a lot like a shell-encased funnel-web spider. But would any crab taste as sweet if it came ready-made on a stick? In these days of cryovac'd, fresh-frozen, nutrient-free and flavour-enhanced food, a good, honest crab is a lesson in the joys of having to work for your pleasure. It isn't a cheap thrill, forgotten as quickly as an icy-pole or a fizzy drink. It is an almost primeval pleasure, full of the crunching of shells, and spraying of juices, and requiring an absolute disregard for one's best tee shirt. As for accomplices, you need little more than a lemon and some good home-made mayonnaise.

May there always be crabs. They keep us messy, but honest.

Crab and sweet corn soup

Real crab. Real sweet corn. Real chicken stock. It's a real shame the corner Chinese take-away has killed the beauty of this simple soup with cans and cornflour.

1 fresh corn cob, cooked
6 cups (1.5 litres or 2½ pints) light chicken stock
1 cup (185 grams or 6 ounces) freshly shelled crabmeat
salt to taste
1 teaspoon corn flour mixed with 1 tablespoon cold water
1 egg
2 spring onions, finely chopped

Scrape kernels from the corn cob with a sharp knife.
Heat the chicken stock to a rolling simmer, and add crabmeat and corn. Cook for two minutes, stirring. Add salt to taste.
   Stir in the cornflour mixture, return to the boil and cook, stirring while it thickens.
   Beat the egg lightly and pour in a long stream into the simmering soup, whisking lightly all the while so it forms strands. Serve in warm soup bowls and sprinkle with the spring onions.
   Serves 4.

Singapore chilli crab with coconut rice

One of the world's truly classic dishes. The Singaporeans like to mop up the rich, lush, sticky juices with slices of fresh white bread. I prefer coconut flavoured rice, and the odd round of Indian roti bread.

- 1 mud crab or 1 king crab, (or 4 small sand or blue swimmer crabs)
- 3 tablespoons vegetable oil
- 1 garlic clove, crushed
- 2.5 cm (1 in) piece ginger, minced
- 3 dried red chillies, soaked, drained and chopped
- 2 tablespoons sweet chilli sauce
- 4 tablespoons tomato sauce or ketchup
- 1 cup (250 ml or 8 fluid ounces) hot chicken stock or water
- ½ teaspoon salt
- 1 teaspoon sugar
- 1 teaspoon cornflour blended with 1 tablespoon cold water
- 4 spring onions, chopped
- 1 egg, beaten
- 1 cup (155 grams or 5 ounces) jasmine rice

Buy live crab if possible, and place in the freezer for half to one hour, hopefully a humane way of sending them to sleep.

Use a knife to lever the shell from the rear, and clean fronds away. Remove claws and crack lightly. Cut the body in half, then cut each half into three, keeping legs attached.

Heat the oil in a wok, and fry crab pieces for three to four minutes, and set aside.

Drain all but one tablespoon of oil from the wok and reheat. Add the garlic, ginger and chilli and stirfry for a minute, before adding sauces, stock or water, salt and sugar. Stir well to mix.

Add the cornflour paste, bring to the boil, and stir until mixture thickens.

Return the crab to the wok with the spring onions, and toss to coat them in the sauce until the crab is cooked.

Add egg and stir until the sauce thickens. Serve immediately with fragrant coconut rice or steamed jasmine rice.

Serves 4.

Coconut rice

- 1 cup (155 grams or 5 ounces) long-grain rice
- 1 cup (250 ml or 8 fluid ounces) coconut milk
- 1 cup (250 ml or 8 fluid ounces) water
- 1 pandan leaf, tied in a knot
- salt to taste
- 2 tablespoons spring onions, finely chopped

Wash rice under cold running water until the water runs clear, not cloudy. Drain well and place in a small pot with the coconut milk, water and pandan leaf.

Bring to the boil, cover, lower heat and simmer until all the liquid has been absorbed.

Remove from the heat and fluff up the rice with a pair of chopsticks.

Serves 4 as a side dish.

Sand crab pasta

Hot with chilli, redolent with the earthy aroma of garlic and alive with the fresh, sweet taste of crab, this is heaven twirled around a fork.

>4 sand or blue swimmer crabs, uncooked
>440 grams (14 ounces) linguine
>3 tablespoons olive oil
>1 chilli, finely chopped
>2 garlic cloves, peeled and squashed
>½ cup (125 ml or 4 fluid ounces) fish or chicken stock
>1 tablespoon butter
>2 tablespoons freshly chopped parsley
>freshly ground pepper

Cook the crabs in plenty of boiling, salted water for six to eight minutes. Allow to cool, then lift off the head shell, and clean away the fronds. Chop each crab into four, and remove flesh, reserving one or two legs per person for garnish.

Cook the pasta in plenty of boiling, salted water until al dente and still firm.

Heat the olive oil, chilli and garlic in a pan. Add the crab flesh and legs, and toss gently to heat through. When the legs change colour, add the stock, then the drained pasta.

Add butter, stir through and serve in four warm pasta plates, topped with lots of parsley and pepper.

Serves 4.

Inner beauty

As a tourist in France, the establishment you choose to eat at will depend largely on the guide book you happen to be using at the time.

If it is the *Guide Michelin*, then you will be looking for one, two or three stars. Devotees of the more adventurous *Gault-Millau* will set their sights on four chef's toques, or a high score out of twenty.

I, on the other hand, look for five A's.

The *Association Amicale des Amateurs d'Andouillettes Authenthiques* must be one of the most eccentric gastronomic societies in the world. Its purpose in life is to promote the authentic andouillette, a sausage made from pig's intestine, veal offal or a mixture of both. Only restaurants serving the best quality andouillettes receive the organisation's blessing and may display the AAAAA sign.

It may seem a lot of fuss to make over a sausage, but then, the andouillette is no ordinary sausage.

With its coarse texture and strong, rank flavour, it is most definitely an acquired taste. But once acquired, it rapidly develops into an obsession.

In France, the obsession is easily fed.

Outside France, however, it's not so easy. More often than not, if you want andouillette, you have to make it yourself. Which, after a fit of Chronic Andouillette Deprivation, is what I have decided to do.

Day one

Finding fresh pig's intestines is no easy matter. Strange, when you consider that there are thirty metres of intestine in every pig, and over one million pigs in the country. That means there are thirty million metres of fresh pigs' intestines running around, and I can't track down a single kilo.

Then I stumble into a suburban Vietnamese butcher, and discover that the intestine is one of the few things in the shop I recognise.

I arrive home with my precious innards, breathless with excitement, and sit down with all my recipe books.

One book advises that if the intestines have not been cleaned, then they should be soaked in cold water for twenty-four hours.

I examine my intestines. Have they been cleaned? How can one tell if they haven't? Can you die from eating uncleaned intestines?

I take no chances. I proceed to the bathroom, where I pull a 3-metre length of intestine over the nozzle of the cold tap. I then turn on the water.

Like a Bugs Bunny Cartoon, the water bulges and surges along the length of the intestine, which is transformed into a living, writhing eel. By the time the water reaches the other end, the entire thing is lashing about like an out-of-control hose.

I am soaked. My bathroom is soaked.

I am suddenly aware of a very strange smell: a cross between head-spinning ammonia and very stale pork.

Day two

After twenty-four hours of soaking, I retrieve the intestines from the refrigerator, and set aside the larger ones for the casings.

Another book suggests I slice the rest of them lengthwise into thin strips, but I would like to see them control three metres of slippery, rubbery intestine while executing the perfect cut. Next, I add a *quatre épices* of cloves, allspice, peppercorns, aniseed, coarse salt, nutmeg and dried herbs (okay, so I can't count), along with carrots, onions, olive oil, garlic, thyme and wine to both lots of casings, and return them to the refrigerator to marinate for a day.

Day three

Unbelievably, the andouillette craving is still with me.

I cut a large piece of pork belly fat into strips about 30 centimetres (12 inches) long and 5 millimetres (¼ inch) square and coat them with a *persillade* of garlic, parsley and salt.

Andouillette fillings are often chopped, put through a mincer, and fed into the casings with a sausage feeder. But according to all the experts, the authentic way, unfortunately, is by hand.

Fillings vary enormously from region to region. The Troyes version contains nutmeg and mushrooms, the Beajoulaise include double cream and Dijon mustard, and andouillettes from Nancy owe their distinctive flavour to the addition of truffles and madeira.

Not feeling particularly regional, nor overly rich, I stick to the classic version of pure pork.

Holding a strip of intestine in one hand between thumb and forefinger, I loosely wind the strip around my hand four or five times. Then I carefully lay the loop down on the bench, and coil a piece of pork fat around it. A length of string is then threaded through the top of the loop, and the loop itself is twisted into a figure of eight until it is the size and shape of a thick sausage.

The larger intestines have already been cut into sausage lengths. I thread the string through one of these, and tug at it. The filling pops snugly into its skin, and I howl with triumph.

When all the sausages have been made, I tie off the ends with string, prick them all over and place them in a large pan with the marinade and veal stock.

Placing greaseproof paper over the top, I leave them to poach for four hours, and go away to pray.

After three and a half hours, I can wait no longer. I peep under the paper. Each perfectly formed sausage has shrunk to about one-third its size.

I have created the world's first cocktail andouillette. What could I have done wrong? Was the water simmering too rapidly?

Were the sausages too small to begin with? Can one die from eating andouillettes that are too small?

I lovingly transfer my charges to a shallow dish and cover them with the strained cooking liquid. I'm not giving up now.

Day four

The day of reckoning is at hand. After a night in the refrigerator, my andouillettes are ready.

I crumb them and fry them in a pan.

Feeling the excitement welling within me, I pour a glass of '93 Volnay and ceremoniously set the table.

We sit down.

I cut one end of a crumbed, golden andouillette and place it in my mouth.

It is a masterpiece. The flavour is perfect. The texture sublime. Better? Yes, definitely better than the *andouillettes authentiques françaises*. Could it be — I hesitate, but must go on — that the French make their andouillette just a little too large?

Andouillettes

1.5 kilograms (3 pounds) large pig's intestines
salt
black pepper
1 tablespoon *quatre épices* (equal quantities pepper, nutmeg, cloves and cinammon)
½ teaspoon salt
4 tablespoons finely chopped parsley
3 garlic cloves
2 tablespoons shallots, finely chopped
300 grams (9½ ounces) pork fat, cut into 5-mm strips
1 litre (1¾ pints) veal stock
1 large onion, chopped
2 tablespoons olive oil
2 carrots chopped
a little fresh thyme
bay leaf
1 litre (1¾ pints) dry white wine

If the intestines have not been cleaned, rinse each one by placing one end of the intestine over cold tap. Soak in cold water for 24 hours, then clean and scrape.

Set aside larger intestines for the casings, sprinkle with salt and store in the refrigerator. Using scissors, slice the rest lengthwise into long thin strips and place in a bowl along with salt, pepper, half the parsley, bay leaf and the *quatre épices*. Now add carrots, onion, olive oil, one clove of garlic, thyme and wine to both lots of casings, and return them to the refrigerator to marinate for a day. Drain, reserving liquid and vegetables.

Cut a large piece of pork belly fat into strips about 30 cm (12 in) long and 5 mm (1/4 in) square.

Hold a strip of intestine in one hand between thumb and forefinger, and loosely wind the strip around your hand four or five times to make a looped bundle about 15 cm (6 in) long. Carefully lay the loop down on the bench, and coil a piece of pork fat around it. Make a persillade by pounding together the 1/2 teaspoon of salt, the remaining parsley, garlic and shallots in a mortar and pestle, and coat the pork-fat strips. Thread a length of string through the top of the loop, and twist the whole thing into a figure of eight until it is the size and shape of a thick sausage.

Cut the larger intestines into sausage lengths a little longer than your bundles, then thread the string through each casing, tugging sharply, allowing the filling to pop into its skin.

When all the sausages are made, tie off the ends with string, and prick them all over. Bring marinade, vegetables and veal stock to the boil, then reduce the heat and add the sausages. Simmer gently for three hours. Leave the sausages to cool to room temperature in the liquid.

Transfer them to a shallow dish. Degrease the stock, bring to the boil, then strain and pour over sausages and leave in the refrigerator until needed.

To finish, simply coat in fresh dry breadcrumbs and fry in a little olive oil, or slash three or four times and grill under a very gentle heat. Serve with French mustard, a little salad and some crusty bread.

Makes 8 to 10 sausages.

I can't guarantee the size of them.

Playing with fire

It's his party trick.

One minute, he is the charming, affable, intelligent film editor, relating a long and cleverly edited story of his recent trip to Bangkok. The next minute, his designer clad arm reaches lazily out, his hand grasps a large fresh chilli pepper from a bowl on the restaurant table, and he pops it, whole, into his mouth.

Grown men quake and swoon, women shriek, and dogs run quivering under tables. There couldn't have been more of a fuss had he pulled the pin from a grenade and thrown it down his throat.

And yet, he just sits there, smiling and chewing.

The entire restaurant goes deathly quiet.

Suddenly, his face changes. A cheek muscle twitches. An eyebrow shivers. The corners of his mouth tighten. His skin takes on the glow of a ripe tomato, then just as quickly, fades to a pale avocado green.

The people at our table watch, fascinated.

At the next table, mouths hang open like slack drawbridges.

Waiters have lined up behind him with jugs of iced water.

From somewhere hellishly deep inside him comes a strange noise that sounds like a blocked sink treated with a belt of Drano.

He starts to drip. Tears fall from his eyes. A single droplet of sweat trickles down his cheek.

He's hit the big one, and he's off and running. And so is his nose.

Just as the assembled audience is discussing the relative merits of an ambulance or a stomach pump, he sits bolt upright, straightens the Versace tie, brushes down his Commes des Garcons jacket and smiles sweetly. 'Divine', he says.

It could be that he was one of a large family, and had to resort to devious measures in order to get attention. Whatever the cause, this man is a lost soul. He is a chilli junkie. A hopeless addict, as sad in his own way as the drugstore cowboy who lives in dark alleyways and spends his last dollars on dope.

This man is so gone, he shares spoons. He snorts chilli powder. They say he does a line of paprika spiked with cayenne powder at parties. Like many seemingly normal, responsible citizens, he can now only find true pleasure in the exquisite pain of chilli after-burn. The hotter the chilli, the deeper and longer lasting the euphoria. Food that once seemed full of flavour and subtlety is now merely insipid and bland. There is no joy for him in mashed potatoes, morning muesli, or innocent afternoon teas.

The sad thing is that he is not alone. You find chilli junkies in almost every walk of life. You may work with one. You may live with one. You may even be one yourself and not even know it.

For your own benefit, try to answer as honestly as possible the following questions:

1 Do you find it difficult going a whole day without eating chilli?

2 Have you ever felt remorse after eating chilli?

3 Have you ever eaten chilli before midday?

4 Do you ever eat chilli alone?

5 Have you seen *Some Like It Hot* more than five times?

6 Do you lose time from work due to your chilli eating?

7 Have you ever been to a hospital or an institution as a result of your chilli eating?

8 Do you crave chilli at certain times each day?

9 Do you find it impossible to stop after just one chilli?

10 Do you like to wear a lot of green and red?

If you answered yes to even one of these questions, it's possible that you are in the early stages of chilli addiction. But it's not too late for you to salvage something of your life. If you scored five or more, you are a certified chilli junkie and are totally beyond help. You may as well go out on a blindingly hot masaman curry with a chilli con carne chaser and go directly to hell where you will feel quite at home, especially around meal times.

Chilli junkies are the Evel Knievels of the food world. They are ever-hungry for greater daredevilry; always ready to gun their throbbing tastebuds over one more double decker bus of adrenalin-pumping chilli heat. They will crash and burn over a particularly vicious sambal telur or Madras curry, but they will always leap up again, in plaster and on crutches, ready to get back into the hot seat with bandaged hands on the throttle, aiming higher and farther than ever before.

Hooked on the alkaloid capsaicin, the heat-generating substance found mainly in the white-seed bearing tissues of chillies, they seek a rapid, immediate bite on the back palate and throat, followed by a long, low-intensity burn on the tongue and middle palate.

Undeterred by the fact that capsaicin is widely used in anti-mugger sprays and anti-dog products, they journey farther down the path to chilli nirvana.

Some psychologists call this condition a constrained risk, or a high-security adventure. Although our bodies tell us immediately, by way of such elementary signals as runny eyes, extreme mouth burn and sniffy noses, not to continue eating, we like the shock of the burn and the fact that we can ignore the signals and get away with it.

People this far gone know their stuff. They go for the slimmer, smaller, and more pointed chillies every time — and they leave the seeds in. They have their own dealers, one for the common or garden *Capsicum annum* species, and a special one for the *Capsicum frutescens* to get their daily dose of the Louisiana tabasco chilli pepper. Alas, familiarity leads to higher resistance and bigger doses, and they have to pay through the nose to support their habit, a fact that has led to an alarming increase in chilli-related crimes.

Of course, there are different types of chilli junkie. The cayenne chilli junkie, who lives for chilli con carne, knows at a sniff whether his cayenne pepper was indeed made from cayennes or not.

There's the Scotch bonnet or habanera junkie, who sails around the Caribbean, stopping at every port for the local version of West Indian jerked pork, fragrant with allspice, hot with chilli and heady with dark rum.

Next is the jalapeno cowboy junkie, whose hand is permanently curled around a Mexican taco, not to be confused with the pasilla, ancho or mulato chilli junkies who also hail from south of the US border.

Finally, there are the birds' eye chilli junkies who frequent Thailand, Indonesia, Vietnam and Malaysia. Fortunately these are rarely seen in public, and most of them have had to be kept under lock and key.

These people are mad. They buy and eat two dollars worth of mixed chillies as if they are ju-jubes.

How do I know this? I have been there and done that.

Yes. I was a chilli junkie. It helps to be able to say it. I have gone through the baptism of fire and survived. It all started with a Thai meal, at which my future mother-in-law kindly offered me a prawn that was so hot, it bit me before I could bite it. Not wishing to show a lack of manliness in a crisis, I took another prawn. And another.

Soon after that I was taking the odd day off work, hanging around the markets in dawn's early light. I was hiding serranos in the sock drawer and jalapenos in the laundry basket.

When questioned about it, I would act surprised. One or two chillies never hurt anyone, I would say. After all, I only really ate them to be sociable.

I soon discovered that people took no notice of my 'problem' if I pretended to be a gourmet. They weren't to know that I only ordered the Malay curry puffs for the dark, powerful sambal that accompanied them. That I cooked giant Moroccan feasts of couscous and tajines just so I could eat the harissa sauce. Or that those tiny Vietnamese spring rolls wrapped in mint and lettuce only existed for me once they were dipped into a sweet, chilli flecked nuoc cham sauce.

I travelled widely so people couldn't trace a pattern in my eating habits.

On a business trip to London, I had to live for three days on Alistair Little's mashed potato, the Savoy Hotel's roast beef and Yorkshire pudding, and Anton Mosimann's bread and butter pudding.

Suddenly, something wild and uncivilised snapped inside me. I fled into the Bombay Brasserie's lunchtime buffet and overdosed on pork vindaloo and curried goat.

I have been to Bangkok many times and have never seen a kick-boxing match and never had a single shirt made. But the red duck curry at the Bussaracum I can lovingly describe in minute detail.

It was in Bangkok that I had my first lost weekend, on the wild boar chilli dip at the Tan Ying. I remember taking my first bite, and the next thing I knew, I woke up down at the wharves three days later.

That's when I knew I had to do something.

I now limit myself to one chilli vodka at the start of the meal, and only order pizza with triple chilli once a month.

It's no problem. I can give up any time I want. Any time at all.

Cha gio with nuoc cham
(little spring rolls with chilli dipping sauce)

These tiny Vietnamese spring rolls are no bigger than your little finger, but dip them in the sauce and they pack a whole handful of punch.

- about 30 grams (1 ounce) cellophane noodles
- 5 dried wood-ear mushrooms
- 300 grams (9½ ounces) minced pork
- 200 grams (6½ ounces) fresh crab meat, shredded
- 2 shallots, minced
- 2 garlic cloves, minced
- ½ cup (60 grams or 2 ounces) fresh bean shoots
- 1 tablespoon fish sauce
- 1 pack rice paper wrappers, or spring roll wrappers
- flour and water for paste

Cook the noodles in boiling water for two minutes or until soft. Drain and cut into 2.5-cm (1-in) lengths. Soak the wood-ear mushrooms for 30 minutes, then cut into fine strips. Combine noodles, wood-ears, pork, crabmeat, shallots, garlic, bean sprouts, and fish sauces and mix well.

If using rice paper, dissolve two tablespoons of sugar in two cups of hot water and transfer to a deep, wide plate. Soak each wrapper briefly until it softens, then transfer to a dry towel.

Place a heaped tablespoon of the filling just below the centre of the spring roll wrapper or rice paper, and roll tightly into a thick, compact cigar shape, folding in the sides as you go. Seal the final flap with a little of the flour and water paste.

Deep fry a few at a time in peanut oil until golden brown.

Traditionally the rolls are wrapped in pieces of fresh iceberg lettuce with a few Vietnamese mint leaves or Asian basil leaves and dipped in a little bowl of nuoc cham.

Makes about 20 rolls.

Nuoc cham sauce

- 2 tablespoons palm sugar
- 2 tablespoons boiling water
- 1 garlic clove, crushed
- 2 tablespoons fish sauce (nuoc mam or nam pla)
- 2 tablespoons lime or lemon juice
- 1 slice lime or lemon, segmented
- 2 red chillies, sliced
- 1 tablespoon white vinegar

Stir sugar into water until dissolved, then combine with garlic, fish sauce, lime juice, lime pieces, chillies and white vinegar. You can strain it if you like, but I prefer to leave all the bits in.

Serve as a dipping sauce for fresh spring rolls, grilled chicken, lamb and pork, meatballs, and so on.

Makes 250 ml (8 fluid ounces).

Moroccan chicken with tomato, olives and preserved lemon

I've fiddled with the more traditional recipe, adding tomatoes and making it nice and soupy. Fresh lemon peel can be substituted for preserved lemon, but it won't have the same zing.

- 1 chicken, cut into 8 pieces
- flour, to coat
- salt and pepper
- 3 tablespoons butter
- 4 tablespoons olive oil
- 1 large brown onion, peeled and finely chopped
- 2 garlic cloves, peeled and flattened
- ¼ teaspoon powdered saffron
- ½ teaspoon sweet paprika
- ¼ teaspoon chilli powder
- ¼ teaspoon powdered cumin
- ¼ teaspoon powdered ginger
- pinch cayenne pepper to taste
- 300 grams (9½ ounces) chopped tomatoes
- 2 cups (500 ml or 16 fluid ounces) chicken stock
- ½ preserved lemon (peel only), cut into strips
- 15 green olives
- 1 tablespoon chopped parsley
- 2 tablespoons green coriander
- extra preserved lemon peel, chopped for side dish

Dry the chicken pieces with paper towelling, then dredge them with flour that has been heavily seasoned with salt and pepper. Melt the butter and oil in a heavy-based pan and fry the chicken on both sides until golden and crusty.

Remove chicken to a warm place. Add onion to the pan and cook over slow heat until it turns a translucent golden colour.

Add all the dry spices and garlic, and heat through until the smell is warm and high.

Transfer onions and chicken to a casserole, adding tomato, chicken stock, and preserved lemon.

Simmer gently for one and a half hours. About ten minutes before the finish, add the olives.

Garnish with parsley and coriander and serve with couscous, harissa (recipe follows) and a bowl of extra, chopped, preserved lemon peel.

Serves 4

Harissa

- 4 dried red chillies
- 1 teaspoon caraway seed
- ½ teaspoon cumin seeds
- ½ teaspoon coriander seeds
- 1 teaspoon dried mint
- 2 garlic cloves, crushed
- ½ teaspoon salt
- 1 tablespoon water
- 3 tablespoons olive oil

Soak the dried chillies in hot water for one hour. Grind the spices together in a coffee grinder reserved for your spices.

Drain chillies, pat dry and chop. Blend chillies with garlic, spices, and salt until a thick paste forms. Add water and olive oil, mix well and store in a well-sealed jar in the refrigerator.

Makes 1 jar.

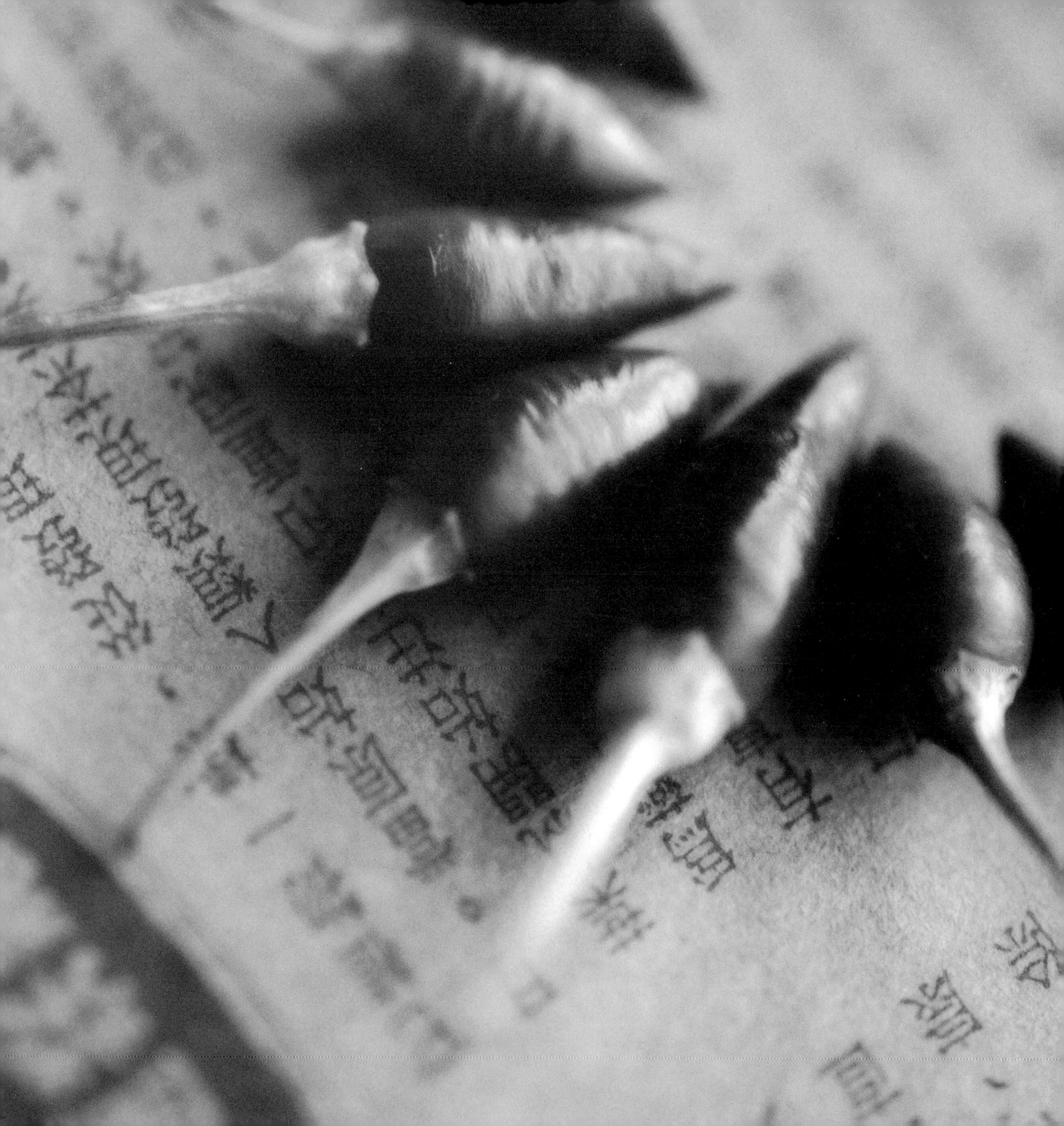

Fish cutlet with Thai sweet chilli sauce

The fish is really just an excuse to make the sweet chilli sauce. Still, it's a very nice excuse.

   1 red capsicum
   1 cucumber
   2 spring onion greens
   125 grams (4 ounces) bean shoots
   2 tablespoons coriander leaves, washed
   2 tablespoons flour
   salt and pepper
   4 thick cutlets of any firm, white flesh fish
   vegetable oil for deep frying
   8 tablespoons sweet chilli sauce (see recipe)

Core and seed the capsicum and slice into long, thin slivers (around 7 cm or 3 in long). Cut the cucumber lengthwise into slices, then again into long, thin matchsticks. Cut the spring onion greens into long matchsticks and soak in ice-cold water to make them curl.

Mix the capsicum, cucumber, spring onions, bean shoots and coriander and set aside.

Season the flour with salt and pepper. Press the fish cutlets into flour on both sides and on the skin.

Heat the oil until a pinch of bread browns easily, then add one cutlet and cook until golden, turning once. Check that it is cooked by inserting a knife next to the bone. The flesh should peel away from the bone easily, yet still be faintly pink. Drain on a paper towel and keep warm while you cook remaining cutlets.

Serve each cutlet leaning on a mound of jasmine rice. Quickly toss the capsicum, cucumber, bean shoots and coriander in a little of the sauce and pile them high on top, then drizzle sweet chilli sauce over the lot.

Serves 4.

Sweet chilli sauce
   2 red chillies
   250 ml (8 ounces) white wine vinegar
   70 grams (2½ ounces) white sugar
   2 tablespoons lime juice
   1 tablespoon Thai fish sauce (nam pla)
   1 tablespoon rice wine vinegar

Blend chillies, wine vinegar and sugar. Add lime juice, fish sauce and rice wine vinegar. Store in an airtight jar in the refrigerator until required.

Penne all'arrabbiata

When in Rome, do as the Romans do. Double the amount of chilli in this recipe.

    4 slices bacon
    2 tablespoons olive oil
    1 onion, finely chopped
    1 garlic clove, finely chopped
    2 red chilli peppers, finely chopped
    400 grams (12½ ounces) canned roma tomatoes
    500 grams (1 pound) penne
    1 tablespoon butter
    1 tablespoon grated Pecorino or Parmigiano

Cut bacon into matchstick strips. Heat olive oil in a heavy-bottomed frypan, add onion, garlic, chilli and bacon and cook until golden.

Add tomatoes and cook gently, stirring occasionally, for 15 minutes.

Cook pasta in plenty of boiling, salted water until al dente, tender but firm to the bite.

Drain the pasta and add to the sauce in the frypan, stirring well. Add a ladleful of the pasta cooking water if the sauce seems too dry.

Serve with grated cheese.

Serves 4.

Char kueh teow

Kueh teow or hor fun noodles, as they are known in China, are sold in large, flat white sheets, and will apparently keep in the refrigerator for a couple of weeks, although I've never had the chance to find out.

1 pack (about 1 kilogram or 2 pounds) rice noodles
1 tablespoon vegetable oil
2 cloves garlic, crushed
2 dried red chillies, soaked, drained and chopped
2 eggs, beaten
1 tablespoon dark soya or mushroom soya sauce
1 tablespoon light soya sauce
1 tablespoon oyster sauce
300 grams (9½ ounces) green prawns, peeled
250 grams (8 ounces) squid, sliced
2 lup cheong Chinese sausages, steamed and sliced thinly
125 grams (4 ounces) bean shoots
4 spring onions, chopped

Cut noodles into strips 2 cm (1 in) wide. Place in a bowl, and pour boiling water over them, while gently separating the noodles with a pair of chopsticks. Drain and rinse under cold water to stop them from overcooking.

Heat the wok until it is very hot, add the oil, then heat it. Add the garlic and chilli and stirfry for two minutes. Add the noodles and toss.

Push the noodles to one side, pour the egg in the centre, cover with the noodles and toss to distribute the egg.

Add the sauces, prawns, squid, lup cheong and bean shoots and stirfry until cooked, without overcooking. Top with spring onions and serve hot.

Serves 6.

Curry puffs

Whoever said good things come in little packages was probably either a Malaysian or chilli freak, or both.

1 potato, peeled
1 carrot, peeled
1 onion, peeled
1 tablespoon Malay curry powder
pinch of chilli powder
½ teaspoon sweet paprika
2 tablespoons oil
4 curry leaves
1 dessertspoon finely chopped ginger
200 grams (6½ ounces) minced lamb
pinch of sugar
½ teaspoon salt
6 sheets of store-bought puff pastry
vegetable oil for deep frying

Chop the potato, carrot and onion into very small dice.

Mix curry powder, chilli powder and paprika with a little water to form a paste.

Heat the wok, add two tablespoons of oil and heat. Add curry paste and leaves, and stir for two minutes. Add vegetables and ginger and stir for two minutes, then add meat and cook for about four minutes. Add 125 ml (4 fluid ounces) of water, cover and cook over gentle heat until mixture is soft and reasonably dry.

Add sugar and salt, stir through and cool.

Cut circles out of pastry sheets using a small Chinese bowl as a guide.

Place a spoonful of filling in the centre of each round.

Moisten the edges with water and fold them over to form a plump half-moon shape. Press the edges together to seal, then pinch and fold small sections of the rim over one another so they form a braid all around the curved edge of the puff.

Heat the oil in the wok and deep fry the curry puffs until golden. Drain well, and serve.

Makes 12.

Curry laksa

Everybody likes a laksa. In Northern Malaysia, they like a tart, tangy broth flavoured with tamarind and pineapple, full of noodles and studded with fish, known as Penang or Assam laksa.
But the laksa I adore is the curry laksa, or laksa lemak from Malacca; a magical, spicy potion rich with coconut, yellow with turmeric, and overflowing with rice vermicelli noodles, prawns, fish balls, tofu and chicken.

Curry paste
- 1 onion or 6 shallots, finely chopped
- 1 tablespoon ginger, grated
- 1 tablespoon galangal, grated
- 2 garlic cloves, crushed
- 2 stalks lemon grass, white part only, finely sliced
- 6 dried chillies, soaked, drained and chopped
- 4 candlenuts or macadamia nuts, crushed
- 1 tablespoon blachan (shrimp paste)
- 6 laksa or Asian mint leaves
- 1 teaspoon coriander, ground
- 1 teaspoon paprika
- 1 teaspoon turmeric powder
- 1 teaspoon cumin, ground

Soup
- 2 tablespoons vegetable oil
- 1.5 litres (2½ pints) chicken stock
- 2 teaspoon palm or brown sugar
- 1 teaspoon salt
- 2 cups (500 ml or 16 fluid ounces) coconut milk
- meat from one cooked chicken breast and one cooked chicken thigh, sliced
- 8 fish balls (from Asian groceries)
- 8 raw prawns, peeled but with tails intact

Noodles
- 100 g (3½ ounces) dried rice vermicelli
- 300 g (9½ ounces) fresh Hokkien egg noodles
- 1 cup (125 grams or 4 ounces) bean shoots, washed
- 4 squares fried beancurd puffs
- 1 cucumber, peeled and cut into matchsticks
- fresh mint and coriander

To make the curry paste, pound or blend the onion or shallots, ginger, galangal, garlic, lemon grass, chillies, nuts, blachan, laksa leaves and spices to a paste. If using a mortar and pestle, start with the wet ingredients, and gradually add dry ingredients, pounding steadily for ten to fifteen minutes.

Cook dried noodles for five or six minutes in boiling water, then drain. Cut the beancurd puffs in half diagonally.

To make the soup, heat the wok, add the oil and heat it through. Fry the paste for five minutes until fragrant. Add the chicken stock, sugar and salt and bring to the boil, stirring, until the sugar dissolves. Reduce the heat, add the coconut milk and gently heat through. For the last minute of cooking, add the chicken, the fish balls and the prawns and cook just until the prawns change colour.

To serve, pour boiling water over both types of noodles in a heatproof bowl, drain and rinse. Pour boiling water over the bean shoots in a small bowl, and drain immediately. Distribute noodles and beancurd puffs among four warm, deep, soup bowls. Add hot soup, then divide the fish balls, prawns, and chicken fairly between the bowls.

Arrange the cucumber and bean shoots in little piles on top and scatter with mint and coriander.

Serves 4.

Cashing out

It was a typical day.

I introduced myself to my wife over breakfast, a meal generally eaten in one hand while rushing out the door to the car in order to catch some conference or other.

We exchanged diary dates as I leapt into the car, and she enquired politely as to my health as I reversed back into the street. Later that morning, in between meetings, I rang her just as she was finishing her conflict resolution workshop, and we went over the mail and telephone messages.

That night, as we met in bed and introduced ourselves to each other again, I realised that there was something missing from our lives: time. We were spending all our available time working, so we could afford to pay for all our labour-saving devices.

I looked around me, at my friends slaving in jobs they had started at eighteen, at my expensive, glossy, green, status symbol car, at the economy, at horrible, evil things like the old tool cupboard that still needed clearing out. It was time to do something drastic.

'Darling, I think we should talk.'

'I can fit you in Monday week', she replied.

We decided to go and live in Italy for a year. To get to know each other again, and to get to know a different, slower rhythm of life. We would give ourselves twelve months to get organised, then we would pack in our jobs, pack up our lives, pack our bags, and just go.

Home would be an atmospheric, marble clad, evocative little apartment in Bologna, or Modena, or Verona.

Mornings would be spent drinking espresso in atmospheric, marble clad, evocative little cafés, while at night we would stroll in the night air, listen to music and read books. Best of all, there would be no tool cupboard.

'But why Italy?' demanded my father-in-law, in that where-are-you-taking-my-daughter tone.

'Because it has history', I blurted. 'Because the people are still in touch with the earth, and the seasons still count for something. It's everything: the pale golden colour of the piazzas, the painterly afternoon light, the reassuring calm of siesta time.'

He nodded, but I could feel I was losing him.

'Italians take life by the throat as if it is their God-given right', I persisted. 'They have music in their hearts and fire in their souls. They dress well, they eat well, and they live well. Not only that, they know how to drink coffee.'

The nod became a head shake, and I decided not to tell him about the tool cupboard.

To my friends and colleagues however, I suddenly became a hero. I was doing what everyone secretly wanted to do. They threw parties for me. Bought me drinks. Called me a lucky dog. Turned up with open diaries suggesting the following July as the most convenient month for them to come and stay.

'So when is the book coming out?' people would ask.

'Book?'

'Yeah, you know. *A Year in Bologna. A Taste of Emilia Romagna. Stuffed Pig's Trotters I Have Known...*'

Of course! The book! Move over Peter Mayle-order, I'm coming through. First, though, some homework. I signed up for Italian lessons with the wonderful Milena, who in just four months had me reading newspaper reports of Cicciolina's love life. The Italian political news took a little longer, but Milena assured me many Italians don't understand it either.

I spent hours propped up against the window at my local espresso bar, practising looking bored and worldly. I got to the point where I could sit on a ristretto for an hour and a half, wearing a meaningful expression like a Romeo Gigli jacket, and saying things like beh! and allora!

I listened to way too many Umberto Tozzi records, and practised walking like an Italian man. You keep your head down, hunch your shoulders, put your hands in your pockets and walk slowly, as if unemployed, feeling the sun on the back of your head.

The next thing I knew, we were off. I leapt on the plane with a copy of Tim Park's *An Englishman in Verona: Italian Neighbours* to give me a stranieri's (foreigner's) insight.

Somewhere over the wide blue ocean, up to my neck in the colourful locals, quaint customs and strong coffee of Parks' life, I got the shivers. Flat-hunting, according to Parks, is sheer torture. The neighbours are certifiably crazy. Government officials corrupt. Council by-laws baffling. Tradesmen are a protected species, with those who actually get things done, all but extinct.

As for the language barrier, if Parks, a trained linguist, can't make himself understood, what chance does my beh! and allora! have? I can't spend all day chatting about Cicciolina's love life. (Although, in Bologna, you probably could.) And then there are the strikes.

At that point, the pilot informed us we couldn't land in Italy because of nationwide industrial action. *A Year In Zurich*? *Airports I Have Known*? My novel was getting thinner, as we journeyed by train from Zurich into Italy, via the tradesman's entrance.

Stranded at the awe-inspiring Milan railway station, we took temporary refuge in the cafeteria, where a warm beer, a cold coffee and two bread rolls cost four times as much as it did on my last visit.

The hotel room was small, cramped and ugly, with *non funziona* air-conditioning, but costing only a little more than a room at the Regent Beverly Wiltshire.

And so it went. I added up what one dollar got me: five seconds of a seat at an outdoor cafe; the froth from the top of a cappuccino; two licks of a gelato; or one twirled fork full of linguini al vongole.

Trying to get a taste for our new home before finally settling down, we travelled north and south, pausing only for a mighty bollito misto lunch at the renowned Fini restaurant in Modena, a swoon-inducing creamed polenta with fresh porcini mushrooms at Trattoria alla Coa near Verona, and a remarkable lunch of rigatoni with calves' intestines, and carciofi alla giudia (deep-fried artichoke flattened and fried to resemble a flower) at the atmospheric Giggetto al Portico d'Ottavia in Rome's Jewish quarter.

After three weeks, I had eaten my rent. My wife was wearing her share. All we had was our return ticket, and an ability to say *non gassata* when asked how we wanted our mineral water.

There were also several things I was beginning to miss about home. Like plumbing. Like a telephone system I could understand. Like whole grilled fish I could afford. Like lighting you could actually see by, instead of the dim, dark rooms that Italy's high electricity rates demand. No wonder they all wear those nice Giorgio Armani glasses.

We sat down and had a strong espresso in an atmospheric, marble clad, evocative little café, and decided to go home. Not because Italy was too much for us, or too expensive. Not really. More, because we had made a mistake. We loved our home, our space and our sunshine. We just had to make our life work in our own world, rather than buy into someone else's.

So home we went. We now sit down to breakfast together every morning. We talk. We work hard, then go out for a long, leisurely coffee together. At night, we stroll in the night air, listen to music, and read books.

I can buy all the whole, flapping fish my heart desires, pull some vegetables out of my garden, and smother them with great olive oil.

I can park my own car outside my own house, and sit under a tree with a beautiful woman I am madly in love with, a bowl of home-made pasta and a glass of fabulous, locally grown wine.

Then I can sit down at my computer in a well-lit room and almost make a living out of what I love doing.

You have to sort out your own tool cupboard sooner or later.

Bollito misto with salsa verde

This is a dish of mixed, boiled meats. Doesn't sound fabulous, does it? But it is, especially when prepared with split-second timing by the impeccable Fini restaurant in Modena. This is my down-home, back-to-stay version.

- 1 veal tongue or small ox tongue
- 20 parsley stalks
- 2 bay leaves
- 3 onions studded with cloves
- 4 celery stalks, roughly chopped
- 3 carrots, roughly chopped
- 12 black peppercorns
- 1 kilogram (2 pounds) beef brisket or silverside
- 1 fresh, free-range chicken, about 1.5 kilograms (3 pounds)
- 1 cotechino sausage, cooked
- 1 zampone (stuffed pig's trotter), cooked
- 4 potatoes
- bunch of baby carrots

Soak the tongue in cold water overnight. Drain, then place in a very large saucepan, with the herbs, onions, celery, carrots, pepper and water and cook for one hour.

Add the brisket and continue cooking for another hour, then add the chicken and simmer for half an hour. Add extra liquid as needed. Wrap the pre-cooked cotechino and zampone in muslin, prick all over, and simmer for the final half an hour. Remove the tongue and carefully peel the skin away. Remove the sausage and zampone and unwrap. Return to the pot.

Carve slices from each of the meats, and arrange on a large platter moistened with strained broth. Serve with mostarda di frutta (glazed sweet mustard fruits) and salsa verde. Accompany with boiled potatoes and baby carrots.

Serves 10.

salsa verde

- 2 tablespoons chopped parsley
- 20 to 30 basil leaves
- 4 anchovy fillets, mashed
- 2 garlic cloves, minced
- 2 cornichons or 50 grams (1½ ounces) salted capers soaked and rinsed
- 6 tablespoons extra virgin olive oil
- 2 tablespoons red wine vinegar

Blend the parsley, basil, anchovy fillets, garlic, and cornichons or capers together in a food processor. Add the olive oil in a slow trickle, with the motor still running. Add vinegar to taste.

Carciofi alla Giudea

One of Rome's most ancient and traditional dishes, this is a spectacular presentation of deep-fried artichokes, the leaves curling out to resemble the petals of a flower.

    8 small, young artichokes
    juice of 2 lemons
    salt and freshly ground pepper
    olive oil for deep frying

Remove the tough outer leaves of the artichokes, and trim the tops of the remaining leaves. Trim the stem, leaving about 5 cm (2 in). Soak the artichokes in a bowl of very cold water with the lemon juice for three to four hours, then remove them and drain well.
    Carefully pull each leaf down slightly to form the shape of a flower. Be careful not to snap them off. Season the inside with salt and pepper. Heat the oil, add the artichokes and cook slowly over a gentle heat without browning, turning frequently until the inside is tender. When cooked, remove from pan, and press the leaves gently down to make them spread out more. Return to the oil and deep-fry quickly over a high heat to crisp the outer leaves.
Drain well and serve.
    Serves 4.

129

Polenta con funghi

If anything could change my mind and make me want to go and live in Italy all over again, it is the magnificent fresh porcini mushrooms that feature in Trattoria Alla Coa's magnificent dish of soft polenta and mushrooms. I have little packets of dried mushrooms, but it's not quite the same…Nevertheless, this recipe that I adapted from a dish by London's most famous funghiphile — Antonio Carluccio — gives you a pretty good idea.

300 grams (9½ ounces) fresh mushrooms (eg slippery jack, orange fly cap, abalone, shitake, field)
2 tablespoons dried porcini (ceps)
2 tablespoons olive oil
1 onion, finely chopped
1 can of roma tomatoes
salt and freshly ground black pepper
6 cups (1.5 litres or 2½ pints) light chicken stock
1 cup (185 grams or 6 ounces) polenta
2 tablespoons butter
2 tablespoons freshly grated Parmigiano

Wipe the fresh mushrooms clean, and slice thickly. Soak the dried mushrooms in just-warm water for 15 minutes. Heat the oil in a heavy-based frypan, add the onion and cook until it starts to soften. Add mushrooms and cook for five minutes, stirring.

Add the tomatoes and their water, breaking them up with a fork. Cook until the tomato water evaporates and the mushrooms are cooked. Season with salt and pepper.

To make the polenta, bring the salted water or stock to the boil and very slowly add the polenta in a steady stream, stirring continuously. Lower the heat and keep stirring until the grains dissolve and the polenta starts to come away from the sides of the pan — around 20 minutes. Add the butter and half the cheese, and stir well. Pour the polenta into warmed pasta bowls, and pour some sauce over the polenta.

Serves 4.

Swordfish with lemon and herb sauce

I adapted this from a recipe given to me by Maria Battaglia, a vivacious, dedicated cooking teacher who regularly holds classes in Verona and Sicily. This is a simple, uncluttered dish, yet still special enough for easy entertaining.

- 1 cup (250 ml or 8 fluid ounces) extra virgin olive oil
- 2 tablespoons fresh lemon juice
- 1 teaspoon salt
- 2 garlic cloves, crushed
- 1 fresh chilli, finely chopped
- 1 tablespoon finely chopped fresh basil
- 2–3 tablespoons finely chopped parsley
- 2 tablespoons finely chopped pine nuts
- 1 teaspoon fennel seeds
- 6 sword fish (or tuna or marlin) fillets, about 150 grams (5 ounces) each

Combine all the ingredients except the fish, and leave at room temperature for one hour.

Brush the fish with a little extra olive oil, and place on grill. Cook for two or three minutes on either side, leaving the middle just rare. Serve with a bowl of the herb sauce, and a good salad.

Serves 6.

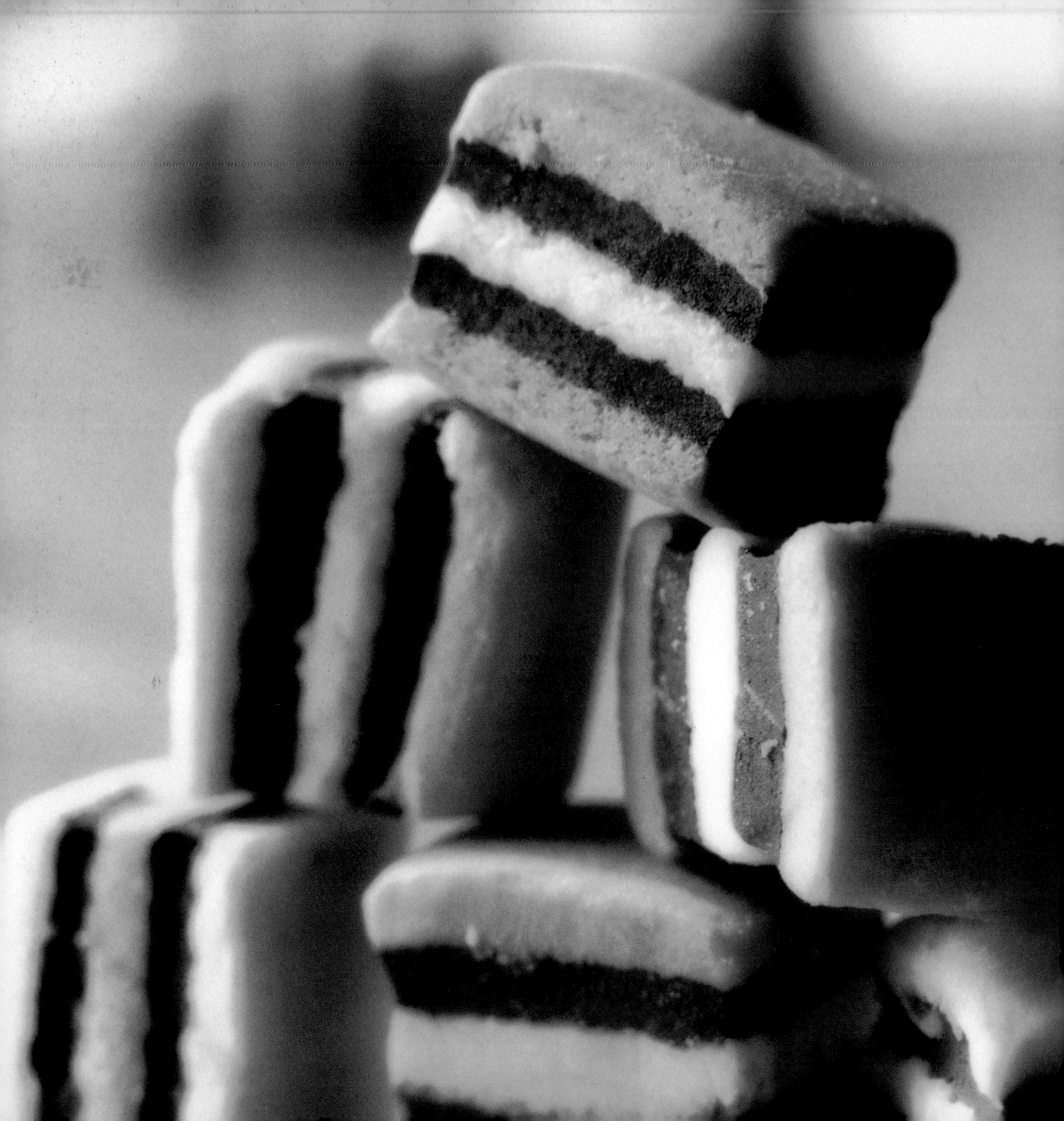

Survival of the fattest

There is nothing quite like the first day of a diet, with all the promise of svelte slimness and social success stretching tantalisingly before you. Unless, of course, every day is the first day of your diet.

Yes, I'm afraid there is now a word that is found on my lips more often than Cantonese double-cooked belly pork.

The time has come to lose a great deal of the gains I have made over the past few years, a fact that has been confirmed by my near and dear. Eyes that once stared lovingly into mine now drift downwards, as if against their will, to settle on my stomach.

Friends who always used to ask me how I could eat so much and remain so slim now only ask me how I could eat so much.

Even my chiropractor seems more worried about my middle front than my lower back. He recently tucked a little list into my hand and mumbled something that sounded like death knell. On reflection, it could have been de-tox diet.

I thought his list of foods didn't look too bad for an average meal. Then it dawned on me that the list was of things I was *not* to eat.

No meat. No coffee. No tea. No chocolate. No milk. No butter. No cheese. No poultry. No seafood. No chillies. *No chillies!!* No sugar. No alcohol. No eggplant. No capsicums. No way.

About all that seemed to be left off the hit list were bananas and nuts, which is exactly how I would have wound up after two weeks.

I attached it to the fridge door in the hope that I would shame myself into doing it. Instead, every time I laid eyes on it, I just had to have a restorative beer, a few slices of cloth-bound cheddar, a chunk of spicy salami, and a dill pickle.

But now the time has come to put my fork down.

The thought is depressing. I must be one of those baby boomers who were taught from an early age to equate food with love. Like most kids, I was bribed with sweets and fizzy drinks into making life liveable for my parents. Parties and other good times where everyone had fun came to be represented by an excess of pink icing and jellybeans. The die was cast. Food meant happiness, and presents, and pin-the-tail-on-the-donkey. No wonder I find myself craving fairy bread whenever I am upset, tired, stressed, hungover or all four.

There is also a vague gnawing in my stomach when I think about dieting that can only be identified as resentment. We can rule out hunger. I don't think I've felt hungry, really, truly hungry, since I was a skinny eighteen year old who smoked his way through his weekly pay cheque. I resent the fact that I have to stop eating what I like, when I like. It's not my fault that I'm overweight. It's this silly sedentary society. It's a twentieth-century disease. It's in my genes. It's because I'm a writer. And anyway, who says I have to be skinny? And so on.

I have tried before, you know, and failed. In the early Eighties, Michel Guerard's *Cuisine Minceur* was as seductive as any drug. 'I wanted to produce a complete festival of light meals for slimming,' wrote Guerard, 'with salads as fresh as children's laughter, gleaming fish, the heavy scent of forbidden peaches, and roast chickens as deliciously perfumed as those of my childhood picnics'.

But the reality was not quite so idyllic. My breakfast at Guerard's luxurious Eugenie-les-Bains health spa in the southwest of France consisted of a glass of sulphuric spa water, a single boiled egg and a ghastly rice bubble cake. The forbidden peaches must have been forbidden.

Then there was the time I signed myself into a local health care centre for a lost weekend. Things went well until dinner, which began at 5.30 in the afternoon with grace, then went on to broccoli with brown rice and potatoes, and rhubarb crumble. The dinner table conversation revolved around how many kilojoules were in a pat of butter, and if it were true that broken biscuits contained fewer calories than whole ones. I went to bed at seven with a pile of gourmet magazines, and wept into my rosehip tea.

This time around, I look to the experts for guidance. Americans know all about dieting. It's the second most popular pastime in the country, after eating.

Between 1960 and 1980, the mean weight of Miss USA winners dropped by 3.4 kilograms, while at the same time, the mean weight of the average American woman went up by 2.6 kilograms. The gap between image and reality continues to widen, as they invent no-fat fats, and conduct fat-reducing cosmetic surgery live on day time television shows.

Can someone tell me, while I'm at this point, why I have to lust after skinny women? Who started this scam? I don't actually like skinny women. They feel like peanut brittle when you hug them. And they always make me wonder why they are so skinny. Are they ill? Don't they ever order pizza?

I also happen to think that most women like a man with some meat on his bones. Someone that makes a good hug worthwhile. Someone that makes them, by comparison, look skinny.

I reject the idea of a meal replacement diet of any kind because they're not real. It's like being a lab rat, fed a specific diet for a certain amount of time. You don't learn anything about how to eat in the real world, once you stop paying for their food and start eating yours. And as much as I have my doubts about sugar, I also have my doubts about the long-term effects of artificial sweeteners and anything that contributes to the word 'lite'.

I also reject the grapefruit diet, the pineapple diet, the black coffee and lettuce diet and the meat only diet, on the basis of their sheer stupidity. Fat people aren't dumb, you know.

Then there are the heavy duty, whizz bang diets: the low-fat, anti-cholesterol, lite-on-protein, alcohol-is-the-devil-incarnate diets. But I've seen people who have been on these diets. Sure, they're skinny. Their clothes hang off them. But so does their skin. The men all have grand canyons of creases running from their once chubby cheeks to their once dimpled chin. They don't look happy.

What I need is not a diet, but a conscious way of eating and honouring good food. If I enjoy the taste of good natural food, I would be less likely to pervert it with unnatural sauces and fat-based accompaniments.

So I'm not going on a diet after all. I am going to run in the mornings, and cut back on the booze, and allow the butter police to have their way and reduce my intake to three meals a day. Apart from that, I'm really not going to think about it much.

(THUD.) What was that? Did you hear it? I think I just lost something.

yum

Sticky toffee pudding

One of the few old-style English-style puddings to crash through the stodge barrier. Clever enough for dinner parties, yet comfort-zone enough for around the telly.

- 1 cup (185 grams or 6 ounces) dates, pitted and chopped
- 1 teaspoon bicarbonate of soda
- 1 cup (250 ml or 8 fluid ounces) boiling water
- 2 tablespoons butter
- 155 grams (5 ounces) soft brown sugar
- 2 eggs
- 1½ cups (185 grams or 6 ounces) self-raising flour, sifted

Toffee sauce

- 1 cup (155 grams or 5 ounces) soft brown sugar
- ¾ cup (185 ml or 6 ounces) light whipping cream
- ½ teaspoon vanilla essence
- 2 tablespoons butter

Heat the oven to 180°C (350°F).

Mix the dates and bicarbonate of soda in a heatproof bowl. Pour the boiling water on top and leave to stand.

Cream the butter and sugar until pale, then add the eggs, one at a time, beating well after each addition.

Gently fold in the flour, stir in the date mixture, and pour into a lightly buttered 18-cm or 7-in square or round cake tin.

Bake in the oven for 40 minutes, or until a skewer comes out clean.

To make the sauce, combine the sugar, cream, vanilla essence and butter in a saucepan, bring to the boil, stirring, and simmer for five minutes. Set aside until ready to serve, then reheat quickly when needed.

Cut the pudding into squares and place each square in the centre of a warm dinner plate. Pour hot toffee sauce over each square, and serve with fresh cream.

Serves 4.

A load of tripe

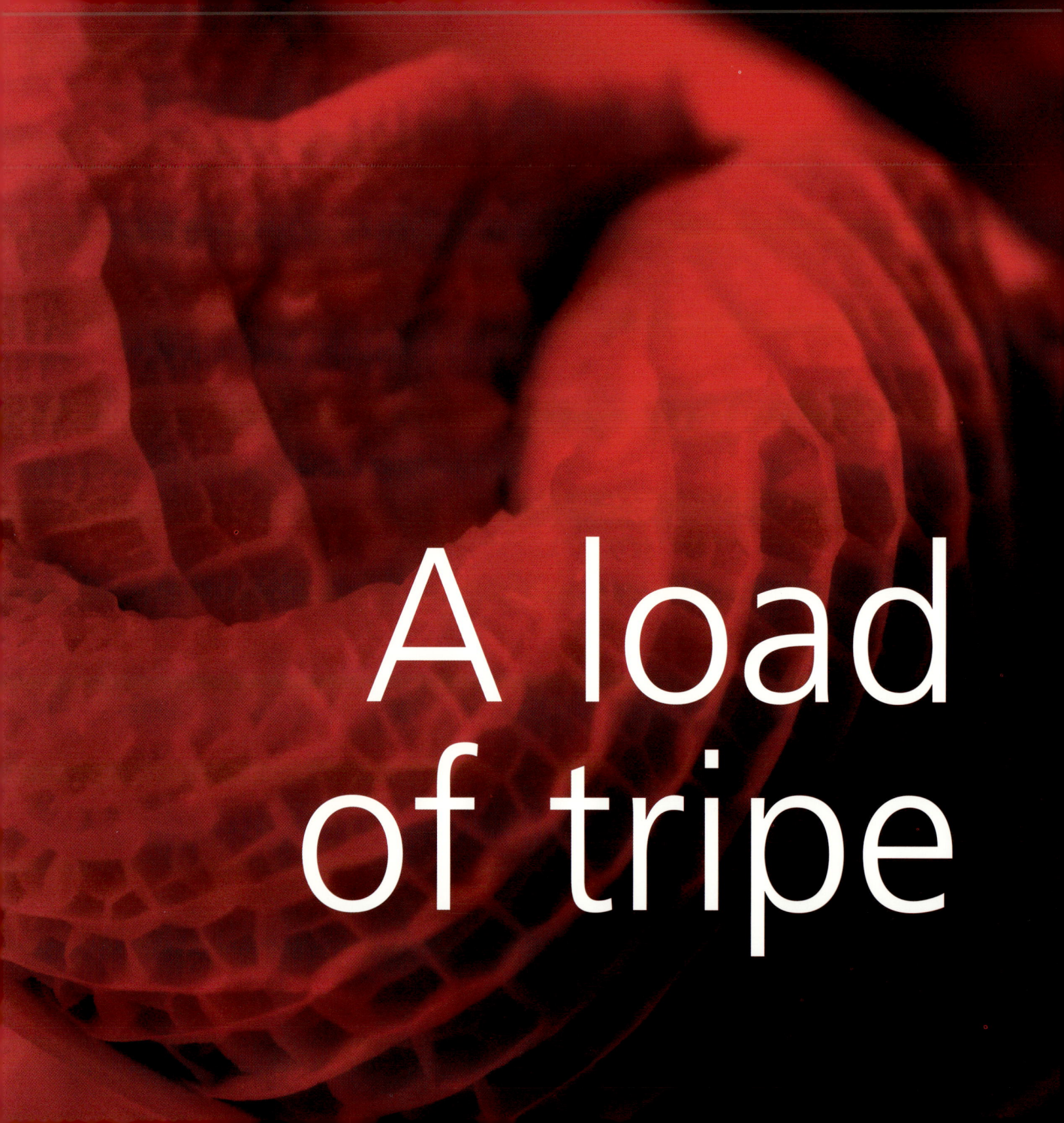

'You don't know what real food is', said Geoffrey. 'I'll show you real food.'

We assemble in his dining room the following week, to feast on rich, creamy dips alive with garlic and herbs, platters of meatballs, chunks of salty fetta cheese, intensely flavoured roasted capsicums, and dark, dank, delicious olives.

No doubt about it. This is about as real as food can get. Then our host bursts into the room carrying the main course on a large silver platter.

We stare with glazed eyes and open mouths at the sight of eight roasted sheep's heads, staring back with glazed eyes and open mouths. From every mouth protrudes a large, dark sausage. An eerie hush falls over the room. It's not every night your dinner watches you while you eat it.

'Unbelievable', mutters someone to my right.

'I know', says Geoffrey apologetically. 'I tried to get them with their tongues still in, but they were all sold out, so I had to use sausages instead. But at least the brains are still there…look!'

He proceeds to wrench back the top jaw of the head in front of him, and dips his fork into the brain.

'Ah', he sighs contentedly. 'Just like Mum used to make.'

Geoffrey is what used to be known in the Eighties as an offal bore. He likes to get to the heart of the matter. And the liver, kidneys, and pancreas. He is part of the growing wave of discerning diners with inside knowledge, who are changing the shape of restaurant menus all over the world.

These are people bored to the back teeth with paying small fortunes for tasteless chicken fillets, lean beef and farmed trout. They are the ones who prefer the bone marrow to the meat in osso buco, and who relentlessly drown out polite conversation with their noisy slurping and sucking. They like to crunch the bones. They always bag the parson's nose, and they argue that the real beauty of most meat goes way beyond skin deep. Give them the naughty bits any day, the strangely shaped odds and ends that most people push around their plates, and try to hide under the knife and fork.

Naturally, I am one of them.

I have loved offal all my life. I even loved that terror of the Anglo baby boomer, tripe with white sauce and onions. I lusted after Tuesday's crumbed brains and bacon, and was first at the table for Thursday's lamb's fry, cooked stiff as a board in the electric frypan and smothered in packet gravy.

Not sharing my passion for offal, my three brothers finally concluded that there was something seriously wrong with me. I was beginning to think there might be something to this theory, until I travelled and discovered the inside story for myself.

The world, I was overjoyed to find, was full of offal bores.

In Florence, I discovered my beloved tripe miraculously transformed into a culinary work of art. Gone were the large chunks and floury sauce, and in their place, meltingly tender, thin strips of perfectly cooked honeycomb tripe coated in a rich tomatoey sauce full of bounce and life. Every country I visited boasted a tripe dish more complex and more satisfying than the last.

There was the French tripe à la mode, rich with cider and sweet with onions; the Cantonese yum cha special of mixed tripe cooked in chilli and star anise scented gravy; and the remarkable Spanish creation, callos a la Madrilena, a witches' brew of chorizo sausages, pig's ears, pig's feet and honeycomb tripe.

But for the serious Italian offal fancier,

all roads lead to Rome's Checchino dal 1887 restaurant at Monte Testaccio, opposite the old Roman abattoirs. Many years ago, the abattoir workers received a proportion of their pay in kind, in the form of intestines, feet, tails and other parts of animals that had no commercial value. They would bring their 'wages' over the road to the restaurant where the chef would invent ingenious, delicious new dishes.

Today, Checchino is invariably packed as tight as a pig's trotter, and you have to pay substantial amounts of inedible lire for the Marianis' magical, marvellous trippa alla Romana (tripe in a meaty gravy.), rich and luscious rigatoni con pajata (pasta with calves' intestines), sublime oxtail stew and irresistible fagioli e cotiche (beans and pork fat). Add a couple of bottles of the local Picchioli wine from the Marianis' miraculous cellar, and you'll never want to say arrivederci to Roma.

Of course, when an offal aficionado dies and goes to heaven, he or she arrives by Star Ferry at Hong Kong.

I have revelled in a late night supper of congee with fresh pig's liver, lost myself in a marvellous hotpot of kidney and abalone, and discovered a new meaning to the word 'crisp', during a typical peasant meal of deep-fried crunchy pig's intestines, the Cantonese snack-attack equivalent of potato chips.

The Chinese are masters at 'making do'. So I wasn't surprised when one restaurant owner sidled up to me, eyes darting left and right. Nervously, he asked in a stage whisper if I would like to try something 'really special'.

'Sure. What?'

More darting of eyes. 'Beef special.'

'Beef Special. Wow!'

'From a very special part of the bull.'

The Hong Kong dollar finally dropped.

Not having eaten bull's penis before, I *was a little tentative, but nevertheless managed to rise to the occasion when the steaming claypot arrived.*

It was a textural cocktail, smooth, slippery, crunchy and rubbery all at once.

The minute I got home, I rang my good friend and fellow offal lover, Loredana, and she went the next night.

'I want the penis', she said, being the direct sort of girl she is.

Excessive eye darting.

'The penis?'

'Yes. My friend had it last night. The bull's penis. In a claypot.'

There was not a single glimmer of recognition in his face.

'Offal. Penis,' she repeated. '*Penis. Offal.*'

'Ah yes! Of course!' said the waiter, and rushed off. Loredana watched him tap the piano player on the shoulder, cutting short a fairly ordinary rendition of 'Hey Jude' in its prime.

'Very sorry', said the waiter, on his return. 'Very sorry for offal penis.'

Trippa alla Fiorentina

While pre-cooked tripe might be faster, it will never match doing it yourself for flavour and control over texture. Most butchers can order raw tripe in for you, if you ask nicely enough. Of course, if you don't have a whole day to kill, you can use the pre-cooked variety. Just forget the first five hours cooking and cut the cooking time to about an hour.

- 750 grams (1½ pounds) raw honeycomb tripe
- 2 onions
- 3 celery stalks finely chopped
- 3 large carrots
- handful of parsley stalks
- 4 tablespoons olive oil
- 2 garlic cloves, peeled and bruised
- 1½ cups (375 ml or 12 fluid ounces) dry white wine
- 6 ripe tomatoes or 1 can roma tomatoes
- 2 cups (500 ml or 16 fluid ounces) stock (chicken or veal)
- 1 sprig rosemary
- salt to taste
- 3 tablespoons grated Parmigiano
- 2 tablespoons butter
- 1 tablespoon chopped parsley

Wash the tripe under plenty of cold running water, then place in a saucepan of cold, salted water. Bring to the boil and blanch for five minutes. Drain and rinse in cold water until cool enough to handle. Cut the tripe into thin strips and place in a saucepan of water with one onion, one celery stick and one carrot, all roughly chopped, and the parsley stalks. Bring to the boil, then simmer for four to five hours or until tripe just starts to turn tender.

Meanwhile, heat the oil in a heavy-bottomed pan and add the garlic, the remaining onion, carrots and celery, all finely chopped and sauté until the onion turns a golden colour. Add the wine and turn up the heat until the liquid is reduced by half. Add the tomatoes, stock, rosemary and the drained, simmered tripe.

Cover and cook gently for two hours, stirring every now and then, adding more stock if needed.

Just before serving, season, add the Parmigiano and butter, and stir through. Sprinkle with the parsley.

Serves 4 to 6.

Tripe à la mode de Caen

This Normandy specialty is tripe nirvana. Not only is it the most famous tripe recipe of all time, it is also probably the most famous offal recipe of all time. Be warned though. There is a lot of work and a lot of time involved, as this is a dish that does not take kindly to short cuts. Traditionally, housewives would take their tripe to the local baker who would cook it for them in an earthenware tripiere. However, a normal domestic casserole dish works as well.

- 1.5 kilograms (3 pounds) raw tripe
- 1 calf's foot, split and cut into 7.5-cm (3-in) lengths
- 2 tablespoons butter
- 500 grams (1 pound) carrots finely sliced
- 500 grams (1 pound) onions finely sliced
- 1 bouquet garni of bay leaf, thyme, parsley
- ½ teaspoon grated nutmeg
- salt and pepper
- 5 tablespoons of Calvados or Cognac
- 1.5 litres (2½ pints) approximately dry cider
- flour and water for paste

Wash the tripe and calf's foot under cold, running water, then place in a saucepan of cold, salted water. Bring to the boil and blanch for five minutes. Drain and rinse under cold water. Where you can, cut the meat from the pieces of calf's foot and reserve. Cut the tripe into 4-cm to 5-cm (1½-in to 2-in) squares.

Rub the inside of a large casserole with the butter. Cover the bottom of the casserole with half the carrots and onions, then add half the tripe and calf's foot pieces. Repeat process, then add bouquet garni and calf's foot bones. Sprinkle Calvados over and add enough dry cider to cover. Add grated nutmeg, salt and pepper, and cover with a lid. Make a paste of flour and water to seal around the edge of the casserole.

Cook in a slow oven (160°C or 300°F) for about eight or nine hours.

Remove the bouquet garni and bones. Add the Calvados and simmer, uncovered, on the top of the stove for a few minutes. Adjust the seasoning as required.

Traditionally, this is accompanied by a 'trou Normande', a glass of Calvados. But a Pinot Noir, or even a good cider is just as nice.

Serves 6.

Callos a la Madrilena

A real lipsticker of a dish, although I must admit I have taken a few liberties with the Spanish original. In this version, I have added beans. Mainly because I like beans.

500 grams (1 pound) raw tripe
2 pig's trotters
1 teaspoon salt
1 tablespoon white wine vinegar
3 onions, peeled
8 garlic cloves, peeled
1 dessertspoon peppercorns
2 bay leaves
4 tablespoons olive oil
2 fresh chorizo sausages
6 thick slices of kaiserfleisch
1 dessertspoon sweet paprika
2 fresh morcilla sausages
1.5 litres (2½ pints) chicken stock
1 cup (220 grams or 7 ounces) cannellini beans, soaked overnight and cooked 45 minutes
2 tablespoons tomato paste

Clean the tripe in several changes of water, then place in a large pot of cold water along with the trotters, salt and vinegar. Bring to the boil, and blanch for five minutes.

Drain and rinse in cold water. Cut the tripe into strips, roughly 5 cm by 1.5 cm (2 in by ½ in) and return to the pot with the trotters, two onions, five cloves of garlic, peppercorns and bay leaves.

Cover with cold water, bring to boil and simmer for five hours. Remove trotters, cool, then take out bones and chop meat and skin coarsely. Strain tripe and reserve the stock.

Heat the olive oil in a heavy, ovenproof casserole and fry the remaining onion, finely chopped, until soft. Add the chorizo sausages (pricked roughly with a fork), kaiserfleisch, three chopped cloves of garlic and paprika. When chorizo starts to change colour, add the morcilla sausages, the chopped trotter, beans, tripe, chicken stock and tomato paste, and simmer for 30 minutes.

Remove the casserole to the oven and cook for an hour at 175°C (350°F).

Serves 4.

yum

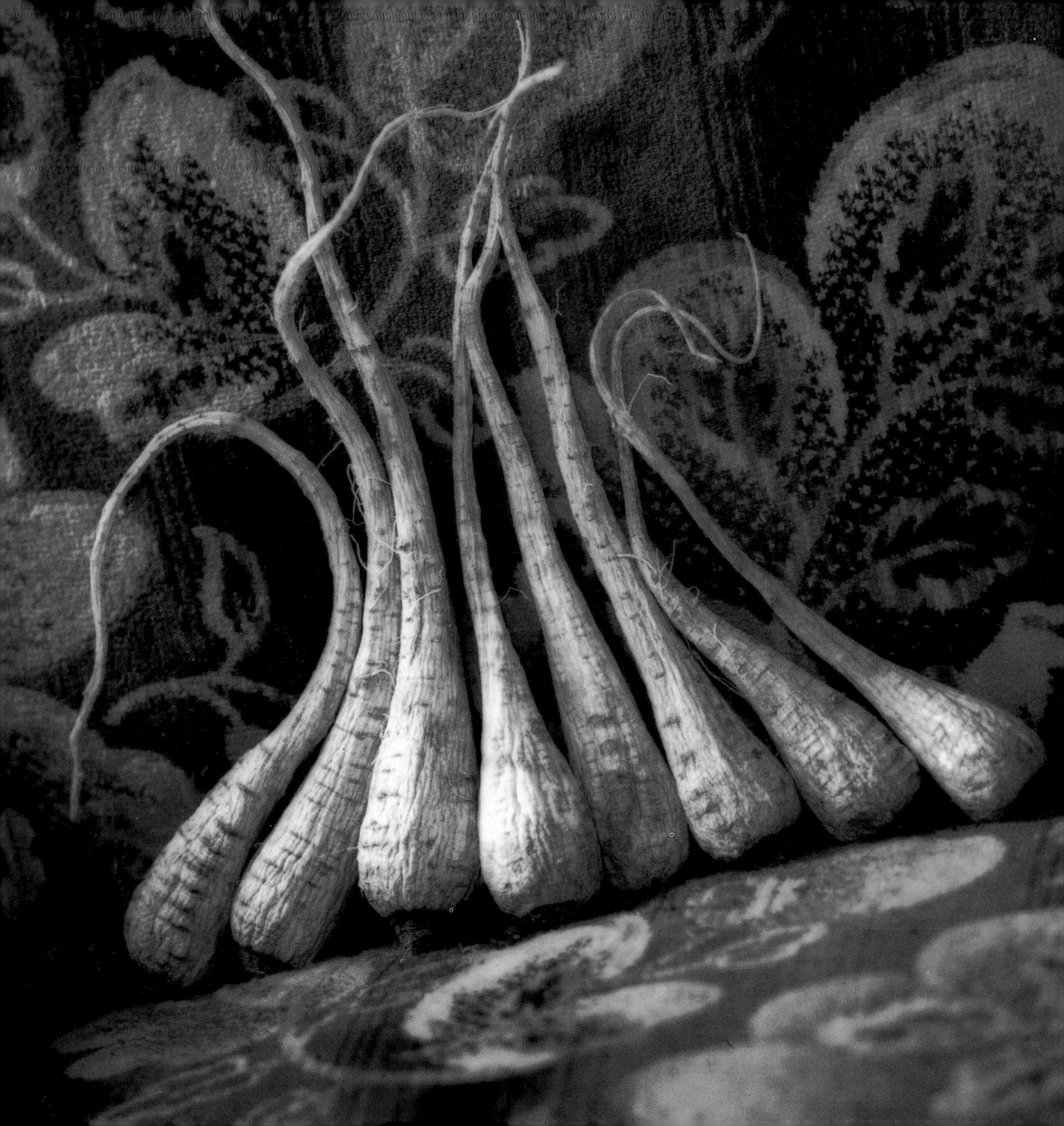

Cold comfort

Summer is a dreadfully over-rated season. The warmer weather is all very well for those free spirits who like to cavort around polluted waterways risking cancer and sunstroke, but it's not for me.

Personally, I relish the idea of not perspiring for another six months, of getting dressed in the morning, rather than undressed, and of slippers by the fire rather than sandals by the back door.

Apart from the fact that you're freezing to death, you really know you're alive in winter. For one thing, you can see your own breath. And while there is far less opportunity to show off one's bare body, this can be a godsend for those of us who happen to look so much more attractive in clothes than out of them.

There is something about the cold that keeps families together too. The heat of summer melts family bonds like butter, and everybody disappears into thin air, to beaches, lakes, parks and outdoor concerts. You don't see families playing board games while huddled around the air conditioner. Six months later, however, the cold acts as a bonding agent. The children turn up again, drawn to roasting chestnuts and toasting marshmallows.

Winter is just so much more civilised. After all, man's greatest leaps forward have all been perpetrated in dismal, overcast conditions. Blue skies and sunshine are more conducive to meeting immediate bodily needs, but grey skies, bitter winds and driving rain keep people indoors thinking, talking, reading, and of course, eating. Which brings me to the very best thing about winter.

Food.

Winter is lovely weather for ducks. It's also great weather for quail, excellent weather for pigeon, marvellous weather for pheasant, and sensational weather for goose. You know winter is upon you when you find yourself suddenly thinking of meals you haven't had for months: roast meat with all the trimmings, life-supporting stews and casseroles, and thick, hearty soups with restorative powers modern medicine can only dream about.

It's no coincidence that the greatest food in the world comes from countries that have a winter. I don't mean your namby-pamby cool tropical season with its few cloudy days and barely discernible drop in temperature. I'm talking about your real, honest-to-goodness frosty, icy, bleak and nasty job.

This is the sort of weather that has produced such classics as the Alsatian choucroute, the Italian bollito misto, the Russian bortsch, the Scottish haggis, the Swiss fondue, the Hungarian gulyas and, perhaps the greatest of them all, the French cassoulet.

Of course, there is more to do in winter than just eat. One can drink.

Red wines, except for the most frivolous, are wasted on summer. The spicy, peppery feistiness of Shiraz demands the company of a beef daube. The fat, rich mellowness of a Cabernet is lost and lonely when not near a hearty, bubbling pot au feu or navarin of lamb. And the subtle, fruity charms of a Pinot Noir fall flat when not flirting with a head-spinning coq au vin, jumping with tiny onions and lardons of smoky bacon.

White wines have a rather special affinity with winter, when they can happily be drunk at room temperature without having their flavour frozen in the fridge. Sweet Sauternes, Tokays, Muscats and ports are all wet weather wonders, and sherry especially comes into its own.

Even Mother Nature, perhaps the

greatest foodie of all, seems to love winter as much as I do. Why else would all the things I love suddenly become available?

Everyone should be game to try game in winter, when it has more flavour and character. Pheasant, guinea fowl and partridge replace Thai prawn salads and barbecued octopus at dinner parties. And, in a master stroke of good timing, the new season's oranges, mandarins, lemons and grapefruit, with their vitamin C overload, arrive just in time to help us fight off winter chills and ills.

This is time to get back to your roots, and feast on roasted parsnips, hot, boiled beetroot, and buttery mashed swedes and turnips. And who needs salads when sweet leeks, brussels sprouts, baby cabbages, cauliflower, broccoli are so good? Apples are at their peak, just in time to be stuffed with raisins and baked or layered into pies, or caramelised into glorious, golden tartes Tatin. Pears are perfect for poaching, and short-lived beauties like celeriac, kohlrabi, Jerusalem artichokes and fennel make us rush to sauté and gratin, stuff and batter, bake and boil.

Any food lovers worth their Maldon sea salt know that the only time to visit another country is between late autumn and early spring. That way, you will be in Tuscany in time to feast on hearty boar stews and gorge yourself on delicious, gamey sausages flavoured with fennel. You will be in southern France in time for the best foie gras and the first rush of glorious wild mushrooms like ceps, chanterelles, and pied de mouton. In Hong Kong, you can pig out on the first of the Shanghai hairy crabs. And in northern Italy, you can savour one of the world's truly remarkable flavours: white truffle.

Spring and summer are not without some attraction. Lamb is good, and herbs return to brighten our lives. Sweet basil turns our heads, and fresh lemony thyme stimulates the senses. Oh, and seafood too, now that I come to think about it. Painterly little pipis, scallops on the shell and marvellous mussels come into their own within the reach of the average corporate raider.

I also seem to remember lunches of poached salmon and chilled Semillon. And freshly picked strawberries and cream, and dusky Bellini cocktails made by squeezing luscious, ripe white peaches into frosty flutes of sparkling wines, and the last golden glow of the setting sun, and the sand in my toes, and ripe red juicy tomatoes and basil smashed onto grilled sourdough bread, and icy cold beer.

When, oh when, will this cold, hard winter ever end?

Pea and ham soup

Soups like this is make you realise why winter was invented in the first place.

- 1 ham bone, with most of the ham removed
- 1 smoked pork hock
- 2 litres (3½ pints) water
- 4 carrots, peeled and chopped
- 3 celery stalks, chopped
- 3 onions, peeled and chopped
- 2 bay leaves
- 500 grams (1 pound) yellow split peas, soaked overnight and drained

Put the ham bone, pork hock and water into a large pan and bring to the boil. Skim off any froth that floats to the surface over a few minutes of simmering. When the water is clear, add the carrots, celery, onion, bay leaves and split peas. Cook, partly covered, for two hours over a gentle heat, allowing a few bubbles to disturb the surface. If the water reduces too much, add more. Continue skimming, if necessary.

It is best to allow the soup to stand overnight so you can take off any fat that rises to the surface. Then reheat, remove bone and ham hock, and shred the meat from the bones, discarding skin and fat. Return the meat to soup, reheat, and serve.

For a very fine soup, remove the bones and blend the remaining soup mixture. Push soup through a food mill or fine sieve, and return the purée to the saucepan with the shredded ham to heat through, then serve.

Serves 6.

Old-fashioned oxtail stew

My bone-sucking career began with my mum's oxtail stew. Since then I have graduated to osso buco bones, glazed pork ribs and lamb shanks, but you never forget your roots.

salt and pepper
2 tablespoons flour
2 oxtails, cut into joints
3 tablespoons butter
2 onions, chopped
2 tablespoons olive oil
2 thick bacon rashers, chopped
2 garlic cloves, minced
1 cup (250 ml or 8 fluid ounces) red wine
1.5 litres (2½ pints) beef or veal stock
6 peppercorns
1 bouquet garni
2 carrots chopped
2 turnips, chopped
chopped fresh parsley

Salt, pepper and flour the oxtail pieces. Brown them in the melted butter in a large saucepan, then remove from the pan.

Add the onions (adding more oil if necessary), and cook until golden. Add the bacon and garlic, and cook gently for a couple of minutes. Return the oxtail to the pan. Pour in the wine and, over high heat, reduce to about a third.

Add the stock, peppercorns and bouquet garni. Bring to the boil and skim the fat from the surface.

Cover and simmer gently for about two hours.

Check the seasoning, then add the carrots and turnips, and continue to simmer for another one to one and a half hours.

Garnish with parsley and serve with boiled potatoes.

Serves 6.

Sticky chocolate pudding

If ever three words needed a winter to come alive in, it's 'sticky', 'chocolate' and 'pudding'. This is a lovely old-fashioned pudding all crisp and cakey on top with a lush, chocolate sauce below.

    120 grams (4 ounces) self-raising flour
    2 tablespoons cocoa
    pinch of salt
    100 grams (3½ ounces) soft butter
    ½ cup (100 grams or 3½ ounces)
       castor sugar
    2 eggs, slightly beaten
    dash of vanilla essence
    1 to 2 tablespoons of milk

Sauce

    100 grams (3½ ounces) brown sugar
    2 tablespoons cocoa
    1 cup (250 ml or 8 fluid ounces)
       boiling water

Heat the oven to 180°C (350°F).
    Sift together the flour, cocoa and salt. Cream the butter and sugar until pale, then gradually beat in eggs and vanilla. Fold in the flour mixture and the milk until mixture is soft, and spoon into a buttered ovenproof baking dish.
    To make the sauce, pour boiling water over the cocoa and brown sugar and stir until they are dissolved. Pour the sauce over the pudding, and bake for 30 to 40 minutes until the top has formed a crust, centre is cooked, and bottom is runny.
    Serves 4.

Marriages made

in the kitchen

It was the perfect marriage. They had grown up together, childhood sweethearts, practically entwined about each other from birth. They were the epitome of opposites attracting.

One was plump, round, sweet and docile, while the other was lean and feisty, a volatile sort of character who always made people sit up and take notice.

Nevertheless, they were made for each other.

Compared to tomato and basil, Romeo and Juliet were pen pals and Gable and Lombard were just good friends.

These two soulmates possess what scientists and sex manuals call a natural affinity for one another. Add a little olive oil and you've got the definitive spaghetti sauce. Add grilled bread, and you have a sensational bruschetta. Throw in fresh mozzarella, and you have the perfect pizza topping, or a miraculous insalata Caprese. Combine with fresh garden vegetables, and you have the makings of a minestrone.

Your average backyard herb patch is a hotbed of passion, lust and intrigue.

Dill is simply counting the days until it can be alone with an Atlantic salmon, mint is waiting to kiss a ripe red strawberry, tarragon is dreaming of firm, young chicken breasts, and oregano is biding its time until it can get its hands on some Greek fetta.

Don't let the kids go out there alone. They'll only come back with those darned awkward questions.

To British chef Nico Ladenis, steak and chips, coffee and rum, and cold lobster with mayonnaise are marriages made in heaven. I would add fresh pear and Parmigiano, fig and prosciutto, toast and marmalade, vodka and cranberry juice, beer and pickled onions and blue cheese and Sauternes.

Another expert on the subject is *enfant terrible* turned adult respectable, Marco Pierre White.

Marco insists he is not in the matchmaking business. 'There are too many chefs trying to dream up all sorts of exotic flavour combinations, but you can't reinvent the wheel', he says, drawing deeply on a cigarette and rattling off words like a human Gattling gun. 'The great combinations have already been invented', he says. 'Beef and red wine, cabbage with pigeon, gin and tonic.'

So what is the ultimate food partnership?

'Oysters and caviar', he says. 'That has to be the sexiest combination in the world.'

Sometimes you have to work at a marriage, to make it succeed. As Shelley Winters said: 'In Hollywood, all marriages are happy. It's trying to live together that's difficult.'

A chef with the talent of Lucas-Carton's Alain Senderens can combine roasted lobster with vanilla and get away with it. Roger Verge can toss pheasant with chartreuse and emerge triumphant. Anton Mosimann can even cook eel with sake, honey, soy sauce and yoghurt and still retain his reputation. Just.

But in the hands of lesser mortals, food marriages as reckless as these would doubtless end in an irreconcilable breakdown. In the early Eighties the foodie divorce rate soared, with fairly inept interpretations of nouvelle cuisine by English-speaking chefs who were slow to catch on to the fact that raspberries are not attracted to beef, mango does not want to be seen out with lamb and kiwi fruit is a misogynist perfectly suited to the life of a bachelor.

Also tricky, are mixed marriages. You have only to look back at the unlikely concoctions whipped up in the name of East meets West in the late Eighties. Galangal married beneath it in a sorbet; water chestnuts were unhappy being caramelised, and sun-dried tomatoes hated being seen in a stirfry.

The most successful culinary marriages of all are the marriages of food and wine. The combination of beef and burgundy is as natural as the air we breathe. Caviar and champagne are inseparable, and are far more likely to end up in a bankruptcy court than a divorce court. A fine consommé inclines towards a fine sherry, and oysters are as much at home with a chilled Sancerre as they are with sea water.

Then there is the most glorious and decadent marriage of them all: foie gras and Sauternes. This is more than a marriage. This is love, lust and true friendship all rolled up into one.

As an enthusiastic home cook, it's fun to introduce one flavour to another, just to see what happens. With enough experience, you build up a palate memory, and can actually 'taste' the combination in your head long before you buy the raw materials.

Of course we all make mistakes, which is not the time to bring up the memory of my John Dory and purple cabbage. More the time to remember the words of that wonderful babe, Mamie Van Doren.

'I've married a few people I shouldn't have', she said. 'But haven't we all?'

Insalata Caprese

Not just a neat respectable little marriage, but a nice, juicy ménage à trois. The bocconcini loves basil, but then so does the tomato. As for the basil, it just can't choose between them.

> 6 small ripe tomatoes
> 6 small fresh bocconcini (mozzarella) cheeses
> fresh basil leaves
> sea salt and freshly ground black pepper
> fruity extra virgin olive oil

Slice the tomato and the cheese into roughly matching slices. On a large plate, overlap the slices, alternating cheese and tomato, and tuck fresh basil leaves in between each slice.

Sprinkle with salt and pepper and drizzle with olive oil. Leave for an hour before eating, for the flavours to fuse.

I also love a few drops of sweet and sour balsamic vinegar on this, and often pile it up into a pyramid, layering tomato and cheese on the way.

Serves 2 as a small course or 4 as a salad.

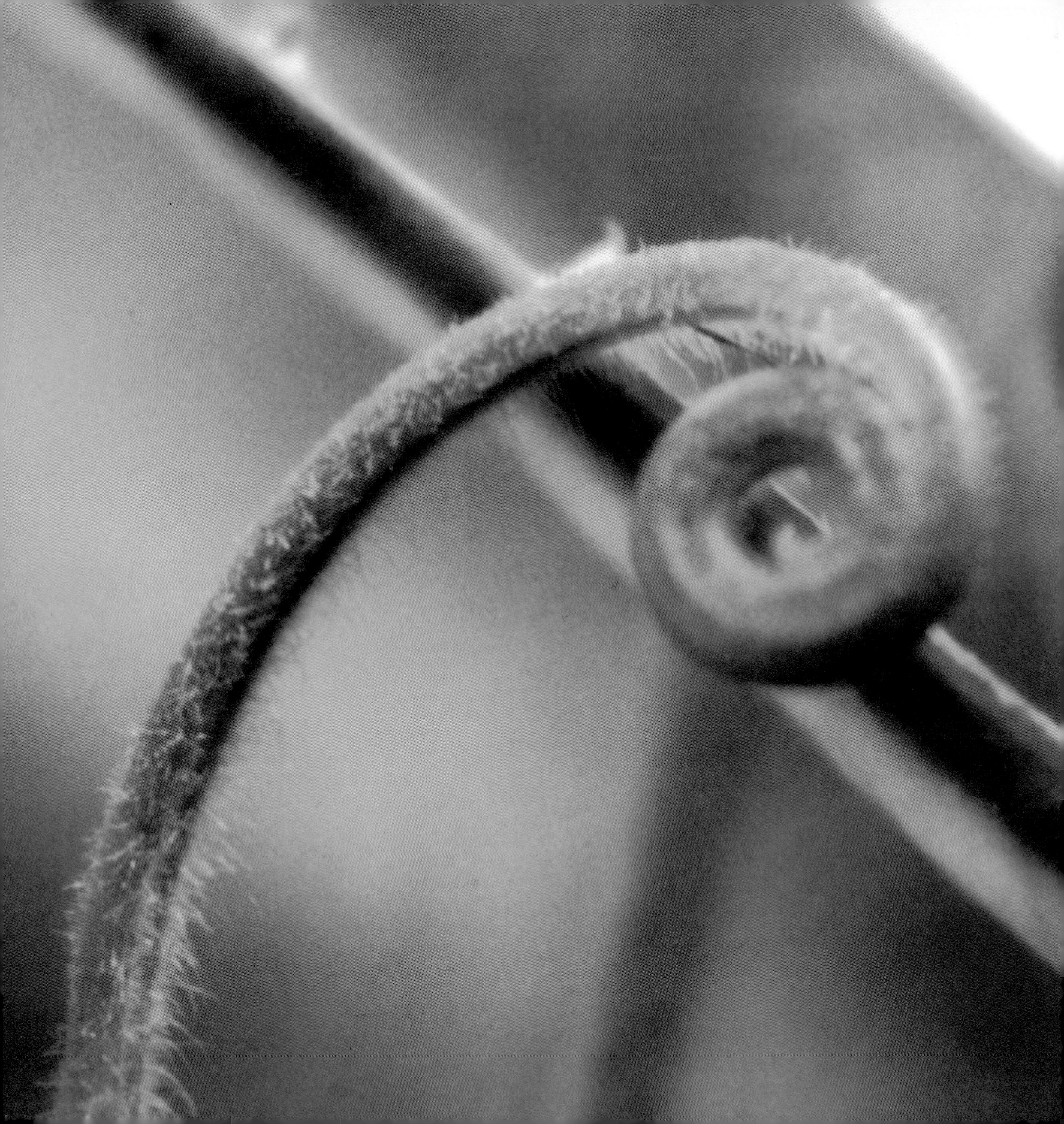

Tagliatelle with tomato and basil

The only cooking involved in this simple dish is boiling the pasta. The 'sauce' is a natural result of the tomatoes, garlic and basil macerating in the oil. The riper the tomatoes and the fresher the basil, the better the sauce.

6 ripe tomatoes
4 tablespoons fresh basil leaves
2 garlic cloves
3 tablespoons extra virgin olive oil
salt and freshly ground black pepper
500 grams (1 pound) tagliatelle

Dunk the tomatoes in boiling water for ten seconds, remove and peel off skin. Cut in half, squeeze out seeds, and roughly chop the remaining flesh.

Mix the tomato with the basil leaves, garlic cloves, olive oil, salt and pepper and leave to marinate in a cool place for two hours.

Cook pasta in plenty of boiling, salted water until al dente, tender but firm to the bite. Drain and toss with the tomatoes in olive oil. Remove the garlic cloves, if you remember. Serve immediately, as the heat of the pasta 'cooks' the tomato sauce. It's not a hot dish, but more a comfortable room temperature dish.

Serves 4.

Note: For a truly sensational pasta dish, make the insalata Caprese on page 158 and dump the whole lot on top of freshly drained, piping hot spaghetti. The heat of the spaghetti softens the cheese, the tomatoes drop their juices, and the pasta absorbs all the flavours. Divine!

Napoletana pizza with tomato and basil

This is not your normal flat pizza, but gorgeous, golden puffed-up balls brought to life with tomato, basil and garlic.

½ teaspoon dry yeast
5 tablespoons warm water
1 cup (125 grams or 4 ounces) plain flour
300 grams (9½ ounces) ripe or canned tomatoes
2 garlic cloves, peeled
salt
1 tablespoon sugar
3 cups (750 ml or 1 pint) peanut oil
fresh basil

Dissolve the yeast in one tablespoon of the warm water, and add to flour in large bowl. Slowly add the remaining water and mix until the dough is firm and elastic. Knead for a few minutes, then shape into a ball and allow to rise in a warm place, covered, for about two hours.

To make the sauce, drop the tomatoes into a pot of boiling water for a few seconds, remove and peel. Cut in half, squeeze out seeds, and chop the remaining flesh. Cook the tomatoes slowly with the garlic, salt and sugar for 20 minutes or so, until soft.

Scatter some flour on the work bench and roll the dough into a log 2.5 cm (1 in) thick. Cut into 2.5-cm (1-in) pieces and roll each piece flat into a round.

Heat the peanut oil and fry each pizza, turning once, until it is golden and puffs up like a ball. Drain on a paper towel. Heat the sauce, stir in the torn basil leaves, and spoon on top of the pizza.

Makes 12.

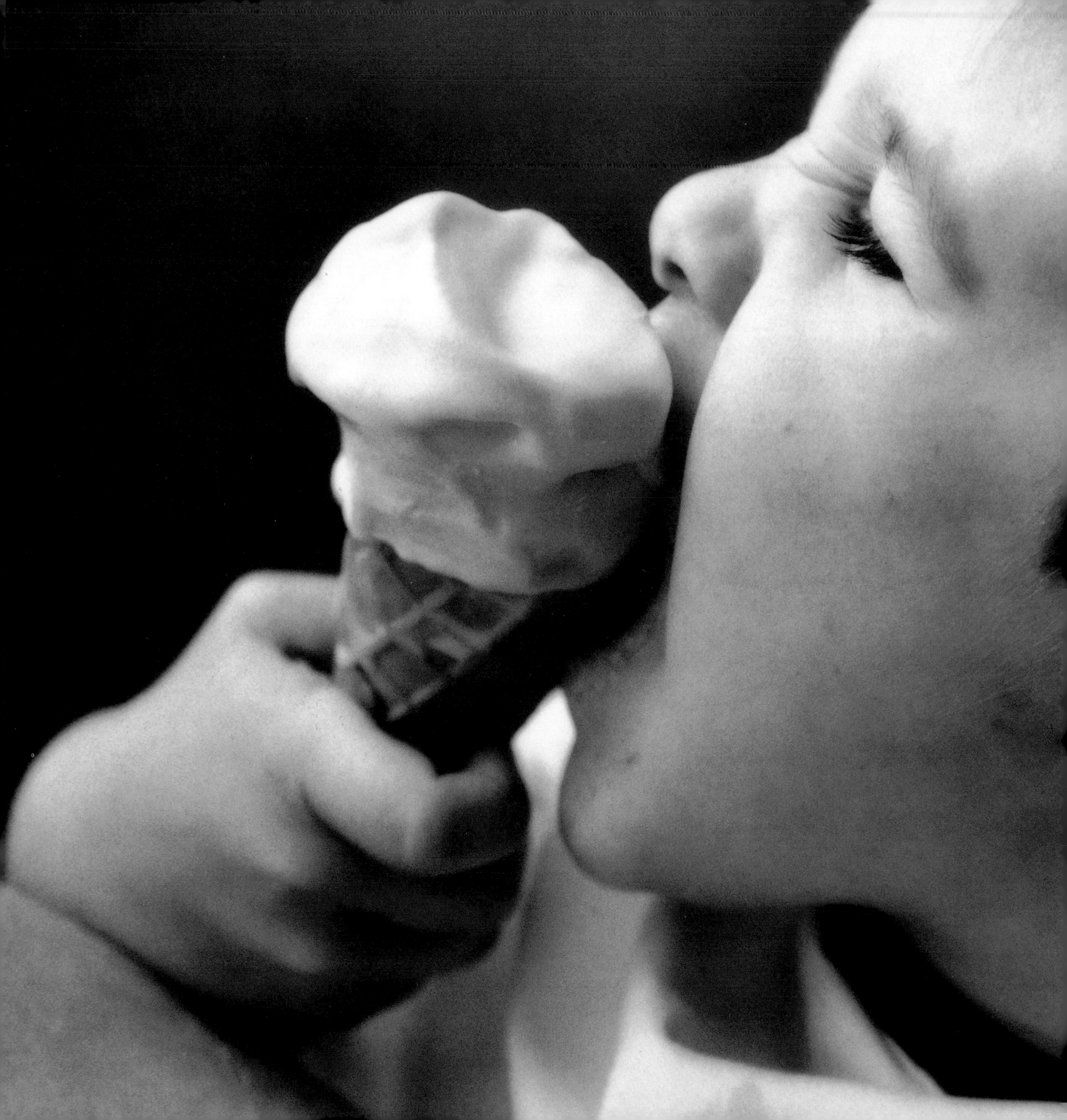

The big chill

We have been driving all of ten minutes when the whingeing starts. It begins as a little whimper here, then a sigh there, until gradually it blossoms into a whole sentence.

'Are we there yet?'

'Still got a fair way to go', I respond cheerfully.

Sigh.

'Can I have an icecream?'

'No, definitely not.' I am firm, but fair. 'You have just had lunch.'

A bored silence descends upon us like a wet fog.

'We just passed an icecream shop.'

'You don't say.'

'Can we stop?'

'No.'

'Awwww...'

'Enn. Ohh. NO.'

Another silence settles in, but this time it's a heavy, resentful type of silence amplified by piercing, accusing stares and a protruding bottom lip.

It's too much for a grown man — even an unfeeling, tyrannical ogre like myself — to bear.

Hating myself for being so weak, I tug at the wheel and park in front of the icecream shop. The car has barely come to a stop when she flings the door open and runs triumphantly into the shop. My wife always gets her way in the end.

Icecream is the safe sex of the food world. Unlike chocolate, we don't even feel all that guilty about eating it.

After tasting icecream for the very first time, the French novelist Henri Stendhal, remarked 'What a pity this isn't a sin'.

According to the family photo album, my own first icecream experience took place when I was about one and a half. The tiny black and white picture shows me sitting on the beach, holding a cone aloft like a glorious trophy. I am wearing a truly smug, satisfied grin, a really cute striped romper suit, and about half the icecream.

It is a curious thing, but when I look at all my other baby pictures, it is as if I am looking at somebody else's childhood. The photographs themselves are my only memories. This picture, on the other hand is different. I swear I can remember the whole thing. I can still taste the icecream (single scoop vanilla) and remember in minute detail the unexpected, chilling thrill that raced to my sandal-clad toes. Pretty remarkable for someone who has difficulty remembering last night's dinner conversation.

So what is the secret ingredient that makes icecream so addictive? According to the icecream makers, there is no secret.

They will tell you icecream is simply a mixture of basic ingredients like cream, eggs, sugar, and milk, whipped and whirled to create the most vital (and cheapest) ingredient of all: air. While it is the egg yolk, or synthetic stabilisers, that give icecream its body and feel, it is the air that gives icecream its softness, and the sensation of disappearing in your mouth. How much air you put into your icecream depends on the quality you want, and the profits you want to make.

Icecream has always had snob appeal. Iced drinks and desserts were cool favourites of ancient China's Imperial Court, while the Arabs, the Persians and the Moghuls supped on a form of icy sherbet between courses, to cleanse the palate.

Among everything else Marco Polo was supposed to have brought back from China was the secret of chilling liquid without ice, by using a mixture of water and saltpetre.

It was to be another two hundred years before the Italians shared this secret with the rest of the world. When Catherine de Medici married the future Henri II of France, her chef, Bernardo Buontalenti astounded the French Court with his ice confections.

For some time, the eating of ices and icecreams remained the domain of the privileged few, featuring at Royal court functions, and select, fashionable cafés. All that changed when America finally got its hands on icecream late in the eighteenth century and set it smack dab next to mom's apple pie as a symbol of all that was good and god-fearing in the good old US of A. In 1846, an American, Nancy Johnson, invented the icecream churn, and the food of the courts became the food of the shopping malls.

By 1917, Americans were so in love with icecream that it was declared an essential foodstuff, and considered such a morale builder it became part of everyday army rations. It was even served to immigrants arriving at Ellis Island to show them what a wonderful, advanced country they had come to.

In 1919, a way was found to make chocolate adhere to icecream and the amazing I-Scream bar was introduced. Later it was to be re-christened the Eskimo Pie, and find its way into immortality.

In 1923, one enterprising company decided to adapt a disposable throw-away drinking cup for icecream use, and the mighty Dixie Cup was born.

While nobody ever really got tired of vanilla, this didn't stop America from searching for new and more tempting flavours.

Rocky Road made its first craggy appearance in 1945, closely followed by chocolate fudge in 1946. 1951 saw fresh pumpkin make a brief, but memorable appearance, while 1962 belonged to banana bongo, 1964 was the year of the Beatle nut, 1969 was Lunar Cheesecake and 1978 heralded the long-awaited Goody Goody Gumdrop.

But in spite of all the American ingenuity, the one truly classic way to eat icecream is still the smooth, mammary-like scoop, settled gracefully upon a simple crunchy cone.

It is this basic form of icecream eating that divides the world into lickers, biters, suckers, kissers and drips.

Lickers can lick an icecream to death in five minutes. Suckers, blessed with asbestos lips, are able to place them firmly against the icecream and draw in a great amount in one go.

Lips drawn back in a ferocious set of teeth, biters attack their icecreams with a series of savage bites. Then there are the kissers, romantic types who smooch their icecreams fondly with gently parted lips. Finally, there are the drips. These are usually under ten years old, and seated in the back of a brand new car, minutes out of the showroom. Their icecreams will drip long before anyone else's, first dripping onto the drip's hand, then when the drip goes to lick the back of the hand, they will drip onto the back seat. Dogs tend to idolise drips.

I am somewhere between a sucker and licker myself, as is my wife. Perhaps it is that which truly cements us together, cryogenically preserving our relationship for all time.

Hot chocolate sauce for icecream

This is the shortest, quickest recipe in the book. I couldn't keep you away from your icecream for too long.

> 150 ml (5 fluid ounces) pure cream
> 200 grams (6½ ounces) dark cooking chocolate or couverture

Heat the cream and chocolate together in a heatproof bowl set into a pan of simmering water and stir with a wooden spoon. Arrange your scoop or scoops of icecream in a bowl and pour hot chocolate sauce on top.

yum

Lemon and sugar crêpes

Of course these are perfectly wonderful without any icecream on the side, but you don't have to tell anybody I said that.

> 1 egg
> 4 teaspoons castor sugar
> 175 ml (6 fluid ounces) milk
> 70 grams (2½ ounces) flour
> pinch of salt
> 3 teaspoons butter, plus extra butter for cooking
> 1 lemon
> 2–3 teaspoons of sugar

Crack the egg into a bowl and beat vigorously with the sugar. When the sugar dissolves, whisk in milk.

Sieve the flour and salt into another bowl, then gradually whisk in the egg mixture until the batter is smooth. Pass it through a fine conical sieve.

Heat three teaspoons of butter until foaming, then whisk into the batter mixture. Leave to rest at room temperature for one hour.

Brush a small non-stick frypan (or crêpe pan) with melted butter and heat until very hot. Pour in a small ladleful of batter and rotate the pan until the bottom of it is totally covered with a thin layer of pancake mixture.

Cook for one to two minutes until air bubbles appear in the mixture and the underside just begins to brown. Flip it over and cook the other side for about a minute.

Keep warm while you make remaining crêpes.

Sprinkle a little sugar and squeeze a little lemon juice on each crêpe. Roll them into long thin cylinders and squeeze a little more juice over the top, and finish with a final sprinkling of sugar. Serve hot.

Makes 4 pancakes, roughly 20 cm (8 in) in diameter.

The invisible man

The problem had to be me. When a waiter complained that he had no record of my booking, it never occurred to me that he might have forgotten to write it down. I would go home cursing myself for having rung the wrong restaurant.

When other restaurants insisted on seating me at the table nearest the lavatory, I reasoned that I must look like someone with a severe bladder problem. And when waiter after waiter kept bringing the wrong order to my table, I signed up for a six-month elocution course to help me e-nun-ci-ate more clearly.

I also suffered a severe case of bad timing, showing up at restaurants on the one night of the year when the special of the day had sold out early, or when the fresh bread hadn't been delivered, or when the chef had suddenly taken ill.

Not wanting to embarrass anyone, I'd chew on a day-old bread roll, drink my warm Chardonnay, surreptitiously wipe the smudge marks from my plate, and eat the char-grilled octopus I hadn't ordered.

Usually, I would decide to finish the meal with as little fuss as possible and leave, which would have been fine, except for my...um...other little problem.

After finishing the last sip of coffee, I would become totally invisible. Maybe it was just my metabolism, or perhaps it was a reaction to the caffeine. But whatever it was, I would suddenly disappear.

It did me no good at all to motion to a waiter, or to call for the bill. The floor staff simply couldn't see me, and would walk straight past my table without even glancing around.

After about half an hour, this mysterious affliction would begin to wear off. I'd regain my visibility, and a waiter would suddenly arrive with the bill.

Naturally I was worried, so I decided to discuss my problems over lunch with my remarkable friend, Les Luxford. Les is Chinese and a film director, but that's not what makes him remarkable. He is one of the few people alive who can walk into a restaurant for the first time, and be treated like royalty.

While I was explaining my predicament, I couldn't help but notice that we were seated at the best table in the restaurant, and that Les had only to raise his left eyebrow a millimetre and waiters would come running. Not only did the headwaiter ask Mr Luxford for his opinion of the meal, but he actually waited for the answer.

Oh, and neither of us disappeared after the coffee.

'You don't have the art', said Les.

'Art? What art?'

Of complaining, apparently. He lifted a brandy balloon to his nose and every waiter in the room came to a standstill. As soon as his lips softened into a smile, they sighed, and went about their work.

'You wouldn't put up with bad service in a bank, or a service station, or a supermarket, so why put up with it in a restaurant?'

I leaned forward and spoke softly. 'So how does one acquire this...art?'

'I was born with it', said Les. 'It's one of the privileges of being Chinese.' With that, he produced a tattered piece of paper from his wallet and recited the words of Yuan Mei, an eighteenth-century Chinese poet and gourmet.

'If something is not right, this is due to carelessness, and it is the cook's fault. If something is good, say why, and when it is bad, pick out its faults. If one does not keep the cook in line, he becomes insolent. Before the food comes, send down word that the food tomorrow must be better.'

He folded the paper up again and picked up a Cristofle knife and fork, holding them like chopsticks. 'Say you're going to a Chinese restaurant', he said. 'First you have to walk in as if you own the place. When the waiters bring you the menu, act as if you are insulted and ask for whatever is special that night.'

He brandished his silver 'chopsticks' and smiled an evil smile. 'When they tell you, tell them it's not good enough. If all else fails, ask for what the staff is having for dinner.'

I was embarrassed just thinking about it. 'I don't think I could...'

'Of course you can', said Les. 'There's nothing to it. And remember to have an argument with the head waiter. Try to have it as early as possible and, for heaven's sake, try to win it.'

'What about?'

'It doesn't matter', roared Les. 'The position of the table, the air conditioning, the tea, the food. But the sooner you're prepared to stand up and be counted, the sooner you're going to be respected.'

I was still uncertain. 'What if I don't want to eat Chinese?'

Les raised his right eyebrow half a millimetre and the bill appeared from nowhere. Slapping down a wad of notes, he stood up to leave.

'Why don't you come and eat with me a few times?' he suggested. 'Just sit there and watch. You'll pick it up in no time.'

I did. The man is an art form. In a restaurant neither of us had been to before, he asked for his usual table. Once when the day's special was sold out, he invited the chef to create a new special. And when we were eating in the lushest, plushest restaurant in Chinatown, he asked the owner what the kitchen was having for dinner.

'Malaysian fish head curry', came the reply.

'Fine, we'll have that', said Les, and the large bowl of fish head curry was removed from the table in front of the astonished staff, and placed on ours. It was the best meal I had ever had there.

After a few weeks, I went solo. And was seated by the toilet. 'Excuse me', I said. 'Could you possibly move the lavatory a few metres so I can smell my wine?'

Profuse apologies followed, and I was soon sitting at the prize table, sipping perfectly chilled champagne, eating beautifully prepared food and experiencing meticulous, well-honed service. The waiter asked me how I enjoyed the meal, and I told him about the lack of acid in the beurre blanc, and the slight predominance of sage in the poultry farce. He actually thanked me.

I glided through the evening like a galloping gourmet. But now, the moment of truth was at hand. I was down to my last sip of coffee. It was time for the bill.

I raised my hand from the table just as the bill was slipped under it.

I paid. I tipped. I felt dizzy with delight.

Outside, on the street, ready to hail a cab, I felt a momentary need for reassurance and turned back to the restaurant. There, in its smoky glass windows, stood a perfect reflection of my body. As I gazed at it, the side of a cab slid into view behind it.

Malaysian fish head curry

Somehow you have to find a way to break it to the cat that his fish head days are over. Once you've tasted this rich, dreamy curry, there is no looking back. Try to choose good, meaty heads.

- 1.5 kilograms (3 pounds) fish heads split lengthwise (1 large head, such as schnapper or 6 small heads, such as salmon)
- salt to taste
- 6 shallots, finely chopped
- 3 garlic cloves, chopped
- 10 dried red chillies, soaked overnight, drained and chopped
- 2.5 cm (1 in) fresh ginger, minced
- 1 stalk lemongrass (inner white part only) minced
- 3 tablespoons Malaysian curry powder, mixed with a little water
- 3 tablespoons tamarind
- 1 cup (250 ml or 8 fluid ounces) warm water
- 5 tablespoons vegetable oil
- 3–4 cups (750 ml–1 litre or 1½ pints) thin coconut milk
- 1 tablespoon sugar
- 6 small okra cut in half
- 2 tablespoons tomato paste

Wash the fish heads well and rub in a little salt.

In a mortar and pestle, grind together the shallots, garlic, chillies, ginger and lemongrass until a thick paste is formed. Combine with the curry paste.

Mix tamarind with warm water and let stand for 15 minutes. Squeeze and strain tamarind liquid through muslin, and reserve.

Heat the oil and fry the chilli paste, stirring on and off, for about five minutes. Gradually add the coconut milk, the tamarind water and the sugar and simmer uncovered for another five minutes.

Fry the okra in a little oil, then add to curry, along with the fish heads and tomato paste.

Simmer uncovered for ten to 20 minutes, depending on the size of the fish heads. Serve with white rice.

Serves 4 to 6.

yum

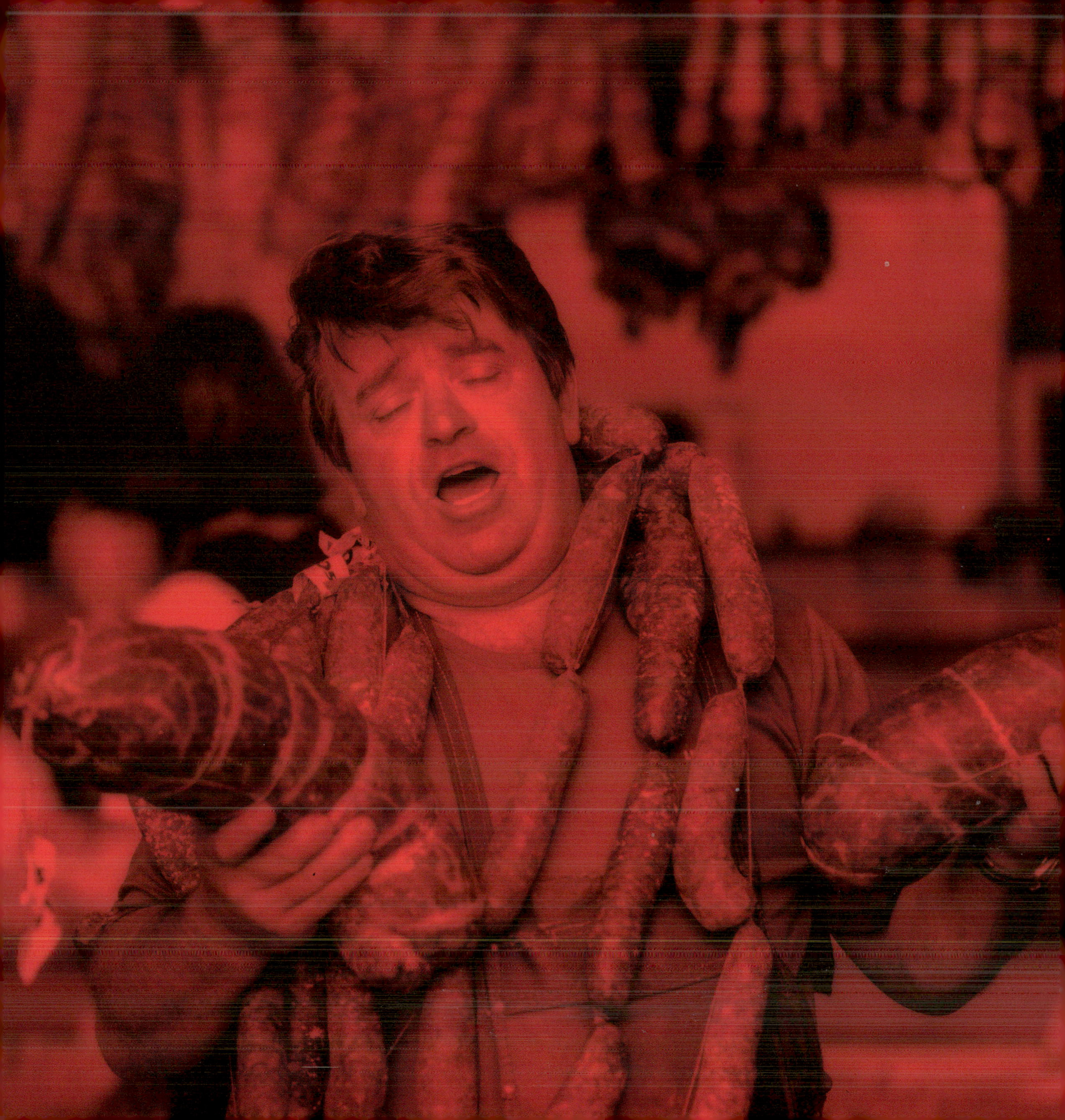

The missing link

Sausages have always had a mixed public image. Ever since they were invented around 3,500 years ago, they have been subjected to some pretty shoddy treatment.

In ancient Rome, the popularity of sausages in various free-spirited Bacchanalian feasts led the elders of the early Christian Church to publicly condemn them. They even managed to convince Constantine the Great to ban the eating of sausages altogether during important national festivals.

To add insult to injury, Emperor Leo V later spoke out against the black pudding, known then as the canabae. 'We have been informed that blood is packed into intestines, as into a coat, and set before man as an ordinary dish', complained Leo, outraged. 'Our Imperial Majesty can no longer permit the honour of the state to be tarnished by these abominable devices of the gluttonous.'

Things worsened in Victorian times. The author of the *Illustrated Manners Book*, published in 1855, not only counselled that talk of diseases, injuries, and deformities should be avoided at the dinner table, but went on to add, 'You would do well not to be talking of dogs when people are eating sausages'.

But perhaps the most serious problem to beset the beleaguered sausage took place in living memory, with the outbreak of a vicious, hitherto unknown yuppie virus known as The Gourmet Sausage. This resulted in the evolution of such unnatural mutants as the Tropical Hawaiian, the Pork, apple, and blackcurrant, and the low cholesterol, ten per cent less fat, sodium-reduced sweet and sour beef, soy and apricot variety.

Sausage-makers lost the art of sausage-making, and instead, put everything inside the sausage skin that one would normally serve on the plate next to a sausage.

Maybe you think I'm taking all this a little too personally. I know my wife does. She claims that men like sausages more than women, that it's a typical male-bonding type of thing.

Nevertheless, I'd rather bond with a sausage than with other men, unless of course, it's around a barbie.

My wife has a theory on that too. She claims that men like to fashion things in their own image.

Who buys the sausages around here? she asks (I do). Who cooks sausages when he's home alone? (I do). Who grew up on a solid diet of pub-counter lunches of curried sausages (I did). And who stole all the cocktail frankfurts at his own son's fourth birthday party? Er, sorry kids — eat the fairy bread.

Okay, I admit it. I would rather have a good sausage than a hunk of steak any day. I suspect it is because we invented the sausage, that for us it is a symbol of our ingenuity and inspiration.

Anyone can cut a hunk off the side of a cow and throw it on the fire, but the first person who saved all the dangly bits and the leftovers of the beast and chopped them, blended them, seasoned them, prepared the casing, did the salting and the smoking, and ended up with a sausage greater than the sum of its parts — now, there's a hero for you.

Sausages are a recipe, after all, and not just an ingredient. They are the epitome of comfort food, because they are difficult, exacting things to make but are designed so that they are quick and easy to cook.

Their complexity and depth of flavour serve as direct links to specific regions, cultures and times throughout history. So why doesn't my wife like them very much?

Too much fat, she says. Too high in sodium. Think of the nitrates. Nevertheless, the odd one still manages to slide down her pretty little golden throat, usually when she thinks I'm not looking.

When she does cook them, with that tight-lipped look on her face, she virtually stabs them to death in a re-enactment of the shower scene from *Psycho*. Once they are filled with more holes than your average pin cushion, she grills them on a rack, so all the fat can run out. Where's the fun in that?

Surely, more things have been turned into sausages than have not.

Germany has no less than 1,500 different varieties of sausage, including pale, smooth weisswurst, meltingly soft leberwurst, kochwurst, rotwurst, bierwurst, blutwurst, mettwurst and teewurst.

Anyone who has sampled a spicy, fiery chorizo with its head-spinning aroma of marjoram and garlic has tasted the very essence of Spain.

In Scotland, the haggis, a sausage made of oatmeal onion and offal stuffed into a sheep's stomach, is practically a national symbol, honoured in verse by the great Robbie Burns, commemorated by distinguished army regiments in full regalia, and the centre of many a memorable New Year's Eve celebration.

In the creamy melting heart of a boudin blanc, you touch the true soul of the Parisian bistro.

In Rome, the New Year is ushered in with a midnight snack of yet another great sausage. The cotechino is a big awkward lump of a sausage made from pork rind, pork meat and back fat, flavoured with salt, pepper, cloves and cinnamon, all stuffed into pig's casing. Forget what it sounds like, it tastes fabulous, and when eaten with boiled lentils, the symbol of wealth, it assures believers of prosperous times ahead.

For me, sausages have formed the most delicious, invisible links in my memory, transporting me back in time to some of my happiest, and simplest, eating experiences.

Like the gargantuan choucroute of local sausages and sauerkraut at La Truite, a comfortable little auberge in Alsace.

Like the deeply dark, intensely flavoured wild boar sausages flavoured with fennel that begin my every meal at Rome's Girrarosta Toscana.

Like my first New York hot dog, buried under mustard, onions and sauerkraut and eaten on the street outside Sachs Fifth Avenue.

Like Taillevent's delicate, ambrosial Cervelas de Fruits de Mer aux truffes et aux pistaches, sliced at the table by the three-star restaurant's owner, Jean-Claude Vrinat.

And like the glorious home-made salami that had been made and hung in the cellars of one of Verona's foremost Amarone makers, forging yet another powerful, airtight bond between food and wine.

Snags like these are not bangers, nor snorkers, but sensitive, new age gastronomic delights, wonderfully crafted produce whose very existence symbolises our wit, integrity, resourcefulness, history and culture. The sausage is a symbol of all man has been, is now, and will be.

Perhaps my wife was right after all.

Cotechino with lentils

In Italy, this is a traditional New Year's Eve dish symbolising prosperity and good times (the lentils represent coins). It is also eaten all year round, symbolising the Italians' all-out love affair with this gorgeously fatty, porky, over-the-top sausage.

- 1 cotechino sausage
- 4 bay leaves
- 1 onion, finely chopped
- 2 tablespoons olive oil
- 2 garlic cloves
- 2 cups (440 grams or 14 ounces) brown lentils, rinsed
- 50 grams (1½ ounces) pancetta, finely chopped
- 2 cups (500 ml or 16 fluid ounces) chicken stock
- 200 grams (6½ ounces) tomato passato or canned tomatoes
- salt and freshly ground pepper

Prick the sausage all over with a fine skewer, wrap snugly in muslin and place in a large pot of cold water with three bay leaves. Cover, bring to the boil, then reduce to a gentle simmer for one and a half hours.

In a heavy-bottomed pan, fry the onion in the oil until golden, then add garlic cloves, drained lentils and chopped pancetta and cook for a couple of minutes more. Add the stock, tomato passato and bay leaf, then cover and simmer gently for about 30 minutes. Season to taste. Slice the cotechino into 1.5-cm (½-in) slices and serve on top of the lentils.

Serves 4.

Risotto with red wine and sausages

In many areas of life, I am a liberal thinker. Not with risotto, however, where I have spent much time dodging inventive little concoctions containing just about everything from spatchcock to strawberries. This one is different, however. It really works.

- 4 Italian pork sausages
- 2 tablespoons butter
- 1 onion, finely chopped
- 300 grams (9½ ounces) arborio rice
- 1 cup (250 ml or 8 fluid ounces) red wine
- 6 cups (1.5 litres or 2½ pints) chicken stock, kept hot
- salt and freshly ground black pepper
- 1 tablespoon finely chopped flat-leaf parsley
- 1 tablespoon freshly grated Parmigiano

Skin the sausages, and heat a non-stick frypan. Pinch small sections of sausage into the pan. Fry gently until crusty and golden, completely drain off the oil, and keep in a warm place.

Melt the butter in a heavy pan, add the onion and cook until the onion softens. Add the rice and toss until well-coated, stirring constantly. Add the red wine and allow it to bubble and be absorbed for two minutes, stirring all the time.

Add a ladleful of stock to the rice, and stir until it is absorbed, over medium to low heat. Add another ladleful and stir constantly but calmly with a wooden spoon until it is absorbed. Continue for around ten minutes, then add crumbled sausage pieces to the risotto and stir through, then continue the process of adding stock for another ten minutes.

Start tasting the rice now to determine how much more time and stock is needed. Add remaining stock a ladleful at a time and cook for another five to ten minutes, until rice is cooked but not soft, and there is a general creaminess to the sauce. When rice is cooked, which will probably take 30 to 35 minutes all up, taste for salt and pepper, add the parsley and Parmigiano, stir and cover. Bring to the table but leave for five minutes before uncovering. Serve with a little extra grated Parmigiano on top.

Serves 4.

Japan to a tea

After reading this, you may never use a tea bag again. You will have seen the truth and nobility of tea, the homage to earth and heaven in every cup.

But you may not thank me for it, for it is not easy, this path less travelled.

No more whizzing into the kitchen for a meaningless, tea-bagged mug to fuel your morning or lubricate your afternoon. Instead, you will be strolling around your garden, appreciating the sort of world that makes tea leaves possible. You will sit in windows watching rain fall, meditating on the nature of fresh water. You will learn to appreciate how the age-old arts of pottery and painting can add pleasure to every moment.

It isn't drugs that alters your life like this. It is participation in a true Japanese tea ceremony.

My awakening takes place in Uwajima, on the southern island of Shikoku. Uwajima is the home of the mythical Ushioni monster, Japanese-style bullfighting, a remarkable fish cake called kamaboke, and more Mikimoto pearls than you'll see at a debutante's ball.

As a very special honour, it is arranged for me to attend the *chanoyu*, or tea ceremony.

Like many rituals, the four-hour-long tea ceremony has evolved over the years strictly guided by a very formal series of rules that make 'one for each person and one for the pot' look like the work of heathens.

In truth, it dates back to the thirteenth century when Zen Buddhist monks would drink tea to help them keep awake during meditation. These days, say the sceptics, it actually helps to drink tea to stay awake during the tea ceremony.

But the tea ceremony is not about tea. It is about ceremony. This time-honoured tradition has been revered by the upper classes for centuries. It was even practised by Samurai warriors who regarded chanoyu as crucial to their development as swordsmanship.

The multitude of strictly observed rules embrace a severe discipline known as sado, a descriptive that will later return to me unbidden as I kneel on a tatami mat in a highly unlikely position.

These rules cover everything from the ideal size of the tea house, and the ideal number of guests (five) to the ideal topics of conversation, and the ideal order in which food is served. Each dish is to be presented at the precise time that its texture, flavour and temperature will be best appreciated. But the most detailed rules of all are those governing the making of the tea itself, a painstakingly precise ritual that takes many years of intense training to master.

I feel like a vestal virgin as we enter the hand-trimmed, topiaried gardens. 'How soon do we start?' I ask eagerly. 'We already have', replies my interpreter, the diminutive Hiroku, as she urges me to fully appreciate the very essence of the lush gardens. This is, after all, a time for contemplation, an opportunity to catch up on soul-enriching experiences like observing how the fronds of a neat little conifer look like a song bird in flight. I count the leaves on a Japanese maple, which gives me the impression of a man deep in meditation, until it is polite to move on.

After some time, we arrive at what Hiroku calls the rest room, but it's not that sort of rest room. More a room for resting in. I am invited to relax, by squatting stiff-legged on a hard tatami-matted floor, and to admire a framed piece of calligraphy and a simple vase of flowers, which I stare at so hard it takes on a striking resemblance to the Ushioni monster.

A rice paper screen slides open, and our hostess, in traditional dress, presents us with a tray of refreshing, savoury plum tea, then the screen slides silently back. That's it? The whole ballyhoo, just like that? No, not at all.

This is just the tea you have while you wait for the tea you're going to have. I understand perfectly. I tend to do the same thing with Chardonnay.

As we drink, Hiroku gives me a doggy bag for leftovers. This is not about saving food, however, it's about saving face. The portions of food served in this *kaiseki ryori* (the meal served during the ceremony) are deemed to be perfect amounts, and it is considered bad form to leave anything on your plate. She then distributes a washcloth for washing lips and hands, and a handkerchief, to be used to wipe my bowl clean when finished.

Next, we dress for tea, by slipping into special sandals. Mine are the biggest available, but size 6 sandals on size 12 feet are far from a fashion statement. I hobble like an ancient monk down another pretty path leading to a beautiful, old stone well where lips and hands are duly washed, then it is on to the tea house itself.

The first shock is that there is no door. Instead there is a small square hatch, just like the ones they used to push your breakfast tray through at country motels. This is the door, through which all must enter in equally undignified fashion. That's the point, apparently.

Having made it (just) through the mousehole, I sit on the floor with both heels tucked in under me.

In three minutes, pins and needles give way to out and out pain, as my hostess explains that concessions are made for clumsy foreigners. By all means, make yourself comfortable by sitting cross-legged, she smiles.

I don't have the heart to explain to her that sitting cross-legged is not how I make myself comfortable. I can feel my thighs gradually break away from the rest of my body.

Perhaps it's a mind thing. I concentrate on the beautiful selection of bowls, plates and saucers in front of me, laid out on a gleaming black lacquered tray. Thus the ritual begins.

Hiroku is unanimously elected the superior guest (praise the lord), so it becomes her task to respond to the thoughtfulness of our hostess, by contemplating, then elaborately praising the dinnerware. Each item has been selected not only to harmonise with the food, but also with the mood of the guests.

She politely enquires as to the age of each piece, and the artist or craftsman who had created it. It is indeed similar to traditional dinner party conversation. 'Fab vase. Alessi?'

The food itself is so mindblowingly simple in presentation that it immediately takes on a spell-binding beauty.

One dish holds a sashimi slice of local snapper in a sweet sake sauce, another contains a small neatly scooped mound of rice, while a third is a sculptured slice of eggplant in fragrant dashi stock. The tastes are as clear as a mountain stream, the very essence of themselves, while the arrival of each dish is a signal for much bowing between guest and hostess. Being a heathen, I find the excessive formality uncomfortable, although that could have just been the pain in my ankles.

A succession of dishes follow: fish ball in soup, a cross section of lotus root that gleams like precious jewellery, a slice of bright orange Hokkaido pumpkin, a single fried fish ball, a translucent prawn, and an intensely flavoured piece of fish that has been marinated, then grilled.

Finally, we are presented with a bowl of thin soup strewn with toasted rice. It is like an internal finger bowl, that refreshes and rinses what feels like one's whole body.

Incredibly, and completely against all medical history, my feet have stopped hurting, my thighs have stopped complaining, and my scepticism has been reduced to such an extent that I find myself studying everything around me with a new, hungry form of curiosity that I have never before experienced.

I have earned, in other words, the right to observe the making of the tea.

Our hostess kneels in front of a large ceramic brazier on which a large iron kettle sits.

One by one she carefully places down the implements she will need: a simple, earth-coloured bowl, a bamboo dipper for transferring water from the kettle to the bowl, an elegant, glazed tea caddy containing the bright green powdered tea, a slender bamboo tea spoon and a delicate many-pronged whisk fashioned from bamboo.

From her sash she produces a neatly folded cloth, and with extreme concentration cleans the already spotless tea caddy, tea bowl and teaspoon.

Hiroku assumes her role of superior guest and asks about the teaspoon. After a lengthy discourse, it is handed around the room, so we all may examine and contemplate it.

Fascinated, I watch our hostess wipe the tea bowl with long, deliberate strokes. Carefully, so as not to upset the surface of the tea, she scoops a spoonful of powder and deposits it into the bowl, then repeats the process.

She then taps the spoon against the bowl, a movement aimed at helping the minds of the guests to focus on proceedings.

Now it is time to lower the wooden ladle into the water. Lifting it back out, she tips it, in one fluid movement, into the tea bowl.

Now comes, the final, and most dramatic step. Using the whisk, known as the *chasen*, she gracefully whips the liquid up into a vibrant, luminous swampy green froth.

The bowl, or *kobukusa* is then handed to the honoured guest, who contemplates first the bowl, and then the tea, holding the bowl aloft so everyone may study the delicate pattern. Then she gently rotates the bowl, and slowly sips the tea, which is accompanied by a small, delicate sweet.

The tea is like no other I have ever tasted. At once creamy, bitter, impossibly smooth and yet somehow clawing, it feels as old as a wise man, yet as innocent as a new-born kitten.

Now that I'm home again, I often get into trouble at the table for pausing to reflect on the smooth, uniform glass sides and neat rubber top of the salt shaker, instead of just passing it to whoever has asked for it. And nobody asks me to make them a cup of tea any more, after the first few times.

But how many rituals are left in our lives that form an experience for all the senses? Going to the gym? Watching football? We need to nurture the things that can help us attain some measure of enlightenment and a closer harmony with nature, rather than succumbing to so-called convenience foods, convenience music and convenience philosophy.

A life filled with convenience foods is a convenient life. A life resonant with ritual, and filled with accomplishment and appreciation is an accomplished and appreciative life.

Dashi

The following dishes are not really kaiseki offerings, but everyday mealtime favourites. Nevertheless, the stark simplicity of every dish, the single mindedness of the flavours, and the uncluttered composition are very much in the kaiseki tradition. The dashi, or fish stock, referred to in the recipes can be bought in Japanese food stores as an instant mix. Alternatively, you can make your own.

    1 litre (1¾ pints) water
    25 grams (¾ ounce) kombu seaweed
    25 grams (¾ ounce) bonito flakes

Pour the water into a large saucepan and add the kombu. Slowly heat the water, taking out the kombu just before it reaches boiling point. Add the bonito flakes and as soon as the water hits the boil, remove them immediately, otherwise the dashi will turn bitter.
    Strain through muslin and use in the following recipes.

Chawan mushi

A delicious savoury custard studded with goodies. Traditionally, this is made in a special, lidded chawan mushi cup, but you can use a ramekin covered with aluminium foil.

- 1 tablespoon sake
- ½ teaspoon soya sauce
- 1 small chicken breast, cut into small cubes
- salt to taste
- 4 prawns, shelled and deveined
- 4 shitake mushroom caps, soaked and de-stemmed
- 8 gingko nuts
- 4 slices kamaboko fish cake
- 4 eggs
- 2½ cups (625 ml or 1 pint) dashi
- ½ teaspoon salt
- 2 tablespoons mirin
- 2 teaspoons grated fresh ginger

Sprinkle the sake and soya sauce over the chicken, and sprinkle the salt over the prawns. Leave for a few minutes, then cut the mushrooms in half and place in individual cups along with prawns, chicken, ginko nuts and fish cake.

To make the custard, beat the eggs thoroughly, but not to the stage where they become frothy. Stir in the dashi, salt and mirin. Pour the egg mixture into the cups, and replace the lids. Steam for about 15 minutes. Alternatively, the cups can be placed in a roasting dish with enough water to reach half way up the cups and placed in the oven.

When cooked, sprinkle a little grated ginger on the top. Eat chawan mushi with a little porcelain spoon.

Serves 4.

Vinegared carrot and daikon salad

This dish is often served at special festive occasions. Once made, it can be kept for up to a week in the refrigerator.

    10 cm (4 in) piece of daikon (giant white radish)
    1 medium carrot
    a little salt
    3 tablespoons rice vinegar
    1 tablespoon mirin
    2 tablespoons dashi
    1 x 4 cm (1½ in) square piece kombu

Cut the radish and the carrot into the thinnest matchsticks possible. Sprinkle with salt and leave for five to ten minutes. Squeeze the vegetables in your hands until the daikon is soft and pliable, and any excess water has been squeezed out.

Combine the vinegar, mirin and dashi and bring to the boil. Allow to cool, then chill.

Combine two tablespoons of the vinegar mixture with the vegetables.

Place the kombu on the base of a glass bowl. Squeeze the excess vinegar from the vegetables, and arrange on the kombu. Pour over the remaining vinegar, cover and chill.

Serves 4 to 6.

Agedashi dofu

A simple piece of tofu is transformed into edible art by the deep fryer.

    2 cakes fresh tofu (beancurd)
    oil for deep frying
    2 tablespoons plain flour or corn flour
    250 ml (8 fluid ounces) dashi
    2 tablespoons soya sauce
    2 tablespoons mirin
    2.5 cm (1 in) piece daikon radish, grated
    2 spring onions, finely chopped
    10 grams (½ ounce) dried bonito flakes
    10 grams (½ ounce) fresh ginger, grated

Pat the tofu dry and wrap it in a dry tea towel. Place a weight on top (a dinner plate, say) and let stand for about an hour to get rid of any moisture. It is important that the tofu is as dry as possible.

Unwrap tofu, cut each piece in half, and lightly flour. Deep fry each cake separately for about six minutes until a nice, light, golden colour.

To make dipping sauce, mix together the dashi, soya sauce and mirin and bring to a simmer in a saucepan.

Drain deep-fried tofu on kitchen paper and place two halves in each bowl, carefully arranging a little pinch of ginger, daikon and spring onion on top. Pour on a little of the dipping sauce, and scatter a few bonito flakes on top of the beancurd.

The heat from the beancurd will cause the flakes to 'wave' in the wind, as if alive. They are not, of course.

Serves 2.

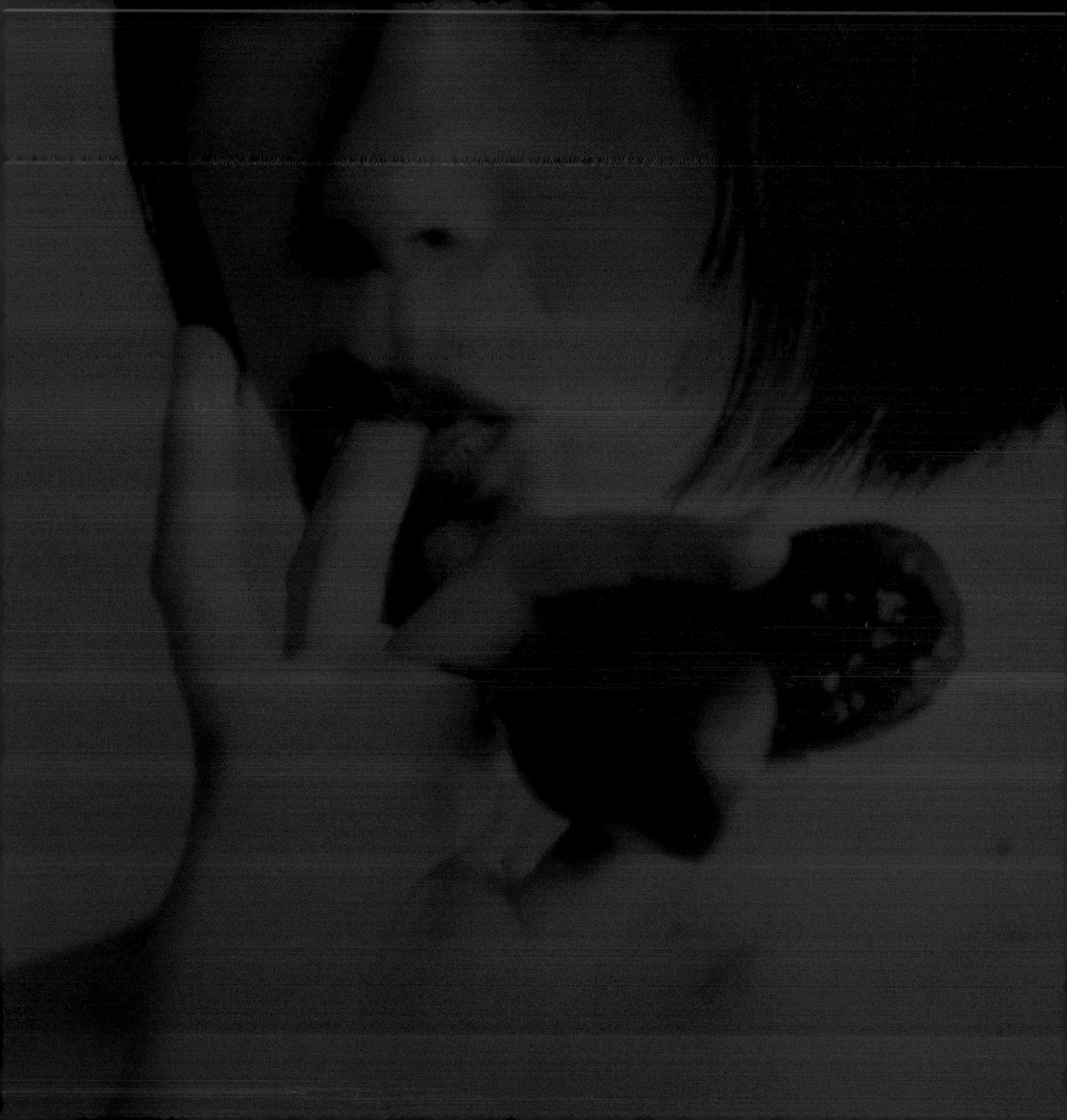

Le grand buffet

There is one social institution that somehow manages to bring out all of the human race's basest and ugliest instincts. It accentuates our anxieties, underscores our uncertainties and puts our basic greed on show for all to see. I refer, of course, to the buffet.

Put a perfectly respectable Doctor Jekyll in front of a spread of soggy pastas, wilted salads, and lacklustre pâtés, and before you know it, the fingers will be gnarling, the hairs will be sprouting and the warts popping up from nowhere.

Just what is it that makes us think those huge mountainous piles of asparagus spears, marinated eggplant and Scotch eggs are all going to totally disappear in the next five minutes? Why do we feel a compulsion to pile our plate so high we can barely see over it? We may have just polished off an entire suckling pig and two litres of icecream, but put us in front of a buffet table and suddenly we're reaching for the stack of plates like a baby grasping for its midday feed.

The basic tenet of the buffet was perfectly illustrated in the film version of the Beverly Hillbillies, when Jethro suddenly found himself at a particularly lavish table loaded with goodies. Barely able to stop himself, he was soon stuffing his pockets and every available space with anything that stood still long enough. Such bounty, reckoned the once-poor country boy, couldn't last. It didn't occur to him that he was poaching from his own buffet.

Not too long ago, I found myself taking breakfast in a rather grand hotel dining room with cook, author, and raconteur Robert Carrier. We quietly sipped our tea, mesmerised by the sight of three young Japanese girls earnestly coming to grips with the concept of the hotel's buffet breakfast. Suddenly, one of them grasped the general idea, grabbed a plate, and merrily circled the table, piling the dry bricks of Vita Brits next to a dollop of Swiss muesli, a Danish pastry, a little scrambled egg, and a couple of chipolata breakfast sausages, and three rashers of bacon. The other two quickly followed her lead.

Before Carrier and I could even think of snickering, it occurred to us that we may both have made similar, separate *faux pas* in Japan while trying to order a balanced meal of dishes we had never heard of before. I passed a small comment on the morally loathsome nature of the buffet, to pass the time, and Carrier replied with alacrity, claiming it to be one of the most physically dangerous forms of dining in the civilised world.

He had once attended a very sophisticated dinner buffet party in Paris, he said, and was standing by the table, carefully deliberating between the homard and the Belon oysters, when a particularly well-groomed, elegant and elderly Parisian woman kicked him in the shins. She, too, had her eye on the Belon oysters, and nothing, not even Robert Carrier, was going to stop her.

I must also admit to experiencing some rather splendid buffets in my time. Perhaps the most memorable was a spectacular breakfast buffet prepared by the Hotel Villa D'Este in Como. There was no limit to the delights that spread out before me, including lightly coddled eggs, jewel-like, paper-thin slices of prosciutto, extravagantly good salami and local bresaola (air-dried beef), about twenty different varieties of breads and sweet rolls, delicate fly-away pastries, pots of wondrous home-made jams, and so on, all capped off by a gigantic, gleaming silver tureen filled with crushed ice and strewn with bottles of chilled Prosecco. By the time I had finished breakfast, it was almost time for dinner, which I swore to take in an à la carte fashion.

I also recall a particularly fine spread of regional Emilia Romagna specialties at the Jolly Hotel in Bologna, and a colourful island feast on Erakor Island in Vanuatu, featuring more coconut crab than the average Vanuatuan will see in a lifetime.

But these are the exceptions.

Most of the buffets in my life have been sad and sorry affairs where the tired and boring food is outdone only by the tiresome and boorish behaviour of the guests.

So whose shins can we kick for inventing the idea of the buffet in the first place?

In England, at formal medieval dinners, the buffet was actually a collection of shelves in the dining hall used to display the family silver, the stuff being far too valuable ever to be actually used.

In later centuries, the shelves were used to display the food to be served later in the evening, in an effort to get the guests excited about the meal that was to come. A noble idea, and one that was destined to go horribly wrong.

In France, buffet restaurants sprang up in all the major railway stations in an effort to feed travellers quickly and well. Some, like the famous Le Train Bleu in the Gare de Lyon were as elaborately decorated and as magnificently appointed as any three-star establishment.

In Italy, the buffet concept was elevated to divine heights in the shape of the antipasto table, a glittering array of all that was fresh and in season ranging from elaborate pre-cooked meat and fish dishes to simple platters of fresh vegetables refreshed with fine olive oil.

But perhaps the true origins of the buffet lie in the noble zakuska, a Russian table of 'small bites' which reached somewhat excessive heights in the nineteenth century.

Originally, this way of eating was devised by large country estates who were called upon to entertain cold, tired and hungry travellers at all hours of the day and night. Whenever they arrived, the zakuska would be ready for them. In more upwardly mobile Moscow mansions, the zakuska table became a permanent fixture, continually restocked in order to cope with that unexpected attack of the midnight munchies. The forerunner, perhaps, to our late-night refrigerator raids.

The zakuska always featured the deliciously plump local herring, which might be presented in a mustard sauce, in sour cream or perhaps with a simple oil and vinegar dressing. Then there would be a variety of other fish dishes, all manner of cold meats and pâtés, and 'caviars' made from eggplant, or crushed dry mushrooms steeped in wine, all washed down with as many as fifteen different types of vodka.

But it was caviar that was the real hit of the zakuska table, and from the amount of beluga, oscietra or sevruga displayed you could pretty accurately work out the worth of the hosts — and of their guests. One noble family was said to keep a cut-glass barrel that held a whopping 20 kilograms (40 pounds) of caviar. In a wave of unbridled hospitality, it was duly filled to the brim every single day. The memory of this makes me feel rather ill, as I drop to the floor to pick up any miniscule stray beads of caviar that may have fallen from my annual thimbleful.

Later, as the zakuska became a popular pre-opera snack, hot dishes were added to the repertoire such as highly flavoured meat balls known as bitki, veal kidneys in a rich madeira sauce, and foshmak, a hearty, baked dish of herring, boiled potatoes and onions. This would then sustain one through the longest of operatic acts, without one having to be so common as to eat a real meal.

If the buffet has become the most maligned word in the English culinary language, then smorgasbord comes a close second, a sad state of affairs for which the entire population of Sweden may never forgive us.

In most Scandinavian countries, there is a certain purity about the smorgasbord that totally escapes the coleslaw-munching, plate-balancing habitués of the art in more 'civilised' Western countries.

The true smorgasbord, originally known as a bread-and-butter table, divides itself into four very strict parts, each requiring a fresh plate and a fresh appreciation. The first course concerns itself primarily with herring. It is filleted, chopped, sliced, diced, slivered, salted, smoked, pickled, marinated, dried, oiled, battered, baked, fried and boiled, often in consecutive order, but it is still herring.

Next come more fish dishes such as jellied trout, smoked salmon, cod roe and maybe a dish of fagelbo, a salad of sprats, capers, beetroot and raw egg. After a course of cold and pressed meats, one finally proceeds to the final course of lush and rich hot dishes including the famous Jansson's frestelse, or temptation, a rib-sticking casserole of anchovies, potato, onions and cream.

With the food shortages of the second world war, the Swedish government prohibited the serving of smorgasbord in all public restaurants. Even when the ban was lifted in 1949, the feast had lost its popularity being seen as too dear, too fiddly, too excessive and too just-about-everything else. Alarmed that Sweden could lose one of its most important cultural icons, a restaurateur called Tore Wretman set about renovating and restoring the smorgasbord. The iced swans and ornately carved decorations were the first to go, as he devised a set of specially designed serving platters that fitted snugly together. Almost single-handedly (an appropriate term, recognising the way in which one eats while clutching a plate and a glass) he revived the tradition. Today, the smorgasbord — the *real* smorgasbord — is once again, a beautiful thing.

With the finely honed ability to take any worthwhile culinary idea and turn it into something totally unrecognisable, it didn't take America too long to get into the act. It soon perfected (if that indeed is the appropriate term) the self-service restaurant.

The first of these intriguing institutions was the Exchange Buffet, which opened in New York on September 4 in 1885. Unfortunately, it was a men-only affair, and the food had to be eaten standing up. Women had to wait until 1893 before they were given the right to serve themselves, at an establishment in Chicago run by a certain John Kruger. While he based the idea on the Swedish smorgasbord, for some reason known only to himself, he decided to call it a cafeteria after the Spanish word for a coffee shop. At the time, the establishments were better known as 'conscience shops' as Mr Kruger allowed the customers to tally their own bills. This is not a concept one sees in widespread usage today.

In 1898, the Childs Brothers introduced the tray to the caffeteria, enabling Americans to choose their desserts and drinks at the same time as their savoury dishes, while in 1902, Joseph Horn and Frank Hardat took self-serve to new technological heights with the introduction of the automat. This removed that annoying human element from the gathering of nutrition: one simply walked up to a wall of gleaming glass boxes filled with pre-cooked, pre-heated, pre-sliced food, dropped a coin in the slot and removed the meal of your choice.

Today, the buffet mentality rules our lives to the point where there is now a whole generation who think that lettuces grow in all-you-can-eat salad bars and that pasta is a generic term for anything that sits all day in a gluggy sauce under warming lights.

Even our shopping habits embrace the buffet ideals with our supermarket olive bars, cheese bars, salad bars, this-that-and-the-other bars. Life is a smorgasbord. Artistic and cultural pursuits are in many cases reduced to video boxes displayed on shelves, friends appear so many and varied we can pick and choose among them as if they are stuffed cherry tomatoes.

We help ourselves wherever, and whenever we can, with only the slightest panic growing in the back of our minds that one day the bounty may run out, that quite possibly there might be something wrong in the fact that twenty per cent of the world's population keeps on using eighty per cent of the world's resources.

No wonder we say God helps those who help themselves. If this keeps up, He or She might have to.

The antipasto table

Whenever I'm dining in the restaurants of Italy, the table I most want to be seated at is the antipasto table: a glorious explosion of colour and movement, and food so fresh you expect it to keep on growing. What you won't find on this table are slices of boring dried-up salami and mortadella, tired old tasteless olives and commercial giardiniera pickled vegetables so vinegar laden, your lips hurt for days after.

The word 'antipasto' literally means 'before the meal', but a well-planned selection of these appetisers *is* a meal. On the following pages are a selection of antipasto recipes to serve six hungry people.

Roast capsicum salad

Roast four red or yellow capsicums under a grill or over a flame until they are black and blistered. Cool, peel off the skin, remove the stalk and seeds, then cut the capsicums lengthwise into strips. Be sure to retain any juices. Combine these juices with three to four tablespoons of extra virgin olive oil, one finely chopped ripe tomato, which has been peeled and seeded, one finely chopped clove of garlic, and some basil leaves torn into strips. Add salt and pepper to taste, then combine with the capsicum strips. Serve at room temperature.

Mushrooms in oil and vinegar

Wash and dry a kilogram (2 pounds) of small button mushrooms. Fry two garlic cloves in 85 ml (2½ fluid ounces) olive oil until they begin to brown. Remove the garlic and add the mushrooms, one tablespoon of capers, one finely chopped red chilli and fry together for a minute. Add 125 ml (4 fluid ounces) white wine, cover, and simmer for about 15 minutes. Remove the lid, add 1½ tablespoons of red wine vinegar and a dessertspoon of chopped fresh oregano. Turn up the heat and boil for five minutes. Serve at room temperature.

Mussel salad

Scrub and de-beard 2 kilograms (4 pounds) of live mussels that have been soaking in several changes of cold water for five to six hours. Heat two tablespoons of olive oil in a thick-bottomed pan and fry two cloves of garlic until they colour. Add a few black peppercorns, a sprig of basil, some parsley stems, two bay leaves and 250 ml (8 fluid ounces) of white wine. Boil until the wine reduces by half, then put in the mussels, cover with a tight-fitting lid and turn up the heat.

After about two minutes, give the pan a big shake, remove the lid, and begin removing the mussels that have opened with a pair of tongs. Cover for another 30 seconds, then remove any more that have opened. Repeat process four or five times, discarding any mussels that don't open. Remove the mussels from their shells, cool and dress with the juice of half a lemon, two tablespoons of extra virgin olive oil, some ground pepper and a tablespoon of chopped parsley

Suppli

Before you can make this dish, you first need to have made risotto the night before (no hardship). I love this with a pumpkin risotto but any variety will work. Combine two beaten eggs with 1½ cups of risotto, then press a tablespoon of the mixture into the palm of your left hand. Place a cube of bocconcini in the middle, and cover with another spoonful of rice, rolling your hands together to form a ball. Roll the ball in breadcrumbs and place on greaseproof paper. When all the balls are made, refrigerate for an hour or two before deep frying until golden.

Crostini di fegatini

Clean and trim 500 grams (1 pound) of chicken livers and cut into small pieces. Heat three tablespoons of butter and three tablespoons of olive oil in a pan and fry three tablespoons of chopped onion until golden and translucent. Add a few sage leaves, a tablespoon of capers and the livers. Sauté over a medium heat for five minutes until lightly browned. Meanwhile, grill six thick slices of tough sourdough, or Italian casalinga bread.

Roughly mix the livers together with a fork into a coarse, lumpy paste, and spread thickly on the toast. Pop the slices into a warm oven for a minute and serve.

Turn over

a new leaf

A salad is not an easy thing to love. It's a mess, really, a madcap concoction of all sorts of things in a bowl, the culinary equivalent of a migrant's hostel. Everything looks as if it would rather be someplace else.

It doesn't have the sizzle of a steak, the ruby orb of a ripe tomato, the golden goodness of a cob of corn, or anything solid and sensible and real that you can bite into and understand.

Which is why I had long regarded salads as things you ate when there wasn't any decent food around.

My theory was that lettuce — particularly of the iceberg variety — contained some sort of weird, untraceable enzyme that enabled it to side-step the normal human digestion process. Whatever this remarkable property was, it manifested itself into a substance capable of avoiding any contact with the taste buds. It was also able to entirely eliminate any sensation of tangible food matter hitting the stomach.

How else can you explain a food that gave you no feeling that you had eaten anything, and no sensation of taste? It was such a yawn, that I wasn't at all surprised to learn that the ancient Greeks used the sap from lettuce as a cure for insomnia.

Scientists put this sleep-inducing quality down to lactarium, a hypnotic property similar to opium. But we lettucephobes knew better.

As for the Egyptian belief that the things were powerful aphrodisiacs capable of promoting fertility in males, I imagine this far-fetched little theory was started by some down-on-his-luck Upper Nile lettuce farmer. The only green rustly stuff that gets most guys going is cash.

I was at one with Apicius, the Roman cookbook writer and social commentator, who firmly maintained that lettuce was indigestible. This opinion was later shared by Fagon, the medical advisor to Louis XIV. Horrified by the king's voracious appetite for salads, Fagon eventually succeeded in banning lettuce and cucumber altogether from the royal table.

Oddly enough the original 'zelada' or salad was not a cold dish at all, but a soupy ragout popular in the fifteenth century. The sauce for this dish included pungent, pickled greens, which were later replaced by fresh, raw greens.

By the seventeenth century, the romantics had taken over and the salad was suddenly presented as the culinary way of the future.

In his enlightening writings of 1614, Giacomo Castelvetro spoke long and longingly of the pleasures of the salad.

More salad advice came in 1664 in the form of John Evelyn's *Acetaria, a Discourse of Salletts*.

Evelyn maintained that in composing a salad, no plant should be allowed to overpower another, and that each should fall in place naturally like musical notes.

With the popularity of salads came the search for the perfect dressing.

Of course, the one, the original vinaigrette recipe had already been documented by the French, who steadfastly maintained that it required 'a miser for the vinegar, a spendthrift for the oil and a wise man for the salt'. There is also a version that adds 'and a mad woman to toss it all together'.

While vinaigrette became popular in England due to the world's first door-to-door salad rep, a French emigré called d'Albignac, it was soon to lose its virginity and nobility.

The English transformed it into a soggy, vinegary mess, while the Americans simply didn't know when to stop. They believed if a little salad was nice, then a lot of salad must be twice as nice, and kept adding nuts, fruits, cheese, gelatine, and even meats with generous abandon. While a few of these concoctions, like the Caesar and the Waldorf, managed to keep some semblance of harmony, many, like the Butterfly Salad, the Candlelight Salad and the Santa Claus were travesties, as gaudy as confetti, rich with sweet mayonnaise and as cloying as a brandy Alexander.

I grew up thinking that salad was a saggy baggy iceberg lettuce dotted with tomato wedges, some vinegar-soaked cucumber slices, and several discs of canned beetroot, sploshed with commercial thousand island dressing, the lot sitting in a round wooden bowl that reeked of stale garlic. On special occasions, there were orange segments in it as well.

Then salads went warm. Someone thought it was a good idea to fry up lots of bacon and chicken livers and toss the whole lot onto some delicate green leaves instead of onto a sturdy piece of grilled bread. Result? Soggy green, fat-drenched leaves.

I was about to toss the whole concept of salads out the window, when I experienced my salad epiphany. Until this day, I was an extra virgin. It was my third consecutive day of eating at Alain Chapel near Lyons, so I already had under my belt the master's gateau de foie blondes, his Bresse chicken 'en vessie', his milk-fed lamb with young vegetables, and his grilled langoustine. What next? I shivered with anticipation as the covered dish arrived. As the gleaming silver cloche was removed, my face fell like a shaky soufflé.

It was full of lettuce leaves. Funny little green ones, curly little white ones, and odd, wild, stringy ones. But as the salad was composed in front of my eyes, bound with two different dressings, and linked with a tender pigeon breast, a sweet Breton lobster and a small black truffle, I could feel a tingling warmth spread through my body.

With my first bite, it was as if a bright sun suddenly rose.

This was not a salad, but manna from heaven, oiled with sparkling vinaigrette, sharp with mustard and sweet with onion. It took me forty minutes to eat, and I loved every mouthful.

I felt the same way as I felt when I finally got around to reading Shakespeare, not as a crash-course student, but as a curious, consenting adult.

More salad days followed, the most memorable being at Robuchon in Paris, where the simple salad that followed a spectacular main course of whole roasted guinea fowl stuffed with a full lobe of foie gras made me see more than three stars.

Here was an amazing thing: a pile the shape of a dariole mould of frisée (curly endive) that were so fresh, they were practically brittle, spiked with the purest of vinaigrettes enriched with the juices of the guinea fowl, then powered into a fifth dimension with the addition of fresh, chopped truffle.

The real joy of salads — and their downfall — is that they are completely dependent on their maker. Fail to wash the leaves free of grit, and you've ruined everything. Fail to dry them sufficiently and the dressing will run off the leaves like water off a duck's back. Add three too many things, and you've got a side show, not a salad. Not enough sea salt, and it's lifeless. Too many edible flowers and it's horsefeed.

But get it right on the night, with its brilliant alchemy of greens, oil and vinegar and you will be a soul lost to the magic of salads. Try it yourself, in the privacy of your own home.

I knew that my life had changed when I was sitting in the downstairs dining room of Chez Panisse in San Francisco.

While I was ploughing through a five-course menu chockers with anchovy-studded lamb, sweet scallop linguini and cep and potato tarts, Alice Waters entered, sat at a table with friends and slowly, very slowly, ate her dinner.

All she had in front of her was a large plate of salad leaves of virtually every shape and size. She picked up the leaves in her fingers and ate dreamily, serenely, and carefully. I would willingly have swapped my entire five courses for her single salad.

Black pudding and glazed apple salad

It may just be some kind of culinary blood lust, but black pudding is a craving that has stayed with me all my life. Yet, even I have to admit that the stuff can be just too rich and heavy, which is why this dish is so terrific. The rocket lightens, the apple sweetens, and the vinaigrette lifts it into the realm of a higher being.

- 2 Granny Smith apples, peeled, cored and sliced
- 2 tablespoons butter
- 1 tablespoon brown sugar
- 1 tablespoon olive oil
- 1 horseshoe black pudding, sliced into 2 cm (1 in) rounds
- 3 tablespoons extra virgin olive oil
- 1 tablespoon balsamic vinegar
- salt and pepper
- 2 bunches of rocket leaves, rinsed and dried

Fry the apples in the butter for three or four minutes. Add the sugar and toss well, to coat. Cook over a low heat until the apples soften and turn a golden brown with little crispy bits.

In a non-stick frypan, heat the olive oil and fry the black pudding until both sides are crisp and crunchy.

Whisk together extra virgin olive oil, vinegar, salt and pepper and lightly dress the rocket .

Distribute the leaves between four plates, topping each thatch with slices of caramelised apple and crisped black pudding.

Serves 4.

Salade Niçoise

This is my favourite salad in all the world. While canned tuna is acceptable, a fresh piece of tuna, lightly grilled so it's still rare in the middle, can turn it into the stuff of which legends are made.

4 small fresh tuna steaks
1 tablespoon extra virgin olive oil
mixed salad greens
4 ripe tomatoes, quartered
1 small cucumber, peeled and sliced
1 green capsicum, seeded and sliced
2 hard-boiled eggs, quartered
handful of black olives
fresh basil leaves
8 anchovy fillets
salt and freshly ground pepper
2 tablespoon lemon juice
1 garlic clove, smashed
6 tablespoon virgin olive oil

Brush the tuna steaks with olive oil and grill quickly on both sides. Leave tuna to rest for ten minutes before cutting into sashimi-like slices.

Arrange the greens on a large plate. Top with the tomatoes, cucumber, capsicum, tuna, eggs, olives, basil and anchovy fillets.

Mix salt, pepper, lemon juice and garlic, then whisk in the olive oil. Discard the garlic, and pour the dressing over the salad, tossing very lightly.

Serves 4.

Greek salad

My friend Christos Vafeas makes a mean (and generous) Greek salad. He specifies that the cos lettuce should be roughly chopped into large strips not left whole, that the fetta must be Bulgarian not Greek, the onion must be white, not purple, the anchovies must be left whole, not chopped, the herbs must be fresh, not dried, and that the end result must look rustic, not sophisticated. It's that sort of passion and discipline that makes the Greek salad, well, Greek.

   1 cos lettuce
200 grams (6½ ounces) fetta cheese
1 cucumber, peeled and seeded
3 ripe tomatoes
1 white onion
10–12 anchovy fillets
80 grams (2½ ounces) kalamata olives
a little fresh oregano
a little fresh thyme
125 ml (4 fluid ounces) extra virgin olive oil
3 tablespoons white wine vinegar
1 garlic clove, crushed
pinch of salt
1 teaspoon oil from the anchovies

Wash the leaves thoroughly, then spin dry and cut into large strips. Place in a large bowl. Cut the fetta and cucumber into rough, bite-sized pieces, and cut the tomatoes into quarters and add to the bowl. Halve the onion and slice thinly, break the anchovies up with a fork, and add to the bowl along with the olives and fresh herbs.

Whisk together the olive oil, the vinegar, and the oil from the anchovies until it emulsifies. Add the garlic and a pinch of salt, and pour over the salad. Toss well with your hands. It shouldn't look too well groomed, but rough and rustic.

Serves 6.

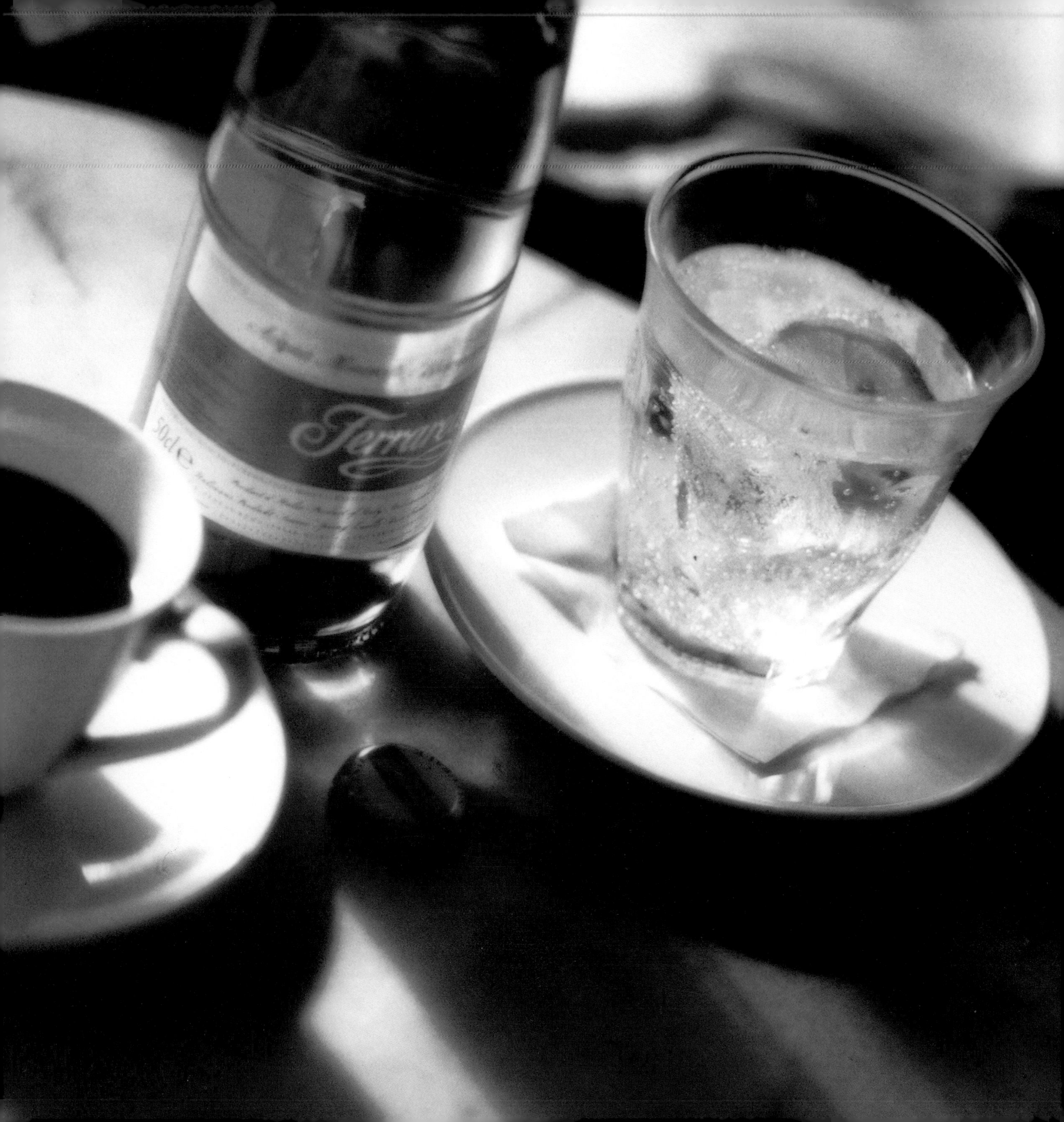
50cl

Blue jackets, grey pants and white truffles

Not everybody loves Milano. 'Prosaic and winterish', wrote Matthew Arnold in 1865. 'Like a slice of hell', said Edmund Wilson in 1947, the same year that Dylan Thomas called it 'a giant nightmare city'.

'Beastly Milan, with its imitation hedgehog of a cathedral, and its hateful town Italians, all socks and purple cravats and hats over the ears', wrote D.H. Lawrence in 1913.

In truth, Milano is a large industrial city that closes down if there is no trade fair on. There is always a trade fair on.

At the time of my first visit, there are fourteen trade fairs on. Nevertheless our travel agent manages to find a hotel. 'It's right in the shadow of the Duomo', she says chirpily.

On our arrival, we find that it is also in the shadow of a large amount of scaffolding and safety netting. We lug our suitcases into a lobby that looks like a run-down community medical centre. A sign warns against taking women into one's room. When we see the room, we know why. It's not nice enough. It is tiny, depressing, dingy and smelly, with a panoramic view of the light shaft that runs down the centre of the building.

I trudge the sixteen kilometres of winding corridor back to reception and ask the snooty concierge for a better room.

'Eemposseebala', sneers Signore Snooty. 'Dee 'otel, she ees full.'

'Then we'll find another hotel.'

'Eemposseebala. Milano ees full.'

'Milan is full?'

'Signore', he sighs, 'don't you know what time of year dees ees?'

'Of course I do', I say. 'It's white truffle and porcini season.'

More sighing. 'Eet is fashion season. Dees week, all the fashion designers, they release their new fashions. There ees no 'otel room in the whole city.'

We do the only thing possible, and head for the Galleria Vittoria Emanuelle, where tables of Japanese and American tourists watch other tables of Japanese and American tourists for vital clues to the authentic Milanese style. Armed with a Michelin guide and a street map, we hit the streets in search of a hotel room. Five hours and twenty-seven hotels later, there is only one hotel left on our list to try. By now, I have no pride left. I will beg. I will cry. I will bribe. 'Buongiorno, signore', I say nervously. 'Avete uno room?'

I am already walking out the door, when he pushes the register across the counter. 'Sign here.'

Home is now room 'due vente nove' of the Windsor Hotel, a well-run establishment with smiling porters, a lively bar and a trolley stop right outside the front door.

I want to celebrate our good fortune by going out for a coffee, but I have reckoned without the signora. She takes me by the credit card and drags me into a boutique with an unpronounceable name. In a flash, my designer jeans, expensive T-shirt and running shoes are disposed of, never to be seen again. Instead, I am wearing a navy blue jacket, a navy blue and red striped tie, and soft, grey, full-cut pants with cuffs that drape softly over black leather slip-ons.

'That's better', she says, straightening her tight black skirt and tweaking her cashmere. 'Now we can go for coffee.'

All of Milano has apparently decided to do the same. Every little hole in the wall is a café, the bar lined with pasticceria and men in blue jackets, red and blue striped ties, grey trousers and black shoes, sipping little cups of black coffee and tall glasses of water. My wife joins them on her return from the lavatory, obviously confusing the Marcello Mastroianni type with myself.

She engages in animated conversation without even realising her mistake, poor thing.

For my part, I can't help but notice the style and poise of the Milanese women. They are superbly dressed in an almost flashy way. Their skirts are tight, heels high, stockings sheer, and sweaters cashmere. Their coats are flaunted, rather than worn, their scarves are Hermes, their hair is immaculately swept back from their flawless made-up skin, and their jewellery gleams gold, nestled in just about every place one could possibly nestle.

I am in Milan to meet with the Accademia Italiana della Cucina, a respected world-wide society of food lovers founded in Milano in 1953 by writer and gourmand Orio Vergani. The purpose of the Academy is to rediscover and safeguard the most genuine traditions of Italian regional cooking. In other words, to protect the world from strawberry risotto and éezee-mix polenta.

Senior delegate Signore Enzo Lo Scalzo, dressed in blue jacket, grey pants and black shoes, makes us welcome. Immediately, he sets about telling us why the food of Lombardy is so good. He describes the influence of the Spanish, the French and the English, the geography and the climate. It all boils down to beef, fish and poultry, with rice thrown in. A lot of rice thrown in.

The Milanese eat two hundred tonnes of rice a year, and are famous throughout the world for their risotto alla Milanese. We are introduced to the definitive version at the venerable Hotel Marin, where it is rich with stock and laced with more red-gold threads of saffron than I have ever seen on one plate.

After lunch, the food keeps coming in the shape of a visit to the famous Peck's, a vibrant jewel box of a food hall alive with newly arrived porcini mushrooms, orange egg-shaped ovoli mushrooms, cutely clustered chiodini mushrooms, and the all-precious white gold: the magnificent tartufi bianchi, or white truffles of Alba.

In Peck's fish shop across the road, the place is literally crawling with flapping, squirming, wriggling, slithering creatures. There are live frogs, feisty crabs, and Neanderthal-looking razor fish. A huge swordfish hangs in the window as proudly as if it were designed by Gianfranco Ferre. I lose my wife at this stage to something that sounds suspiciously like Moschino earrings.

Next door, is the Peck's macellaria, where a baby suckling pig lies in cruel imitation of life against its mother's enormous carcass.

Around the corner is Peck's pasticceria, and the spuntino bar, where more blue jackets consume glasses of red wine and plates of pasta.

I arrive back at the hotel with a bag of ovoli mushrooms, not quite knowing what to do with them. My wife comes back with a bag of Moschino earrings. I set about giving her every opportunity to wear her new wardrobe, but find Milan a difficult city to get to know.

Like most working cities, its restaurants are formal, power-broking establishments, rather than casual glam trattorie.

The whipping wind and incessant traffic keep social life behind stone walls and huge wooden doors, not easily accessible to the tourist. But I persevere, and discover a lighter-than-air pizza topped with rocket and cooked in the huge wood fired oven at the mega-trendy Paper Moon Café on the Via Bagutta. This is followed by a classic osso buco at Peck's formal restaurant, which is presented with a long spoon known as the 'tax collector', for extracting the marrow from the bones. At Boeucc, in the Piazza Begiosa, I fall upon an exotic salad of wild mushrooms, truffles, and Parmigiano that is heaven itself.

My finest meal in Milan was one of my finest meals of all time.

Aimo e Nadia is a good half hour taxi ride into an unfashionable outer suburb.

Flanked by factories, the simple security door opens to reveal Aimo Moroni himself, dressed in his chef's whites.

If this man were a wine, he would be frizzante, with a natural, bubbly enthusiasm that makes me feel perfectly content to place my stomach in his hands.

Originally from Tuscany, Aimo does most of the marketing while his wife Nadia does most of the cooking. It's an arrangement that has been successful since the early Sixties, when they used to serve four hundred meals a day to local office workers.

Aimo agrees to arrange a meal of tiny tastes that showcase the finest local produce from the market that week.

We begin with a spoonful of cannellini beans spiked with wild mint and flavoured with tiny pork sausages. Then comes a linguini with black truffles, and a mirepoix of tiny vegetables, a baby calamaretti with more truffles, and a plate of fresh porcini mushrooms brushed with a little olive oil and grilled. Aimo insists that we try his signature dish — handmade spaghetti alla chitarra with sweet, golden onion and a heat haze of fresh, hot chilli.

Then comes the highlight. To celebrate the arrival in the market that very morning of the first of the new season's white truffles from Alba, he has created a mound of triple-cream cheese whipped up into a light confection, with thin slices of rocket leaves and slivers of truffle. The taste explodes in the mouth like a sherbet bomb, then lingers like the perfume of a fine liqueur.

Our enthusiasm is now as infectious as his own, and he slips away from our table to reappear with a tiny serve of risotto covered in shaving upon shaving of Alba truffle, like a frail white igloo.

'Food is life', says Aimo Moroni. 'It is the heart of civilisation.'

Nobody bothers to argue.

Obviously Lawrence, Thomas, Arnold and Co. did not lunch at Paper Moon, dine at Aimo e Nadia, shop at Peck's, nor get the very last room at the Hotel Windsor. Of course, they thought Milan was a dump. They probably weren't even wearing blue jackets, grey pants, or gold earrings.

Osso buco Milanese

A gorgeous, glorious, lip-smacking, bone sucking, gravy slurping dream of a dish, enhanced by a gloriously zesty concoction known as 'gremolata'.

- 6–8 slices of veal shin, 5 cm (2 in) thick, with marrow bone in the centre or 12 slices of 'baby' veal shin
- seasoned flour
- 5 tablespoons butter
- 1 tablespoon olive oil
- 1 onion, peeled and chopped
- 2 celery stalks, strings removed and chopped
- 1 carrot, peeled and chopped
- 1 garlic clove, crushed
- 250 ml (8 fluid ounces) dry white wine
- 250 grams (8 ounces) canned tomatoes, chopped
- 250 ml (8 fluid ounces) veal or chicken stock
- 2 garlic cloves, peeled and chopped
- 2 tablespoons parsley chopped
- zest from half a lemon, grated

Coat the veal lightly with the flour, then melt the butter and oil and fry the veal until browned all over. Remove the veal, cook the onion, celery, carrot and garlic until the onion is soft and translucent. Return the veal to the pan, add the wine and reduce to about a third. Add the tomatoes and stock, then cover and simmer for one and a half hours.

Mix together the garlic, parsley and lemon zest to make a gremolata.

Scatter half of the gremolata on top of the osso buco for the last five minutes of cooking. Serve with risotto alla Milanese, and scatter with the remaining gremolata.

Serves 4.

Risotto alla Milanese

Although the traditional accompaniment to osso buco, this warmly colourful, relaxed old friend of a risotto works just as well as a meal in its own right. If you're feeling particularly decadent, slip in a little bone marrow in the last couple of minutes of cooking.

150 grams (5 ounces) butter
1 onion, finely chopped
½ teaspoon ground white pepper
small piece of beef bone marrow
1 cup (250 ml or 8 fluid ounces) dry white wine
2 cups (375 grams or 12 ounces) arborio rice or carnaroli rice
salt
6 cups (1.5 litres or 2½ pints) beef or chicken stock, heated
¼ teaspoon saffron powder (real saffron, not imitation)
100 grams (3½ ounces) Parmigiano

In a heavy pan, fry the onion, pepper and marrow in half of the butter until the onion is golden and translucent.

Add the rice and a pinch of salt and stir until the rice is well coated. Add the wine and saffron, and cook over a high heat, stirring until about a third of the wine is left. Start adding the stock, a ladleful at a time as the rice absorbs it, stirring continuously for the next 25 to 30 minutes.

When the rice is cooked, with no starchiness but still with an al dente firm bite in the middle, remove from the heat, and stir in the extra butter and cheese.

Serves 4 to 6.

Mascarpone with strawberries

Mascarpone is a satin-smooth cream cheese made by curdling thick cream with citric acid. It originated in the Lombardy region, but now belongs to the world.

1 punnet strawberries
500 grams (1 pound) mascarpone
½ cup (100 grams or 3½ ounces) sugar
3 egg yolks
1 tablespoon Strega
2 tablespoons Cointreau
2 egg whites
3 tablespoons milk
3 tablespoons brandy
400 grams (12½ ounces) savoiardi biscuits

Wash and dry the strawberries. Hull them, then cut in half lengthwise and set aside.

Beat the mascarpone and sugar together with a wooden spoon, and add egg yolks, one at a time, beating constantly. When smooth and satiny, add Strega and Cointreau. Beat egg whites until they form soft peaks, then gently fold into the mixture. Combine the milk and brandy in a saucer. Cut the biscuits in half lengthwise and lightly dip them in the milk and brandy. Line the bottom of a straight-sided one-litre (16-fluid-ounce) bowl with the biscuit halves. Cover with a layer of the mascarpone cream and a layer of halved strawberries, then repeat with a second layer of biscuits, mascarpone and strawberries.

Refrigerate for at least two hours, then spoon into dessert bowls, scooping from the bottom to make sure you get a little of everything.

Serves 6.

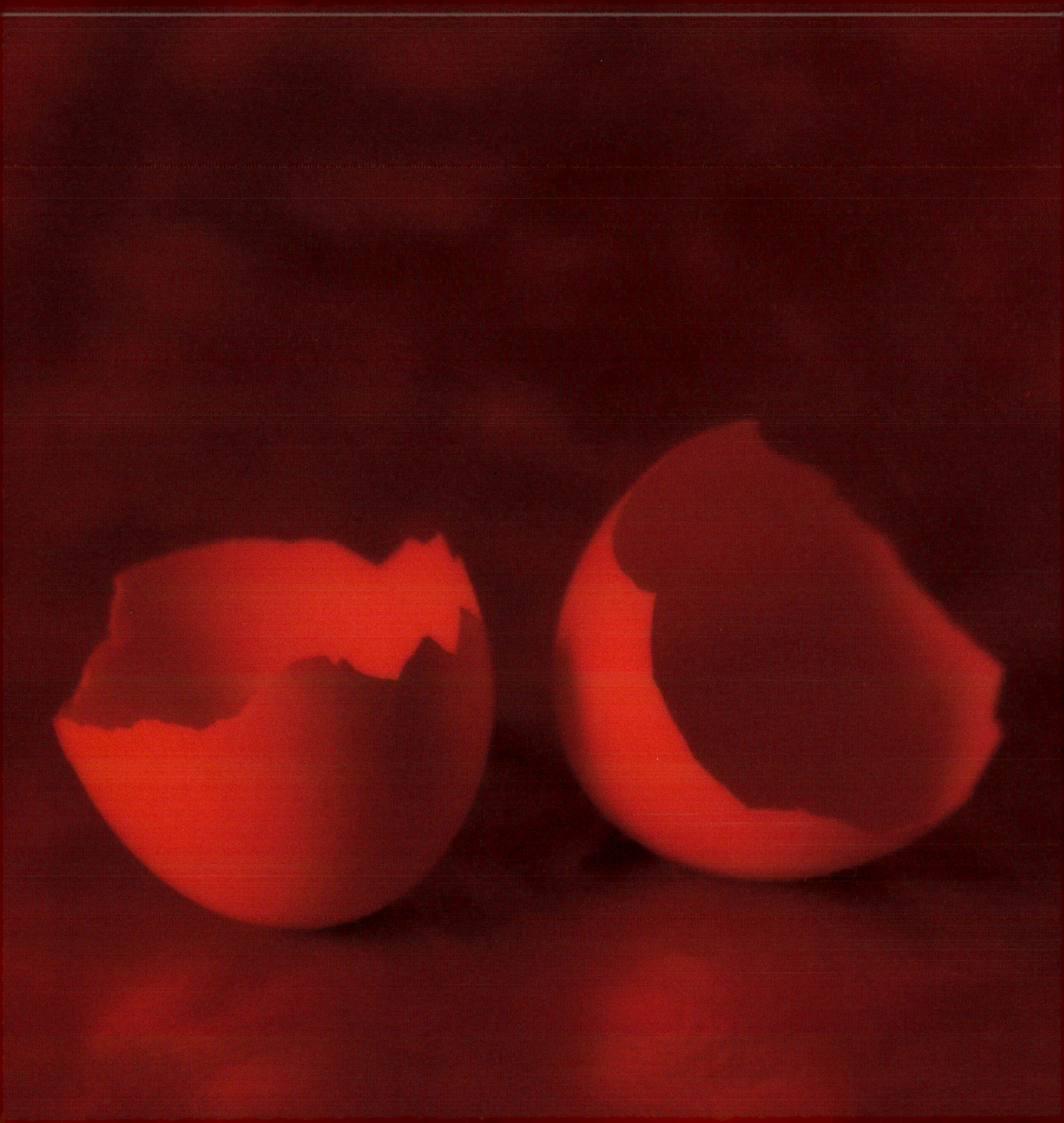

The accidental gourmet

When I first met Joel Robuchon, I was shocked to find that he lacked many of the qualities one would expect to find in a great chef.

As the then owner of the most celebrated restaurant in Paris, and a man who has been hanging around top-class kitchens since he was fifteen, you would think that he would at least have some idea about what makes a chef truly great. But no, he just claimed it had a lot to do with dedication, passion, application and sheer hard work.

How wrong can you be? He even went so far as to say that to succeed, a chef must be thoroughly organised, keep his kitchen in meticulous order, have a thorough knowledge of cooking principles, and work slowly and patiently, using only the very best ingredients.

Trés sorry, Monsieur Robuchon, but I'm afraid you have it all up le spout. If one is to achieve immortality in the kitchen there are certain attributes one simply can't do without.

For a start, you have to be disorganised. You should also be forgetful, clumsy, and impatient. If, at the same time, you can be a little lazy, slightly sloppy and very vague, you are clearly destined for gastronomic greatness.

If you are lucky enough to have a drinking problem or bad sight, you're even more blessed. Above all, though, you must be accident-prone.

Take a look at any cookbook and you will find many examples of food that started life as a culinary blooper. What began as a sure-fire recipe for disaster has often been magically transformed into something of great beauty, and great flavour.

Perhaps the most famous of these happy accidents took place many years ago in the Rouergue district of southern France, a wild and rocky region, pockmarked with numerous, cold, damp and draughty caves. One day, a young shepherd boy sat down in the mouth of one of the caves to enjoy his lunch, a simple meal of bread with fresh sheep curd. Distracted by his flock, the boy left his lunch behind and totally forgot about it until many weeks later when he stumbled upon the very same cave only to find his bread and cheese covered in a curious, dirty green mould. Any sensible, sound-thinking person wouldn't have touched the unsightly mess with a ten-foot shepherd's crook. But this particular shepherd must have been a nerd of the highest order. Not only did he touch it, he ate it, and discovered that his humble lunch had acquired a flavour of incredible depth and beauty. He had just tasted the world's first batch of Roquefort.

And let's not forget the two chemists who lived in the English town of Worcester in the Thirties. One day they were commissioned by a retired English colonel to make a batch of exotic, spicy chutney that he had acquired a taste for during his travels in India.

Guided only by the colonel's hazy memory, the chemists were on pretty shaky ground, but they eventually produced a concoction that consisted of dates, tamarind, black pepper, cloves, raisins, sultanas, currants, chillies, anchovies, ginger, garlic, spring onions, apples, sugar, tomatoes and malt vinegar.

Wisely, the batch was relegated to the dim, dark recesses of the chemists' cellar. Several years later, they stumbled upon the forgotten condiment, and in the pioneering spirit of the young French shepherd who had gone before them, decided to taste it. It was utterly delicious. All they had to do was alter the original recipe by adding the rider: 'Allow to mature for three to four years'. The men's names, by the way, were John Lea and William Perrins.

Unlike Lea and Perrins, George Crum is not exactly a household name. Yet anyone who has ever suffered from snack attack should be eternally grateful that this short-order cook from Saratoga Springs in New York possessed a somewhat short temper and a wicked sense of humour. One night back in 1853, Crum was so incensed when he received a complaint that his French fries were too thick, that he immediately set upon putting the critic in his place. He sliced potatoes so thin, you could almost see through them, and cooked them to an absolute crisp in boiling grease. Then, he sent them out and waited for the fireworks. But instead of fireworks, what he got from the dining room was several more orders for his delicious new-fangled potato chips.

Then there was the story of Tijuana restaurateur, Caesar Cardini, who was caught with his pantry down one 4th of July during Prohibition days. A group of Hollywood patrons had driven over the border to indulge in some serious partying, only to find that Cardini had all but run out of food. Desperate, he instructed his chef to throw together anything he could find in the kitchen. This amounted to little more than salad leaves, bacon, cheese, anchovies (this last, a matter of debate) and a couple of eggs. Almost overnight, Caesar's salad was the toast of the Hollywood set.

And so it went, from accident, to disaster, to catastrophe. There was the gentleman who ran the Minneapolis health clinic in the 1920s who would regularly feed bran to his overweight clients. One morning, as he was stirring the bran a little too energetically, some of it splashed onto the hot stove and formed crisp, delicious little wheat flakes. Single-handedly, the man had invented Weeties, the world's longest-running cereal.

Then we have Frank Epherson, an absent-minded fruit juice manufacturer who left a drink outside overnight, only to find the spoon frozen upright in the glass the next morning. Thus the 'Epsicle' was born. The name was later changed to popsicle.

Maple syrup was invented by a lazy Indian maid who decided to boil venison in nearby tree sap rather than walk to a stream for water. Chocolate chip cookies emerged from an accident in a cookie factory, when a worker inadvertently dropped cooking chocolate into the biscuit dough. And chaud-froid sauce was born when a retainer of Louis XV was called away from his meal of cream-coated chicken to minister to the king. When he returned, his sauce had jelled to form an attractive glaze over the bird.

Compared to the Chinese, however, we Westerners are mere amateurs when it comes to the spectacular culinary faux pas.

Take the case of the Imperial Court's most senior chef, who was busily making the royal family's favourite boiled dumplings. Distracted, the old man completely forgot about them, leaving them with a severe case of burned bottoms. The old chef's son sprung into action. To save his father from Imperial wrath and possible death, he presented the dumplings to the Emperor as a new crisp-bottomed creation called simply 'pot stickers'. Fortunately, the scam worked. The Emperor was impressed, and the old man lived to an even riper old age.

Another Imperial Court story tells of a cook in the royal household who showed up for work one day in a state that can only be described as tired and emotional. The man was so drunk, that while making a traditional prawn dumpling (what is it about dumplings?), he mistakenly used wheat flour instead of the usual rice flour. After they had been steamed, the dumpling wrappers became transparent, revealing the pretty pink colour of the prawns within. The Emperor was most impressed with the dumpling, which became known as 'har gau', and he showered the chef with riches. No prizes for guessing what the chef spent his new-found wealth on.

The grand daddy of all Chinese foodie accidents is Beggar's Chicken, supposedly created when a beggar stole a chicken. Hotly pursued by the authorities, he hid the evidence by wrapping the bird in lotus leaves and burying it in the ground beneath his campfire before making a hasty exit. When he returned for his chicken, he found that the bird was perfectly cooked, moist and fragrant. Modern cooks prefer to procure their chicken through more legitimate means, and there is no evidence that this in any way impairs the flavour.

Perhaps, in all these accidents, there is a lesson to be learned by today's generation of cooks, chained to their Gaggenaus, hog-tied by tradition, and slaves to every single word in their precious little cookbooks.

Until recent times, cooking was a changing, moveable, ever-evolving, oral phenomenon, open to constant interpretation and modification. Changes were never seen as mistakes, but were merely personal translations. With the rigidity of the modern printed recipe, we are now terrified to change a gram of castor sugar in case the God of cooking should strike us down from above.

Painstakingly perfect, deliberate food has no surprises and no history.

It's the same, day after day. But start a recipe on one page and accidentally finish on an altogether different recipe three pages on, as I have done, and you may well be rewarded with a happy accident of your own. Use plain flour instead of self-raising and reap the benefits. Have all the ingredients for Moroccan chicken ready except the chicken, then substitute with glee.

As I write this, grey smoke fills the room. I have just scorched a third tray of peanuts in the oven. It will either be fourth time lucky, or I will make an executive decision that peanuts are highly unnecessary in this particular Thai cucumber and prawn salad. I'm sure I won't miss them a bit.

It was probably a mistake that they were in there in the first place.

Wor tip (pot-sticker dumplings)

The result of braising, steaming and frying techniques, this is a dumpling with the lot: a crisp, delicious bottom, a supple, lush and louche top and a juicy, aromatic and thoroughly irresistible filling. If you're lucky, you may find Shanghai or pot-sticker dumpling skins at your Asian food store. If not, you can always make them yourself.

Filling

- 1 cup (90 grams or 3 ounces) wong buk or Peking cabbage, shredded finely
- 250 grams (8 ounces) minced pork
- 30 grams (1 ounce) fresh pork fat, minced
- 2 tablespoons fresh coriander, chopped
- 1 tablespoon fresh ginger, minced
- pinch of pepper
- 1 teaspoon sugar
- ½ teaspoon salt
- 1 dessertspoon light soya sauce
- 1 dessertspoon Shao hsing rice wine
- 1 tablespoon cornflour

Dough

- 2 cups (315 grams or 10 ounces) plain flour
- 1 cup (250 ml or 8 fluid ounces) hot water

Blanch the cabbage in boiling water. Drain well, then pat dry with paper towels. Let the cabbage cool, then combine with rest of filling ingredients, mixing thoroughly with your hands, then chill the mixture in the refrigerator.

Make the dough by sifting the flour into a bowl, then adding the water a little at a time, mixing until you have a rough dough. On a floured surface, knead the dough for five to ten minutes, until smooth and pliable. Cover and rest for 30 minutes.

Divide the mixture in half. Roll each piece into a sausage about 2 cm (1 in) thick, then divide each sausage into ten pieces.

Press each piece into a circle about 7–8 cm (3 in) across.

Place 1½ teaspoons of the filling on each round, and close the edges to make a semi circle, pinching together at the top. Pleat one side, which causes the dumpling to curve slightly.

Place the dumplings in a lightly oiled steamer and steam for ten minutes, then cool.

Heat two tablespoons of peanut oil in a heavy pan and cook the dumplings, bottoms down until they are golden on the bottom.

Pour half a cup of water into pan, and cover. Cook until the liquid has been absorbed, around four to five minutes.

Remove and serve with a dipping sauce of vinegar and shredded fresh ginger.

Makes 20 dumplings.

Caesar salad

I know forty different chefs who claim to have the one, the true, the original Caesar salad, and they're all different. Here's another one to add to your collection.

    2 cos (romaine) lettuces
    4 slices crusty bread cut into cubes
    1 garlic clove
    1 teaspoon olive oil
    1 egg
    1–2 tablespoons lemon juice
    salt and freshly ground pepper
    1 tablespoon white wine vinegar
    ½ cup (125 ml or 4 fluid ounces) good olive oil
    10 anchovies, rinsed and dried
    1 tablespoon freshly grated Parmigiano
    shavings of Parmigiano

Heat the oven to 160°C (325°F).

Wash and dry the lettuce leaves. Rub the bread with cut garlic clove, brush with olive oil, and bake until crisp.

Lower the egg into a pot of simmering water for one minute, then cool and break open. Combine egg, lemon juice, salt, pepper and vinegar in a small bowl and whisk well

Add olive oil slowly, whisking constantly until it is smooth, then coat the leaves with dressing. Add anchovies and Parmigiano, and arrange in salad bowl.

Tuck the croutons and cheese shavings (best done with a potato peeler) into the leaves and serve immediately.

Serves 4.

Tarte Tatin
(upside-down apple tart)

Long ago in France, the Tatin sisters were renowned for their rustic apple tarts. Ironic then, that they should be remembered for one that fell and broke. The ingenious sisters simply turned it upside down and served it. A lesson for us all.

    8 Golden Delicious apples
    3 tablespoons butter
    $^3/_4$ cup (165 grams or $5^1/_2$ ounces) castor sugar
    shortcrust pastry to fit 20-cm (8-in)
        baking dish

Heat the oven to 200°C (400°F).
    Peel, halve and core the apples.
    Melt half the butter in a 20-cm (8-in) baking dish, sprinkle with half the sugar, and arrange apples, cut side up, making sure to really pack them in, as they will shrink down during the cooking.
    Top with remaining butter and sugar and cook over a medium heat for around 30 minutes. Transfer to the oven and cook for a few minutes just until the apples start to caramelise on top. Leave to cool.
    Roll out the dough, place over the apples in the dish and trim it so that it falls inside. Bake in a hot oven for 20–30 minutes until the pastry is nicely crisp.
    Place a large flat plate over the pan, and carefully turn it over, so that the pastry is now the bottom of the dish.
    Serve warm with pure cream or vanilla icecream.
    Serves 8.

An ode

to udon

I now know how a devout Roman Catholic feels on first stepping into St Peter's Square, or how a Muslim feels arriving at Mecca.

I have arrived in Takamatsu, in the province of Kagawa, on the island of Shikoku, and I am pressing myself against the window of a little glass booth. On the other side of the glass, a man dressed in a pristine white tunic is busily rolling out the dough for a new batch of thick white noodles.

Not just any thick white noodles, but udon.

To an ardent udonite like myself, other Japanese noodles (the nutritious soba, the Chinese-influenced ramen) can seem a little naive. This thick white earthworm of a noodle, however, is a giant-hearted, voluptuous beast.

I could die here, as happily as a truffle connoisseur could cark it in Perigord or a prosciuttophile could pass away in Parma. Because this is Udonville.

While udon flourished in the big cities of Edo, Kyoto and Osaka, nobody has ever taken them quite as seriously as the Kagawans. In olden days, a Kagawan bride was expected to bring udon-making rolling pins and knives as part of her dowry. There is even an official Udon Day in Takamatsu (July 2), when members of the Udon association, a master noodle chef and a priest all gather at a shrine to prepare udon and present it as an offering to ensure a successful wheat harvest.

For centuries, the locals have been prone to saying that if you throw a stone in Kagawa it will land in an udon shop. As if anyone would be silly enough to do that.

With its relatively light rainfall and moderate temperatures, wheat flourished in Kagawa, although with nearly three thousand noodle shops in operation today, as much as eighty per cent of the wheat for udon making now comes from Australia.

With the invention of the noodle-making machine in the Meiji era, hand-made udon all but disappeared, except in Kagawa where, even today, hand-made udon like the ones being made before my eyes are commonplace.

Not that the chef from the Kana Izuni noodle restaurant is making any old udon. He is making Sanuki udon (Sanuki being the ancient name for Kagawa), regarded by noodlephiles as the finest in the world. Sanuki udon are said to have evolved from a recipe brought back from Xian in China by the great Buddhist saint Kobo Daishi in 806 AD.

I watch as the chef effortlessly furls a giant flap of dough neatly around his rolling pin. With lightning flicks of the pin, he rolls one way, then the next, until the dough is the size of a small tablecloth. He then folds it neatly over itself as if folding up the day's laundry.

The folded dough is then placed onto an elaborate guillotine affair, which has been fitted with a spring to regulate the thickness of each cut. With the speed of an electric machine, the chef slices the udon into perfect, uniform strips. Inserting the rolling pin into the middle of the flap, he suddenly produces a rod of finished udon.

I restrain from cheering and clapping, and instead, fling myself up the stairs to the restaurant. My ears are filled with a strange whooshing sound, like wind rushing through maple trees in autumn. Just when it occurs to me that I may finally have lost it, I realise it is the sound of slurping that fills my ears. I am in the right place.

The Japanese steadfastly maintain that to really enjoy noodles, one must eat fast with a cooling intake of breath, and the only way to do this is to slurp. Loudly.

Eat your noodles too quietly, and your host will assume that you are simply not enjoying them. As if.

The delicate question is how best to enjoy my first genuine Sanuki udon.

Perhaps as nabeyaki udon, in a casserole with kamaboko fish cake, tempura vegetables, egg and diced chicken. Or maybe as kitsune udon, in a soup with deep-fried tofu. Or as tsukimi udon, known as moon-viewing noodles, with its floating raw egg looking like a sultry moon, while the white udon noodles resemble the drifting clouds.

I go purist, and order them in a light, clear broth, with no riff-raff.

Carefully, I study the noodles, paying them the utmost respect (something I learned from the cult noodle-western film *Tampopo*), then lift the first silken strands out of the broth.

I pucker up and let the air intake follow. Whoosh!

It is as if I have had a vision.

The first thing my senses absorb is the texture. It is what the Japanese call 'koshi ga aru', firm but not too tough. Then there is a tactile resilience, known as 'nebari ga aru', meaning chewy and elastic, rather than limp and soggy.

Finally, there is the overpowering sensation of 'nodo gashi ga ii', an almost carnal sensation of something sliding effortlessly down the throat.

This is the kind of noodle you would ask for on the last, lingering night before your execution, your wedding, or the end of the world. And the morning after.

This is Sanuki udon.

Tsukumi udon
(moon-viewing noodles)

By responding to the rhythm of the seasons, the Japanese believe that they can be at one with the divine forces of the universe. Every autumn, the gentle art of moon viewing absorbs an entire nation. This obsession has been transferred to a more edible art in this exquisite noodle dish where the egg represents the moon and the udon noodles are the clouds. If you can find fresh udon noodles, so much the better.

   400 grams (13 ounces) dried udon noodles
   1.5 litres (2½ pints) dashi broth
   1 tablespoon sake
   2 tablespoons light soya sauce
   8 slices kamaboko fish cake
   4 dried shitake mushrooms, soaked, stems removed and sliced in half
   4 fresh eggs
   2 large spring onions, sliced thinly on the diagonal

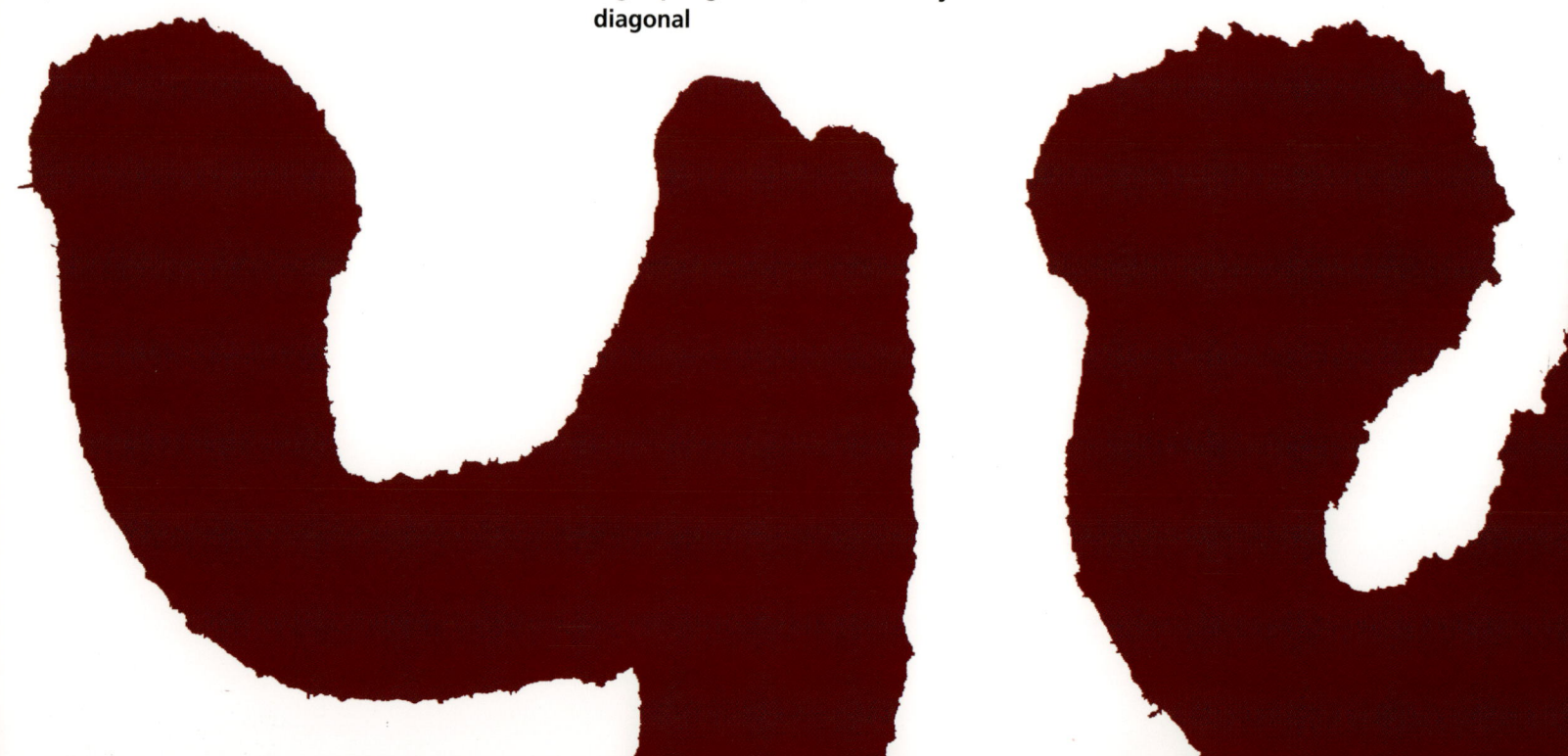

Cook the noodles in boiling, salted water for about ten minutes. Drain and rinse under cold water.

Place the dashi broth, sake and soya sauce in a pot and bring to the boil. Reheat noodles briefly in boiling water, then divide between four warmed serving bowls making a little hollow in each nest.

Add the fish cake and mushrooms, then break an egg into each hollow. Carefully ladle the boiling stock over the noodles, and cover with a plate.

Sprinkle with spring onions.

Toasted nori squares can also be added at the last minute.

Serves 4.

Mum's the word

There I was, driving along the open highway to my mother-in-law's house in the country for dinner. Beside me, Jill was taking a longer, more circuitous journey. Her eyes were all soft and misty-looking. 'Steamed chocolate pudding with chocolate sauce', she purred.

A creamy smile crossed her lips, the sort they used to draw on blonde princesses in children's books. 'You've never tasted anything like it.' The smile creased wider until it had tucked itself around both dangly earrings. 'The pudding itself was deeply dark and deliciously sticky, while the sauce was like molten lava.' She licked her lips and I swear I could see little dribbles of chocolate at the corner of her mouth. 'Or maybe she'll do caramel dumplings in the old electric frypan. I bet you've never had those before.'

Why does everyone insist on believing that their childhood was copyright?

Millions of us have grown up eating caramel dumplings, yet we all believe that we were the only ones.

'Or chocolate blanc mange. Or drop scones, dripping with hand-churned butter.'

The voice was trance-like. I overtook three cars without her even telling me to slow down.

'Egg and bacon pie. Or shepherd's pie. Or (pause for religious silence) roast leg of lamb. Have I ever told you about our Sunday roast lamb dinners?'

'Yes.'

'We used to have roast lamb every Sunday. Dad would stand at one end of the table and pass out little glasses of sparkling wine to us kids. Then he'd start carving. There was always good, thick, brown gravy, peas from the pea paddocks, and piles of roast potatoes, roast parsnips and roast pumpkin. And do you know what we had on Mondays?'

'Yes.'

'Lamb fritters, made from the leftovers. With tomato sauce.' And this is the woman who refuses to eat Paul Bocuse's famous truffle soup outside France because the truffles are canned.

After three hours of this, we finally get to her mother's house, where my wife actually restrains herself from asking what's for dinner.

After pouring us a very good Margaret River Sauvignon Blanc, her mother sits us down at the table and appears from the kitchen bearing steaming bowls of soup. Pea and ham? Chicken noodle? Cream of Tomato? No.

'I hope you like it', she says. 'It's Thai pumpkin soup with kaffir lime leaves, lemongrass and a little tamarind.'

My wife bore up well, but her face seemed to collapse at the arrival of the aromatic Malaysian beef curry and a delicious dessert of Indonesian spiced stewed fruits with cinnamon and cardamom ice-cream. The unthinkable had happened. Her mother had grown up.

This is not something that mothers are supposed to do. Mothers should be snap-frozen in time, or better still, lovingly preserved in hermetically sealed Fowler's Vacola bottling jars, beaming down at us from the top shelf in the pantry. That way, we can reach back into our past anytime we like for an ever lovin' spoonful of warmth and tenderness, mashed potatoes and peas. Isn't that what mothers are for?

At every dinner party, the conversation inevitably regresses into nostalgic longing for one's mother's food. It's like a school-yard contest, with your mum's pineapple upside-down cake being superior in every way to his mum's allegedly light-as-air Yo Yo biscuits and her mum's supposedly scintillating bubble and squeak. Thrust and parry.

'She did an Irish stew you couldn't stop eating.' Countered by: 'What she did with a pound of mince!' Lunge. 'Nobody but nobody did a passionfruit flummery like my mum.'

No one is immune to this affliction.

After a dinner of ouefs à la coque with truffles, turbot with tarragon, and fraises des bois with cream at the lavish Faugeron restaurant in Paris, I woke in my artistically decorated, but physiologically short bed at the Hotel La Villa with a strange feeling in the pit of my stomach that even lemon-flavoured Alka Seltzer couldn't fix. It wasn't the second helping of foie gras, it was an irresistible longing for my mother's baked macaroni and meat ball slice.

If you are ever given a chance to select your own mother, take my advice and go for the French variety. Michel and Albert Roux did, and look where it got them. The two brothers say they not only acquired their love and passion for food from their mother, they also acquired some of their most famous recipes.

The blanquette de veau, fricassée of rabbit, calf's heart with turnips, dandelion salad with fat bacon, and duck with turnips were all hers before they were theirs.

It was easy for Marc Meneau, three-starred chef of L'Esperance in Burgundy, to discover his mother's cooking secrets any time he liked as she worked alongside him for many years in the restaurant kitchen.

Sometimes your mother (and your mother's mother) can be a hard act to follow.

When Georges Blanc received his third Michelin star in 1981, his restaurant was still known as La Mère Blanc, after his grandmother Elisa. In the early 1900s, Elisa was dubbed 'the best chef in the world' by gastronomic legend Curnonsky. Georges' mother, Paulette, turned out to be just as gifted. Fortunately for us, Georges learned to cook as well as he ate.

My mother was no la mère Blanc, but as a resourceful and talented pub cook, her influence on these sensitive tastebuds was no less earth shattering. While you might not find her show-stopping baked spaghetti and meat balls, Wednesday special curried sausages and ultimate with-the-works meatloaf in any cook-book, these were the flavours that formed my basic training as an eater.

But what of the modern-day scenario, where mothers slave all day over a hot computer rather than a stove? Will our kids end up at twenty-first century dinner parties reminiscing over microwaved lean beans and dial-a-pizza's Saturday night special?

It's an awesome responsibility to know that the food we cook or zap today may well become the memories that are savoured tomorrow.

Yes, dear. Even Thai pumpkin soup.

Pock-marked grandmother's beancurd

This is China's answer to Sunday night's savoury mince, but with more class, more bite, and no toast. Grandmother Chen, who had an acne-scarred face, operated a tiny food stall in Chengdu in the province of Sichuan 150 years ago. Her humble dish became so famous that gourmets flocked to her stall, seeing only beauty before them.

- 6 dried Chinese mushrooms
- 6 cakes fresh beancurd
- 1 tablespoon peanut oil
- 3 garlic cloves, crushed
- 1 red chilli, finely chopped
- 1 teaspoon grated ginger
- 225 grams (7 ounces) minced pork
- 3 spring onions, finely chopped
- 2 tablespoons chilli bean sauce (from Asian food store)
- ½ teaspoon sugar
- 1 tablespoon Shao hsing rice wine or dry sherry
- 1 tablespoon dark soya sauce
- ½ cup (125 ml or 4 fluid ounces) chicken stock
- ½ teaspoon Sichuan peppercorns, ground

Soak the mushrooms in hot water for an hour, then remove the stems and cut the caps into quarters.

Cut the beancurd into small cubes, and set aside to drain. Heat the wok, add the oil, then the garlic, chilli and ginger. Then add the minced pork and mushrooms and stirfry for three minutes. Add the spring onions, sauce, sugar, wine, soya and chicken stock and stirfry for three or four minutes. Add the drained beancurd, lower the heat and cook gently for five minutes or so. At the last moment, stir in Sichuan pepper and serve with plain steamed rice.

Serves 4.

Son-in-law eggs

How do you like your boiled eggs — soft or crisp? There are several different stories as to why the name. Some say it has something to do with a mother-in-law who was less than thrilled with her son-in-law, while others claim it was devised by a mother who suddenly found herself with another mouth to feed. Yet another version claims that it came from a young man who tried to impress his future mother-in-law, by making her a dish utilising about the only thing he knew how to cook: a boiled egg. Feel free to make up your own story.

6 hardboiled eggs (boiled for 7–8 minutes, then cooled immediately)
oil for deep frying
2 tablespoons nam pla (fish sauce)
3 tablespoons tamarind water
2 tablespoons palm sugar (brown sugar will work)
2 red chillies, cut into thin slivers
2 tablespoons crisp fried shallots (from Asian food store)
coriander leaves for serving

Peel the eggs, and halve them. Heat the oil in a wok until it just begins to smoke, then deep fry the eggs for a few minutes until they become golden and slightly blistered.

Drain off all but two tablespoons of the oil, then add the nam pla, tamarind water and sugar and simmer for four or five minutes.

Arrange the eggs yolk-up on a plate, and pour the sauce over them. Sprinkle with chilli, fried shallots and coriander.

Serves 6.

It mixes! It stirs!

It blends!

I have just discovered the perfect kitchen gadget. It's not made by Alessi, yet it's ever so stylish and up to the minute. It's not a Zyliss, yet it's ingeniously simple. It's not a Krups, yet it's breathtakingly efficient.

It's made locally, never gets lost, and comes with a lifetime guarantee.

It's the human hand.

This is the kind of implement that tele-marketers would give their right you-know-whats for. 'Introducing the Wonder Hand! It mixes, it stirs, it kneads, it blends, it pounds, it tears, it shreds. And when you're finished, Wonder Hand just washes clean under running water!'

As we watch a close-up of flour-encrusted hands coming remarkably clean under the kitchen tap, the voice continues: 'Buy now and we'll give you another Wonder Hand absolutely free'.

No matter how far modern technology invades our kitchens and our dining rooms, it will never be able to replicate the sensitivity, the subtlety, the versatility, the flexibility, and the manoeuvrability of our own hands and fingers.

Remember your first finger painting at kinder? Remember that heavenly, wet, sticky, luscious feeling of gloriously gooey paint against your smooth little lily whites? The delicious squish of the paint oozing between your fingers? The wonderful sense of power you felt as you swished colour upon colour, and squiggled shape upon shape?

The most exciting sensation of all was just knowing that you were *allowed* to do it. Nowhere else in a child's world is there such an opportunity to make a goddamn awful mess and get away with it.

Finger painting of course, soon leads to bigger things such as play dough and plasticine, the perfect training ground for budding pastry chefs, bakers and pasta makers.

For these people, their hands are their thermometers, their kneaders, their tasters, and their master apprentices. Breads that have been shaped by hand take on a glorious sheen and a life that is unknown in pale, soft, commercial loaves. Old-fashioned pies that have been raised by hand enjoy an upbringing that a modern education can never match; and pasta that is made by hand (using a hand-operated pasta machine is permissible) has an elasticity, and voluptuousness that simply cannot be packaged.

Time and an almost paranoid health consciousness have become the arch enemies of our previously hand-to-mouth existence. We bung things into food processors, and sheath our hands in prophylactic-looking plastic gloves. No wonder Edina's mother mistook Eddy's female condoms for washing-up gloves in the television series 'Absolutely Fabulous'. The result is that, culinarily speaking, we're losing the feeling in our hands.

The girl in the local sandwich shop wears disposable rubber gloves when making sandwiches. I get incredibly nervous as she wields the carving knife, and uses the electric slicer without the benefit of that inbuilt radar of the nerve ends of her fingers. They may (just) be more hygienic than a good scrub with soap and water, but it makes you wonder if they don't promote a false sense of security on both sides of the latex. Recent reports suggest that the more air bags, safety belts and crash helmets we wear on the road, the more accidents we have.

Show me a great chef and I'll show you someone who's not afraid to get their hands dirty.

Arguments of hygiene just don't wash

with Marco Pierre White, for example, who got into hot water for licking his fingers on his Channel Four cooking show.

'If people would spend more time tasting what they are cooking instead of worrying about germs, then the quality of their cooking would soar', he later wrote. 'Licking the cake bowl is a precious ritual of childhood that everyone is familiar with, and if people had seen little Marco on television beside his mother licking the cake bowl, they would have said "how sweet". Instead they saw Big Marco tasting with his fingers and they said "how disgusting". People who can't cope with that lack a passion for life, or for food.'

But it's not just the cook who benefits from the hands-on approach. For the diner too, fingers are by far the most practical, enjoyable and thoroughly satisfying way of eating, even though we have devoted centuries to finding ingenious ways of placing little bits of wood, iron, and plastic between us and our food in the name of civilisation.

The ancient Fijians, for instance, would always eat their day to day meals in their hands. It was only when eating human flesh in ritualistic warrior celebrations, that they used a special wooden fork. It's one of the few times I wouldn't want to get too close to my food, either.

Then there are my own hands-on experiences, like eating a wonderfully pungent, aromatic fish head curry and rice from a giant banana leaf at the wonderful Banana Leaf Apollo restaurant in Singapore, using only my first three fingers and thumb to scoop the delicious morsels of food up to my mouth. Not using cutlery was like cutting out the middle man, and I felt a bond with my food that I have rarely experienced before. The textures and flavours seemed so much more defined and self-contained than those licked off cold hard metal.

In Morocco, I managed to eat a meal of several tagines and copious quantities of couscous in my right hand (the left hand has other important uses of the non-culinary kind). What was memorable about this meal was not that the act of using my hands made me feel closer to the food, but that it made me feel closer to my dining companions. Here was a truly communal act that embodied the very spirit of the sharing of a meal. Not to mention the mess.

Questioning the automatic use of cutlery can lead to some wonderful experiences. Sushi comes alive when your fingers pick up each piece, dipping the fish side in a little soy and laying it flat upon your tongue.

Hand-fed pizzas and even fish and chips taste better, with the added bonus of licking your salty fingers.

So if you have some primal instinct left under those svelte clothes and cyberpunk jewellery, release it before it is too late. Use your fingers to cook with and eat with (barring soups and tirami su), and you'll eat better, feel better and live better.

To this day, I make my own pasta as often as I can. Not because of the heavenly, wet, sticky, luscious feeling of gloriously gooey dough against my not-so-smooth, not-so-lily whites, but because I know this is about the only time left in my adult life that I can make a goddamn awful mess, and get away with it.

How to make pasta

The method behind great egg pasta, or pasta all'uovo, is pretty simple stuff. But the real secret of great pasta depends on the way you use your hands. Don't push and pull and prod, but caress and tease, and tempt the dough. Try to feel what's going on in your dough with your fingertips. Put some music on, and let the rhythm move you.

The golden rule for pasta dough is one egg to 100 grams (3½ ounces) of flour.

So start by tipping 400 grams (13 ounces) of flour (durum wheat or pasta flour) into a mound on a clean bench, and make a crater in the centre of it. Break four eggs into the hole and a scant tablespoon of very good olive oil. Gently beat this mixture with your fingers, gradually drawing in a little flour from the rim. Keep going, and you will soon have a dough that you can push around.

If it feels dry, wet your hands with lukewarm water and keep going. If it feels sticky, keep your hands well-floured and keep going. Keep kneading with good, steady solid rhythm (I do this in time to the Rolling Stones' 'Under the Boardwalk') for around ten minutes. Stop when you have a smooth, shiny ball of dough. Cover in plastic wrap, and let rest for at least 30 minutes.

Set the rollers of your pasta machine at their widest point. Cut the pasta ball into quarters, flatten out a quarter with the palm of your hand, then feed it through the machine twice. Continue the process, changing the notch on the machine to progressively smaller settings. Dust the pasta with flour if it gets too warm and soft.

Cut the pasta into long, thin strips by hand or by guiding it through the cutting attachment on the machine, and hang to dry for an hour or so on a wooden rack.

Pumpkin ravioli with mustard fruits

There's something positively medieval about these sweet-salty-sharp-soft-spicy-herby pillows of niceness. Certainly they're a bit of work, but then so are most worthwhile things in life.

- 500 grams (1 pound) pumpkin
- 1 dessertspoon olive oil
- 1 small egg
- 2 tablespoons mustard fruits, finely chopped
- 2 tablespoons breadcrumbs
- 6 amaretti biscuits, crushed
- ½ teaspoon grated nutmeg
- 60 grams (2 ounces) grated Parmigiano
- pinch of salt
- 400 grams (13 ounces) fresh pasta dough, uncut
- 4 tablespoons butter
- 8 fresh sage leaves
- extra Parmigiano cheese, grated

Peel the pumpkin and cut it into chunks. Toss in olive oil and roast in a moderate oven until tender, about 1½ hours. You want it to be dry, but not burnt. Purée the flesh until it is smooth, adding the egg, mustard fruits, breadcrumbs, biscuits, nutmeg, cheese and salt to taste.

Divide the pasta dough in half, and roll out one half on a floured board until thin. Cut into two equal-sized sheets.

Place heaped teaspoons of filling about 8 cm (3 in) apart on the sheet of pasta. Brush between the filling along the lines to be joined with a little water or beaten egg yolk. Cover with the second sheet and press firmly between the mounds of filling. Cut with a pastry wheel into plump, square little cushions. Repeat process with the remaining half of dough.

Cook the ravioli in a large pot of salted, boiling water for three or four minutes, or until they rise to the surface. While they cook, melt the butter and sage in a small frypan until light golden and sizzling. Drain the ravioli and distribute it between warm plates. Drizzle with hot sage butter and serve with extra grated cheese.

Serves 4.

Tagliolini with lemon and caviar

Purists will argue that the only thing that goes with caviar, is more caviar. But they obviously haven't tried this *molto simpatico* combination of fine, thin pasta, cream, lemon juice and caviar. If the budget doesn't run to caviar, don't worry — the dish is *favoloso* without it.

500 grams (1 pound) fresh tagliolini (thin tagliatelle)
3 tablespoons butter
2 tablespoons freshly grated lemon rind
½ cup (125 ml or 4 fluid ounces) dry white wine
2 tablespoons running cream
2 tablespoons lemon juice, to taste
salt and freshly ground black pepper
50 grams (1½ ounces) Sevruga or Beluga caviar

Cook the pasta in a big pot of boiling, salted water until al dente, tender but firm to the bite.

Melt the butter in a large frypan, and gently cook the lemon zest for one minute. Add the wine and allow it to bubble.

Lower the heat and add the cream and cook, stirring, for a minute or two, without bringing to the boil. Drain the pasta and add to the sauce.

Stir in the lemon juice, salt and pepper, and serve on warmed plates. Top each plate with a spoonful of caviar.

Serves 4.

Pappardelle with chicken livers

Your hands are doubly important when making pappardelle, because the broad pasta strips must be hand-cut. Simply take each flat sheet of pasta and cut it into strips 2.5 cm (1 in) wide. Don't make it too perfect, either. (If you make a right mess of it, just call it 'stracci' instead, which means rags.)

- 400 grams (13 ounces) chicken livers
- 2 tablespoons olive oil
- 2 garlic cloves, bruised
- 1 small onion, finely chopped
- 1 teaspoon rosemary leaves
- a few sage leaves
- ½ cup (125 ml or 4 fluid ounces) red wine
- 250 ml (8 fluid ounces) tomato passato, or 300 grams (9½ ounces) canned tomatoes, well mashed
- salt and freshly ground black pepper
- 500 grams (1 pound) pappardelle
- 1 tablespoon butter
- Parmigiano for grating

Wash and trim the livers, removing any membrane and discolourations, and cut into 2.5 cm (1 in) pieces.

Heat the olive oil, add the garlic, and cook for two minutes. Add the onion and cook until soft. Add the livers, rosemary and sage, and cook, stirring, until livers are almost cooked, about three minutes. Remove the livers, turn up the heat, add the wine, and allow the sauce to bubble and reduce.

Add the tomato, and cook for ten minutes until sauce thickens. Taste for salt and pepper.

Cook the pasta in plenty of boiling, salted water until al dente, tender but firm to the bite. Return the livers to the pan and heat through for a minute or two.

Drain the pasta and toss with the butter in a warmed serving bowl. Pour the sauce on top, toss and serve with freshly grated Parmigiano.

Serves 4.

Fettuccine with Gorgonzola

Combine the tang of aristocratic Gorgonzola cheese, with the lush smoothness of home-made fettuccine and what do you have? Happiness in a bowl. If your Gorgonzola is bit strong, use a mixture of half Gorgonzola, half mascarpone cream cheese, or cream.

> 125 grams (4 ounces) Gorgonzola, chopped
> ½ cup (125 ml or 4 fluid ounces) milk
> 1 tablespoon butter
> salt and freshly ground black pepper
> 2 tablespoons cream
> 500 grams (1 pound) fettuccine
> 2 tablespoons grated Parmigiano

Combine the Gorgonzola, milk, butter, salt and pepper in a heavy-bottomed frypan and cook over a gentle heat, stirring with a wooden spoon until it melts into a thick and creamy sauce.

Add the cream, raise the heat a little and cook, stirring, until the sauce starts to thicken (about five minutes).

Cook pasta in plenty of boiling, salted water until al dente, tender but firm to the bite. Drain well and tip onto a warmed serving platter with the sauce and grated cheese. Toss quickly, and serve immediately.

Serves 4.

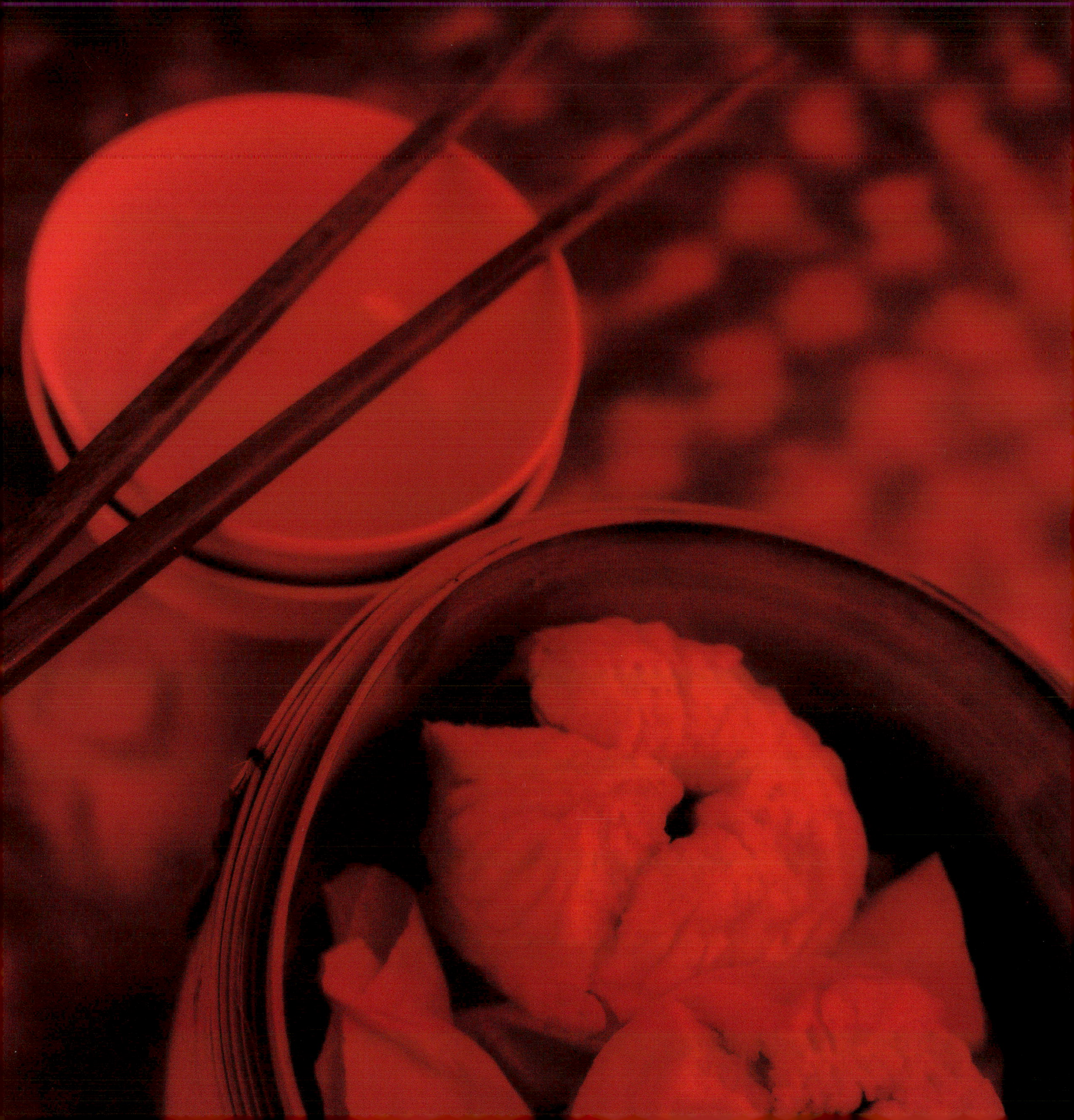

Clang, clang, clang went the trolley

It is a little after midday as we make our way through the Sunday traffic toward Chinatown for yum cha.

In the back seat of the car, Max the mutant teenager is speaking in hushed, serious tones to Kris, his mutant teenage friend.

Kris has never been to yum cha before in his life, so Max is earnestly giving him his briefing.

'Remember', says Max. 'When they bring the tripe and turnips, go for the turnips first.'

'Tripe?' bleats Kris.

'When all the turnips have gone, go for the honeycomb tripe next. Then the dark spongy bits, and then the rubbery transparent bits.'

'Tripe?' repeats Kris. Horror seems to have frozen him in time.

'Yeah, but don't eat too much', says Max. 'You'll need a little room for the chicken feet.'

'Chicken feet?'

Two hours later, Kris emerges from the restaurant, full of prawn dumplings, rice porridge, roast suckling pig, and yes, even tripe. He is a fully fledged mutant teenage convert.

There is something about yum cha that is totally addictive, and no, I'm not talking about MSG.

It's not just the food. It's the whole social event: a relaxed meeting of family and friends over plenty of hot steaming gossip and chit-chat, happily interrupted by little round, steamed things; long, fried, crisp things; and bubbling, aromatic, stewed things.

In China, people have been loyally trekking to yum cha ever since the days of the Song Dynasty (960–1279, but you knew that already), when Canton was a peaceful, cultured province. Travellers would break their journeys at little roadside tea houses that acted as comfort-stop service stations for the soul.

A sip of tea here, a little snack there, and before you knew it, they had invented yum cha, which means 'to have tea and a couple of snacks'. Nowadays, it's more like 'to have tea accompanied by herds of stampeding elephants'.

In Hong Kong, gigantic, five-storey dim-sum palaces attract rich, poor, local, tourist, novice and gourmet to sip, nibble and bite their way through mountains of dim sum.

Waiters carry walkie-talkies to direct the flow of traffic, and gas burners disguised as shining chrome Vespas do slow circuits of every room, frying lor bahk (radish) cakes as they go.

To the uninitiated it is a terrifying sight. But then there was a time when we all looked at our first Italian antipasto, Greek mezes, Spanish tapas or French degustation selection and wondered what on earth to do with it.

My introduction to this peaceful, rhythmic, delicate way of dining was a nerve-wracking, horrendous, torrid affair at the Golden Crown in Nathan Road,

Kowloon, many Sunday lunches ago. The dining room was the size of a football field, and all of southern China had arrived for the first sitting. Trolleys laden with well-worn bamboo steamers and what looked like designer rubbish bins paraded up and down the room, while ancient Chinese faces grimaced over pork knuckles, slurped over bowls of congee and talked through mouths full of rice flour pastry.

A large woman pushing a trolley piled high with bamboo steamers, approached my table, crying out loudly 'Just you bow'. Not wanting to give offence, I bowed madly and received a large steamer containing two fluffy, plump white buns (otherwise known as char sieu bau). After that there was no stopping me. I bowed furiously at every trolley that went by, and managed to assemble an impressive collection of mysterious objects, not all of which, I became convinced, were for eating. In fact, one white rolled-up thing tasted suspiciously like a face washer.

Feeling quite pleased with myself, I summoned the courage to ask the waiter standing behind me for some tea. He smiled, nodded and refused to budge. Eventually, I realised he was not a waiter, but simply a hungry would-be diner who was waiting for me to leave so he could claim my chair. One can only hope this unique method of confirming one's reservation never catches on in some of our more occidental dining establishments.

Things reached their lowest point when two competing trolleys met head-on at my table. 'Gay?' asked one, eyebrows raised. I was beginning to wish I hadn't worn my new Yohji Yamamoto overcoat. Maybe it was just a tad too bright. The other pointed straight at me. 'Aw yuk!' she exclaimed.

While I slid under the table, they continued to offer me gai (chicken) and au yuk (beef balls). Not knowing what to do, I bowed and received a serve of each.

Having eaten enough for three Chinese families, I found a waiter who was a waiter and asked for the bill.

'Bill not work today', he said disarmingly, as he counted the number of steamers on my table and rattled off a sum that would barely pay for a spring roll back home.

I waddled off to the Star Ferry, triumphant. Now perhaps I was ready for that finishing school of tea houses, the Luk Yu Teahouse in Hong Kong's chaotic central business district.

The Luk Yu is Hong Kong's oldest and most traditional tea house. Outside its ornately carved wooden doors, computers are sold on the footpath, while inside, ceiling fans revolve languorously over old mahogany tables, brass spittoons and wooden booths. A very friendly waiter poured tea all over the table, narrowly missing the tea cup, and left me with a cheery grin and an order card filled with Chinese characters.

Under the circumstances, I did the only thing possible. I panicked. What to do? Tick every third one? Mark the date of my birthday? Pick eight numbers and a supplementary? It was like scratch and win, only nobody knew what the prizes were.

At the next table, a giggle of girls was busily circling various things on their order card. Surreptitiously, I copied what they were doing, and felt like a kid cheating in his exams.

It all worked out rather well, although next time I would prefer a little more variety than sweet custard tart, sweet sponge cake, sweet almond jelly, and sweet coconut delight.

It almost put me off my afternoon tea and cakes in the sumptuous lobby of the Peninsula Hotel.

After that sweet and sour experience, I decided there was nothing for it but to learn the names of those little steamed prawn things and tiny fried pork things. Soon came a gruelling intensive research program that lasted three hours every Sunday afternoon.

I learned how to tell a spring roll from a face washer. I learned not to order everything in the first five minutes, but to pace myself, like a runner, to last the distance.

I learned also, that there was as much etiquette involved in a yum cha table as there is in a Sunday roast.

For example one taps one's fingers lightly on the edge of the table to say thank you, and tips the lid of the teapot to one side when it needs more water. I soon tired of jasmine and oolong teas and graduated to bo lei, a hot pungent, grease-cutter of a tea, and gok bo, filled with fragrant dried chrysanthemum petals.

Learning the Cantonese names for things wasn't all that difficult for someone who had mastered spaghetti, risotto, paella and pot au feu.

Soon I knew that pai gwat were yummy pork ribs; fun gwor were fragrant, crescent-shaped dumplings of pork, prawn and coriander; har gau were those highly esteemed and lightly steamed prawn dumplings that are the ultimate test of a good yum cha.

Even the mutant teenager took time off from his heavy metal homework to learn that his favourite pork-filled, deep-fried footballs were called ham sui gok.

So at our very next yum cha, all was going blissfully well, until number one son asked for ham sui gok.

'Sorry?' said the Chinese waitress, blankly.

'Ham sui gok.'

'Sorry, do not know', she said, blushing.

On her next time around, she offered Max an entire tray of you know what.

'That's them', cried Max. 'That's what we call ham sui gok.'

'Oh those', said the waitress. 'That's what we call special fried combination dumplings.'

Rice congee with white fish

Congee, known as jook to the Cantonese, is the ultimate Chinese comfort food. As well as being a yum cha staple, it is often eaten at breakfast, and as a late night supper. After an evening dining on the finest shark fin, the most exquisite duckling and the choicest abalone, even the most hardened Chinese gourmet will finish the night on a back-to-the-nursery bowl of jook.

- 1 cup (185 grams or 6 ounces) short-grain rice
- 2.5 litres (5 pints) chicken stock
- salt to taste
- 200 grams (6½ ounces) white fish, sliced thinly
- 3 spring onions, chopped finely
- ½ cup (75 grams or 2½ ounces) roasted peanuts
- 50 grams (1½ ounces) Sichuan preserved vegetables, rinsed

Wash the rice in cold water, then add to the boiling stock. Reduce the heat to a simmer, then continue to cook for two and a half hours until the rice has transformed into a thick, runny soup with the grains still vaguely discernible.

Divide the fish between six soup bowls, then pour the congee on top. Flavour with spring onions, peanuts and Sichuan vegetables and season to taste.

Instead of fish, you can serve the congee with slices of boiled chicken, roast duck or char sieu red roast pork.

Serves 6 to 8.

Siu mai

These are the classic meat-filled yum cha dumplings; full-flavoured, delicate and surprisingly light, unless, of course you eat four steamer-loads by yourself.

250 grams (8 ounces) shelled raw prawn meat, chopped
100 grams (3½ ounces) minced pork
4 dried Chinese mushrooms, soaked in hot water for an hour, then chopped
4 tablespoons water chestnuts, finely chopped
4 tablespoons bamboo shoots, finely chopped
6 tablespoons spring onions, finely chopped
1 teaspoon salt
1 teaspoon sugar
1 teaspoon Shao hsing rice wine or dry sherry
1 tablespoon light soya sauce
½ teaspoon sesame oil
2 tablespoons cornflour
1 pack of won ton skins

Combine the pork, prawns, vegetables, seasoning, wine, sauce, oil and cornflour in a large bowl using your hands to mix thoroughly. Chill for an hour or two in the refrigerator.

Trim the corners off the won ton skins to make a rough circle, then place a dessertspoon of mixture in the middle of each skin, gather up the sides, letting them form natural pleats. Lightly tap the dumplings on a surface to create a flat bottom, and squeeze the skin around the filling, leaving the top of the dumpling open.

Lightly oil a metal or bamboo steamer and steam the dumplings for 15 to 20 minutes.

Makes around 30 dumplings.

Har gau prawn dumplings

A warning. The dough for these incredibly delicious dumplings can be incredibly tricky to make unless Confucious is smiling upon you, the wind is in the right direction and your luck is in. But don't let me put you off. If things work out right, and you follow the directions to the letter, you will no doubt triumph, and command enormous respect from your neighbours, your friends and your loved ones. A quicker way to command respect of course, is to take them to yum cha.

Filling

- 250 grams (8 ounces) prawns, cleaned; shelled and minced
- 2 tablespoons pork fat, finely chopped
- 2 tablespoons water chestnuts, finely chopped
- 2 tablespoons minced bamboo shoots
- ¼ teaspoon white pepper
- ½ teaspoon salt
- 1½ tablespoons cornstarch
- 1 teaspoon sugar
- ½ teaspoon sesame oil
- 2 egg whites

Dough

- 1 cup (125 grams or 4 ounces) Chinese wheat starch
- ½ cup (60 grams or 2 ounce) tapioca flour
- ½ teaspoon salt
- 1 tablespoon peanut oil
- 1 cup (250 ml or 8 fluid ounces) boiling water

Combine all the filling ingredients, except the egg whites. Mix well, then beat the egg whites until stiff and fold into the mixture. Chill for several hours.

For the dough, mix the wheat starch, tapioca flour, salt and oil together. Bring the water to the boil (covered, so as not to lose any) and stir into the dry ingredients, mixing with chopsticks.

Sprinkle the bench top with tapioca flour, and knead the dough for a couple of minutes until it is a smooth ball. Wrap in plastic and leave for 30 minutes. When ready, lightly oil a clean bench-top. Roll the dough into a sausage approximately 2 cm (1 in) thick, and cut the sausage into 2-cm (1-in) rounds. Flatten with the side of a cleaver, then roll into circles about 7 cm (3 in) circumference, making sure the dough is quite thin.

Place a large teaspoon of the mixture in the middle of each circle, and fold the pastry over to cover the filling. Pinch the top of the pastry at the centre to form two 'ears', pressing the opening together to form a flat lip. On one side of the dumpling make six pleats, pressing the other side so it curves inwards slightly.

Place the dumplings on an oiled steamer, making sure the dumplings don't touch, and steam for 10 to 15 minutes until the wrappers are semi transparent.

Makes about 30.

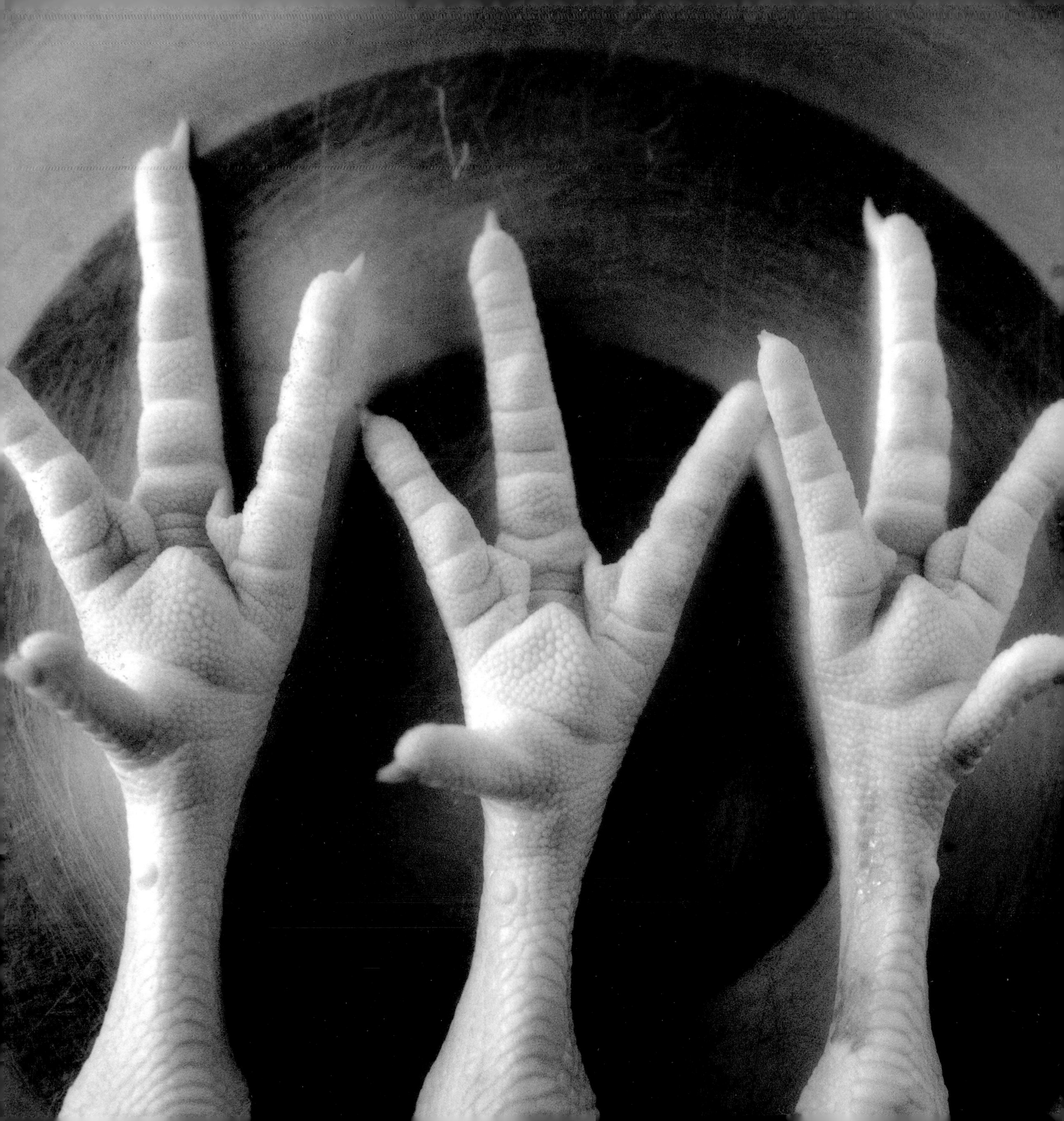

Feet first

There is something about a well-turned ankle that I find totally irresistible. I love feet. So kick me. From the smooth, seductive line of the instep to the tips of those cute little toes, I am irresistibly drawn to this most magical part of the anatomy.

Especially when those coarse, fibrous little hairs have been burnt off first.

I love them all, from chicken feet, steamed Cantonese style, and duck web braised with shitake mushrooms, to calves' feet and pigs' trotters cooked in a daube, the miraculous zampone of bologna, and sheep's trotters à la poulette.

Long before Pierre Koffman and Marco Pierre White transformed the humble pig's trotter into refined three-star fare by stuffing it with morel mushrooms, sweetbreads, and chicken mousse, the good people of St Ménéhould in the Champagne region, as in many other towns of France, boiled their trotters, then crumbed them, and served them with a spicy mustardy sauce. The extraordinary thing about this dish, however, was that the bones were so soft they could be chewed up along with the rest of it.

Nobody except the charcutiers themselves know why the bones are so soft. Some claim it is the twenty-four hours of boiling, but others say a certain vegetable added to the broth produces the right reaction in the trotter. Sceptics hint at pressure-cookers and chemical interference.

Louis XVI, always a bit of a leg man, had a particular weakness for pied de porc St Ménéhould, perhaps the most famous trotter dish in all of France.

While in hiding from the revolutionaries, he insisted on calling into St Ménéhould for just one more foot.

The king was recognised by a member of the convention, apprehended and later beheaded, thus becoming the first man in recorded history to lose his head over feet.

Alas, I have never been to St Ménéhould, but anyone who has ever tried the traditional, don't-eat-the-bones pied de porc so beloved of the charcuteries of Lyons and Paris will have experienced a little of the nirvana that so beguiled the good King Louis.

My most life-changing foot-to-mouth experience took place at that side show of a Parisian bistro, the endearingly tizzy Au Pied de Cochon in the Les Halles district, one time breakfast stop for the market porters and now a compulsory pit stop on the tourist trail.

To know the restaurant's specialty you need only push open a door: grabbing hold of a bright and shiny gilt door handle in the shape of a pig's trotter.

Go in November when the first of the young Beaujolais nouveau arrives, settle into a window table, and count your blessings. Count your bones, as well. I am told the more bones you have left on your plate, the luckier you are.

'Give me a pig's foot and a bottle of beer', sang Bessie Smith with a manic, throaty hunger in her voice that reeked of sex and satisfaction.

Or a pied de porc and a Beaujolais, Bessie, my dear.

yum

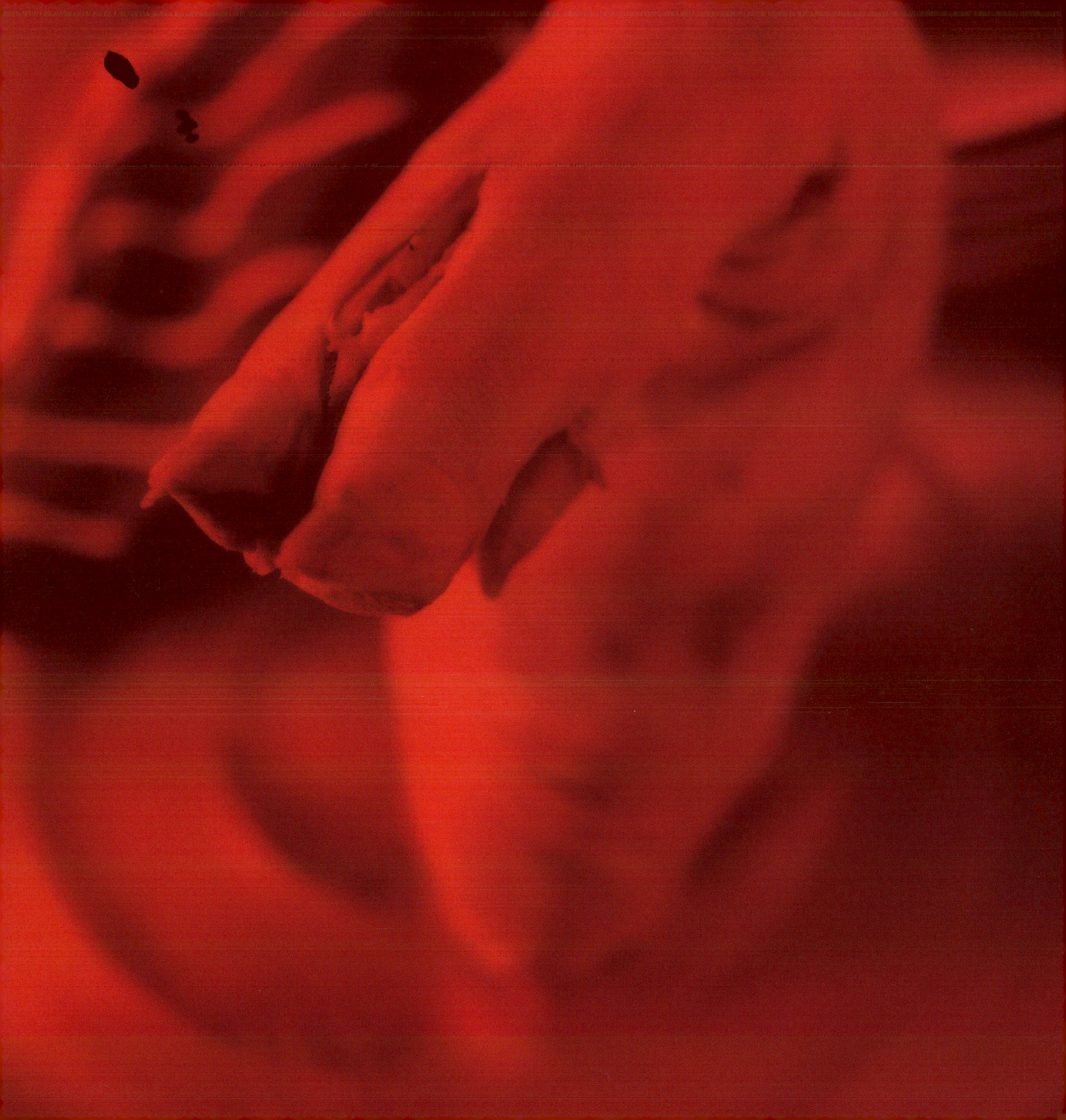

Grilled pig's trotters

I first ate this dish at Pied de Cochon, a wonderful glitzy brasserie in the Les Halles district of Paris, a shrine devoted to the adoration of the pig's trotter.

- 4 pig's trotters, split in half by your butcher
- 500 ml (16 fluid ounces) dry white wine
- 2 litres (3 pints) chicken or vegetable stock
- 2 onions, studded with 3 cloves each
- 2 bay leaves
- a little parsley and thyme
- salt
- 3 tablespoons melted butter
- 2 cups (250 grams or 4 ounces) fresh breadcrumbs
- Dijon mustard for serving

Burn off any hairs from the trotters over a gas flame, then wash under cold running water. Place in a saucepan of cold water, then bring to the boil and blanch for five minutes. Refresh in cold water and drain.

Join the two halves of each trotter together, and wrap each pair in muslin to help hold their shape. Tie with string.

Place the wrapped trotters in a large, clean pot with the wine, stock, vegetables and herbs. Add a little salt and bring to the boil. Reduce the heat so it is just simmering and cook for five hours, skimming occasionally.

Transfer the trotters to a bowl and cover with the drained liquid. When cool, refrigerate overnight.

Remove trotters from the now quite firm jelly, and carefully unwrap them. Cut through with a knife to separate them, then roll each half first in melted butter, then in breadcrumbs.

Place on a lightly oiled baking tray and heat in a hot oven (200°C or 400°F) for about ten minutes. Finish under the grill until lightly golden and crisp.

Serve with lots of Dijon mustard. Serves 4.

Café society:

the long and the short of it

'What's wrong with this city?' said my wife, as she flung open the shutters of our corner room of the Hotel D'Inghilterra and glared out accusingly at busy Via Borgognona.

It was our fourth visit to Rome, and to be perfectly honest, I hadn't noticed anything wrong. In fact, on this rather brilliant autumn day with its painterly light and motherly warmth, everything about this engagingly crazy, wonderfully erratic city seemed exceedingly and excruciatingly right.

'Maybe it's me', she said, eyeing herself critically in the full length mirror, cocking her head first to the left, and then to the right. Suddenly she wheeled around and strode away. Then she stopped, quickly, and darted her head back to the mirror, just to see if she was still watching, which of course she was.

'There must be something wrong with them', she decided, in that fair-minded way of hers that I admire so much.

'With whom?' I asked.

'Those hot blooded Latin lovers out there.' She threw herself on the bed.

'I don't follow you.'

'Neither do they', she groaned.

This time, I was genuinely puzzled.

She continued talking over her shoulder in a rather muffled fashion.

'Not that I want my bottom to be pinched. Of course, I don't. That's unbelievably politically incorrect. And revolting. But how come they don't even try?'

This last, into the pillow.

Being the gentleman I am, I offered to pinch whatever I could, and to follow her around the room darting meaningful Latin glances at her legs, but she said it wasn't the same thing, and eventually we both drifted into our afternoon siestas.

When I awoke, I was dismayed to discover that I felt decidedly unwell. My brow was damp and clammy, and my stomach felt as if it was twirling itself around a fire poker. Perhaps eight meals and sixteen espresso coffees a day was getting on top of me.

Naturally, my wife was very concerned for my welfare.

'Does this mean we can't go to Caffe Greco for coffee?' she said, her eyes wide with worry.

Our days in Rome inevitably began with a coffee and ended with a coffee and an aperitivo in the gloriously decadent Caffe Greco, a glittering, lacquered jewel box of a caffe in the bustling Via Condotti.

To go an entire day without at least one visit was unthinkable.

'You go', I said, feeling secure in the knowledge that she would never leave me all alone and ailing in an alien city.

'Well, if you're sure', was all I heard, before the door closed on her, dressed in the brand new Taverniti cream silk she had found that morning.

An hour and a half later the same door burst open with such energy, I expected it to fly off its hinges.

A woman appeared in the doorway. I knew it was my wife (I recognised the Taverniti), but there was something... different about her. A strange beauty had fastened itself to her skin, and her hazelnut eyes melted like Baci chocolates by candlelight. Even her hair seemed to shimmer.

'It's you', she said, a little breathlessly.

'Pardon?' I squeaked.

'It's not me, it's you. Nobody gave me a second glance because you were always with me. There is this unwritten code that you leave married women alone — well, when in the company of their husbands, at least.'

I thought it was a good time to change the subject.

'How was Caffe Greco?'

She laughed, a deep-throated, almost sexual laugh, if laughs can be sexual.

'It was fabulous', she breathed. 'I've been invited to two movies, three dinners and four parties, and…'

'And?'

'And on the way out of the café, someone tried to grab my bum.'

From that night on, Caffe Greco became even more special to my wife. In one fell swoop, it had managed to restore her faith in Rome, in men, and in her own physical attributes.

From the day Caffe Greco was opened by a Roman inhabitant of Greek extraction named Nicola della Madelena in 1760, this venerable meeting spot has made a habit of enriching and ennobling the lives of the people who frequent it.

The great German poet Wolfgang von Goethe was one of the early regulars, along with the French painter Pierre-Paul Prud'hon.

But not everybody enjoyed the kind of unmitigated amorous success that my wife experienced on that fateful night. In his *Memories*, the legendary lover Casanova writes of the time he went to the 'Caffe di strada Condotti' for an amorous assignation with a beautiful and mysterious young woman who was not his wife. He waited and waited, but alas, the woman in question never showed.

With the nineteenth century came the golden age of Caffe Greco, when kings like Ludwig I of Bavaria and popes like Pope Leo XII rubbed knees and elbows with celebrated men of letters like Shelley, Byron, Keats, Thackeray, Baudelaire, Mark Twain and Nathaniel Hawthorn.

In an average week at Caffe Greco, one would find more composers of note than you could find in a year at La Scala, what with Mendelssohn, Wagner, Rossini, Berlioz, Liszt and Toscanini always dashing in and out. Painters, too, were drawn to the boudoirish rooms of the little building, and local residents were forever brushing up against Jean-Auguste Ingres, Jean Baptiste Corot, Antonio Mancini, and Peter Von Cornelius.

Even today, there is no shortage of artists in Caffe Greco. If you sit still long enough, you may well find yourself etched, sketched, charcoaled or painted for inclusion in a one man show in a Roman back street gallery. Basic requirements for an artist's model are to look extremely thin, pale, beautiful, interesting, very, very rich, or all of the above. Sadly, well-fed, sun-tanned, pleasant-looking, nicely mannered people like you and I are rarely bothered.

With its marble tables, rich gilt-framed paintings, and elegant penguinned waiters in white ties and tails who may or may not decide that you are worth serving, Caffe Greco has the airs and graces of a musty, dusty art gallery.

But this is no sleepy museum, where people sit like stuffed dummies behind velvet ropes. It's a living, breathing, working café where deals are made, bets are laid, arguments are settled and social calendars are adjusted and amended every night of the week. Just ask my wife.

In the crowded stand-up front bar, I've seen an ex Italian President taking coffee and pastry next to a gaggle of gypsies and a couple of handsome caribinieri in full ceremonial uniform.

In the elegant backrooms, anorexic dowager types nibble away at very good chicken sandwiches, and little glasses of wine, while tourists clutching fresh shop-kill shuffle uneasily between the tightly knit tables.

It is Caffe Greco that has taught me that membership of café society is not just a privilege, but a responsibility.

It is not enough to have the time to gawk, or the money to pay for the rent of your table.

You must be prepared to give as well as to take, with your manner and your style. You must dress to be worth looking at (the wearing of a Hugo Boss suit or a Moschino dress can extract the full aroma and elusive depth of flavour from a freshly drawn espresso), develop character in the very lines on your face, or contribute simply by the wit and wisdom of your conversation.

People come to a café not to get away from life, but to immerse themselves in it. They come not to relax and sip coffee, but to work — at being the sort of people they really want to be, reflected a thousand times over in gilt mirrors.

Even the sipping of coffee has its etiquette, and silent codes of behaviour and lifestyle that are as rigid as the laws of the land. A purist will always order an espresso (or simply caffe), a short black coffee with a burnished, golden foam known as crema. A good espresso has so much body that it too is in danger of being pinched.

In cases of extreme emergencies, you may feel the need for the coffee-head's hot-pants, a ristretto, or shorter-than-short black.

Other serious coffees include a macchiato, an espresso stained with a little cold milk and a marocchino, which is not as macho as a macchiato.

A caffe lungo, or long black, on the other hand, is a thinner, taller espresso for people who would probably rather be drinking tea.

In Italy, milky coffees like cappuccino and the even milkier caffe latte are drunk only in the mornings. Of course, the waiters at Caffe Greco will serve you a cappuccino in the afternoon if you order it, but they don't have to like you as they do so.

Back home, we may not have too many eighteenth-century drawing salons or waiters in white tie, gloves and tails, but we can get just as much kick out of going to our favourite little café for some serious people watching and coffee drinking.

Although I must admit that my wife tends towards disappointment when I tag along too.

Tirami sù

This remarkable confection of coffee, cocoa and mascarpone cream was first created at Treviso's glamorous El Toula restaurant. Make it three or four hours before serving to allow the mascarpone to ripen and develop its flavours.

20 savoiardi biscuits (sponge fingers)
100 ml (3½ fluid ounces) strong espresso coffee
4 eggs, separated
3 tablespoons castor sugar
400 grams (13 ounces) mascarpone cream cheese
3 tablespoons cognac or Marsala
2 or 3 tablespoons bitter cocoa powder

Layer the sponge finger biscuits in a glass serving bowl, and drizzle with espresso coffee until they are soaked.
    Beat egg yolks with sugar until mixture is pale and thick. Add mascarpone and liqueur and mix well.
    Beat the egg whites until they form stiff peaks, and gently fold into mascarpone mixture. Pour into serving dish, smooth out the top, and chill for several hours. To serve, dust top with a heavy layer of finely sifted cocoa powder.
    Serves 4.

Roast lamb with coffee

You are hereby ordered to suspend all disbelief until you taste this amazing, if unlikely, combination of flavours.

    salt and freshly ground pepper
    1 tablespoon rosemary sprigs
    1 boned and tied leg of lamb, around 1.2 kilograms (2½ pounds)
    1 tablespoon mustard
    ½ cup (125 ml or 4 fluid ounces) strong black coffee
    1 tablespoon cream
    1 tablespoon sugar
    1 tablespoon brandy
    ½ cup (125 ml or 4 fluid ounces) chicken stock

Heat the oven to 190°C (375°F).

Rub the salt, pepper and rosemary into the lamb, then spread the mustard on top. Combine the coffee, cream, sugar and brandy in a pot over a gentle heat, stirring until the sugar is dissolved.

Place the lamb in a lightly oiled baking dish and pour the coffee cream over it. Roast the lamb for 30 minutes, then reduce the heat to 160°C (325°F) for 15 minutes. Baste every now and then, picking up the caramelising juices at the bottom of the pan and brushing them over the lamb. Remove lamb and rest in a warm place for a good 15 minutes before carving, and it will be soft, tender and uniformly pink.

If your baking dish can take direct heat, add the chicken stock to cooking juices and heat until it is bubbling on top of the stove. Otherwise, scrape the juices into a small saucepan, add the chicken stock and proceed. Slice the lamb into 1-cm (½-in) slices and spoon on the juices. Serve with potatoes roasted with garlic, sage and rosemary.

Serves 4.

Gelato affogato

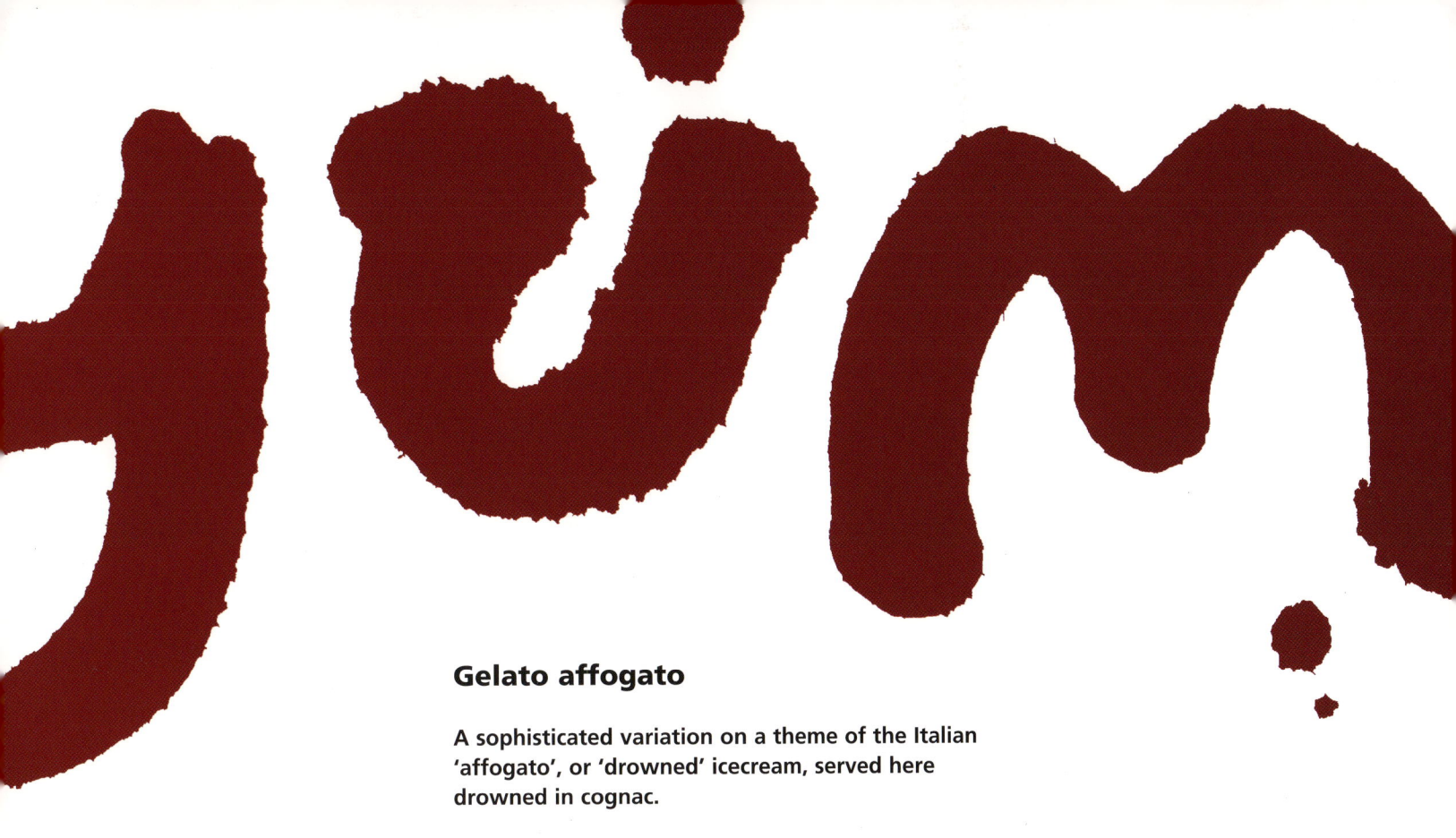

A sophisticated variation on a theme of the Italian 'affogato', or 'drowned' icecream, served here drowned in cognac.

> 8 scoops vanilla or coffee icecream (or a mixture)
> 2 tablespoons coffee beans, finely ground
> 8 tablespoons cognac
> 300 ml (9½ fluid ounces) hot espresso coffee

Divide the icecream between four tall parfait glasses. Sprinkle the tops with finely ground coffee. At the last minute or at the table, pour on the cognac and the coffee.
    Serves 4.

To die for

People who like to eat don't like the idea of dying very much.

To us, death is simply God's way of telling us that we can't have second helpings. Whether we end up in heaven or hell depends on such all-important factors as who has the best butcher, and which venue is allowed to import fresh truffles and foie gras.

It's tricky. One could get very tired of angel food cake and heavenly soufflés. And there's a limit to how many flambés and char grills one can stomach.

Through the centuries, food has both kept us alive, and killed us. In 1135, Henry I of England gorged himself on dozens of lamprey eels and died shortly afterwards from a severe stomach disorder. Lamprey eels have two poisonous filaments in their necks and are also believed to have caused Alexander Pope's demise in 1744.

Even today, poisonous fish still take their toll. Every year, from October 1 to March 31, millions of Japanese play a kind of foodie Russian roulette by eating sashimi of fugu, a species of blowfish with a lethal poison in its liver and ovaries. The poison must be very carefully scraped away, and only licensed fugu chefs are legally allowed to serve the dish. In spite of the laws, about two hundred people die every year from under-the-counter fugu poisoning.

But perhaps the strangest foodie death of all was that of French chef, Henri Vatel, who died not from something he had cooked, but from something he couldn't cook. Vatel had gone twelve nights without sleep, preparing an exquisite banquet in honour of the king of France. The last straw came when his fish order arrived. Instead of the hundreds of fish he had asked for, there were but a handful.

Gripped by despair, Vatel threw himself upon his sword. Shortly after his death by skewer, the rest of the fish turned up. Isn't it always the way?

The history books are full of somewhat unusual last suppers.

The Roman Emperor Claudius died after eating poisoned mushrooms fed to him by his wife Agrippina. Grigori Rasputin, Russia's 'mad monk' died a long and ghastly death after taking a meal of cakes and wine laced with cyanide.

New York racketeer 'Crazy Joe' Gallo was gunned down while eating spaghetti with clam sauce at Umberto's Clam Bar. Pop singer Mama Cass choked to death while eating a ham sandwich. Elvis Presley died after a snack of icecream and chocolate chip cookies.

Of course, at the time, none of these people actually knew they were eating their last suppers.

But imagine if you could plan your last meal ahead of time and that you could choose absolutely anything at all.

This is the last privilege given to the death row prisoners of certain southern American prisons, according to an American newspaper article. And nobody, but nobody, ordered cottage cheese and fruit.

Aubrey Adam Jnr, electrocuted in Florida, wanted a Cajun feast of one pound of popcorn shrimp, one pound of medium-sized shrimp, one pound of jumbo shrimp, one loaf of garlic bread, French fries, pecan pie, pecan icecream and iced tea.

In Georgia, all one William Mitchell wanted was a half gallon of black cherry icecream, to go. Few nutritionists would have approved of Velma Barfield's choice of Coca Cola and Cheez Doodles, but she wasn't following a healthy lifestyle at the time.

It's an intriguing thought, planning your last meal. I mean, what do you do? Pig out on the forbidden fruit of hamburgers, pies and hot dogs? Finally open that bottle of Chateau Margaux 1848 you've been hiding under the stairs? Revert to childhood favourites such as macaroni cheese and golden syrup dumplings? Or put together a five-course banquet of caviar, caviar, caviar and caviar, followed by a little more caviar?

Most food lovers have pretty definite ideas on the subject. The late James Beard always said his final fare would be bacon and eggs. Three-starred kitchen legend, Joel Robuchon told me many years ago that for him, it would be something made with fresh black truffles. 'But only if it were cooked by Fredy Girardet or Alain Chapel.' Sadly, Chapel died shortly afterwards, and on behalf of all those who adored his food, I can only hope that he went out on a meal of his own choice, from his own kitchen.

American chef Jeremiah Tower is another who puts truffles on his wish list. His last supper order is a black-truffled hamburger with a bottle of La Tache. Why La Tache?

'Because I wouldn't be able to afford Romanée Conti', he laughs.

American-born East meets West kitchen wiz, Ken Hom wants a simple bowl of rice with a little Chinese sausage and some stirfried vegetables. London's culinary bad boy come good, Marco Pierre White, has his heart set on an equally simple crab mayonnaise, while legendary Napa Valley vignerons, Robert and Margrit Mondavi are far less modest, having constructed an eight-course menu including a bucket of caviar, Alain Ducasse's truffe en croute, and an assortment of desserts by Gaston Lenotre and wines that range from a 1964 Dom Perignon to a 1921 Chateau d'Y Quem.

As for me, it's easy. My last supper would be a Chinese banquet as served in the Imperial courts. These banquets were usually made up of 365 different courses, including practically every great dish in the Chinese repertoire, and would traditionally last a full three days.

The following are transcripts of letters I have received over the last few years in response to my request for the 'last suppers' of many of the world's finest chefs, restaurateurs and food lovers. My thanks to all who responded so poetically, so amusingly, and so enticingly, and my sincere hopes that we should all go so deliciously.

Michel Guerard

It is Guerard who gets most of the blame for the excesses of French cooking in the Eighties. Yet his Cuisine Minceur was an enlightened, intelligent way of looking at diet food, and his Cuisine Gourmande took the very best of classic French cooking and honed it into something lush and glorious. My experiences at his restaurant at Eugenie Les Bains had all the makings of a perfect last supper in their own right.

You have kindly asked me to let you know what I would choose for my last meal on good old mother Earth.

I would like to think that my selection would give me the strength to go on and enjoy a great number of other meals, but since we have to accept it, we might as well imagine it here and now.

I won't conceal the fact that I have a weakness for caviar, preferably from Iran, but why not Russian?

So as not to appear too extravagant in the eyes of He who awaits me up there — also to the afflicted ones who, alas, will outlive me — I would add some humble pink radishes. These are wonderful eaten with the caviar and a thick slice of toast spread with fresh butter, accompanied by a glass of that delicious white wine of Tursan, 'Baron de Bachen', or perhaps a white Armagnac — superior to all the vodkas in the world.

To keep my feet a little longer on the beautiful soil of the Landes region before departing towards the celestial clouds, I would linger over a fine magret of fat duck from Landes, roasted in the hearth over a fire of vine shoots. On the side, perhaps, some juicy ortolans. With this feast, I would gladly serve a few thick, fried potatoes, roughly cut by hand and browned in a spoonful of the fat from foie gras and sprinkled with a few grains of sea salt.

I would also add a round bread roll into which I would slip, while making it, a big black truffle from our south west. For this occasion, my door would be wide open to a Chateau Petrus 1982, delightfully fruity and artfully fashioned by Jean Claude Berrouet, its talented alchemist. Any that was left would be savoured with a Pont l'Eveque cheese from the Auge country of my childhood.

If that fateful day was taking place when the apricots, bursting with sunshine, were dropping from the trees, I would not hesitate to arrange them in waves on a thin layer of flaky pastry, cooked simply with a few knobs of butter, sugar and lime peel. Thus, it would do justice to a Chateau d'Y Quem 1967, which the Comte de Lur Saluces has been keeping for me for a long time, for this occasion.

On that day, I would drink two big cups of black Arabica coffee, as I would not have to be scared of having a heart attack. In the still warm china, I would pour a little of the best brandy in the world, an Armagnac from the Forties, which I would enjoy religiously while waiting for my departure.

Michel Guerard, *Eugenie Les Bains*

Georges Blanc

The grandson of one of France's greatest woman chefs, 'La Mère Blanc', Blanc has now forged a reputation that eclipses even hers. The family restaurant at Vonnas, which began life as an inn for local farmers now comes with a heli-pad and a waiting list as long as your arm. Like Bocuse, his cooking is very much influenced by the Lyonnais style.

The things I would choose to eat for my last supper reflect my belief that the true art of cooking lies in plain dishes, not necessarily rich, but made with first class ingredients. Only the best is good enough.

On the eve of the great departure, I think we should avoid being too sophisticated. Authenticity, and being faithful to one's principles, is everything.

Consequently, as someone who comes from the Bresse area, I would arrange a meal around a Bresse capon, spit-roasted, with a simple salad into which I would run some of the juices from the chicken, and add a few truffles, if they were in season.

To start the meal, I would choose a lobster cooked in sea water with a simple *sauce vierge*, flavoured with just picked fresh herbs, as I love olive oil and sharp flavours.

For an appetiser, I would take a few slices of an excellent home-made salami, the recipe for which I guard jealously.

For cheese, a Saint-Marcelin from la Mère Richard, perfect with an excellent farm-house bread baked in a wood oven.

For dessert, a soup of perfect white peaches sprinkled with a juice made from raspberries, with a little lemon added.

No coffee, no bill, but the best of wines — Burgundy if possible, and perhaps a Macon Azé of the best vintage from my own vineyards.

For guests, I would like to be with my two sons, so that we can assess together a well-filled life. It is my hope that they will continue in the same way.

Georges Blanc, *La Mère Blanc*

Claude Terrail

La Tour d'Argent is not so much a restaurant, but a monument to the fine art of eating. It is not only the most famous restaurant in the world, it is also one of the oldest, being established in 1582 back in the days when most Parisians were still eating with their fingers. For more years than he cares to remember, Claude Terrail has been the titular head of this gastronomic empire, and as such, has set new and exacting standards for the role of the restaurateur.

This project, so close to the 'flowers and wreaths' does not exactly appeal to me. In fact, it rather puts me off.

Among the gifts nature was generous enough to grant me, I cannot to this day detect a talent for prophecy. Cooking requires a lot of time, and supper a lot of care. Unless playing Banquo's spectre at the feast of Macbeth, this supper would logically take place without me. This last appointment is not one that one can shift with a simple phone call, so my friends must excuse me.

In the circumstances, my provisions would probably be a branch of box tree and a cup of holy water. Let us be sober for an occasion such as this.

Besides, I must tell you a secret. Through incredible luck, I have spent my life cherished by women, and not the lesser ones!

Do I see you smile?

Look at my world, my unique landscape: the Queen of the city, Notre Dame, shines on me. Close by, Genevieve protects me and further on Clothilde teaches me.

From my Tour, I give thanks every day, for they have granted me so many favours.

Shall I tell you the latest?

My seat — yes, my seat — is reserved in the chorus of the chosen ones. I have a chair in my name in perfect surroundings. In that respect there are no problems. They are all worldly people there (I mean of course, from the other world).

What does worry me is that I cannot bear package tours and overcrowded roads. We will have to avoid peak hours, be careful of certain itineraries. I am not particularly keen to land amid hopping imps through stupidly taking the wrong route.

Having arrived without incident (my protecting ladies will see to that), I can now, on this assurance, give you some details, not of a last supper, but the first I will organise to celebrate my meeting with my new friends.

As a welcome, a squad of chubby cherubs (renaissance style, it goes without saying) will fill our flutes from methuselahs of well-chilled champagne. It is a feast. Music please — the seraphs are always in the clouds. Take the violas d'amour, the harps and the celestas. The concerto I choose is *To the Memory of an Angel* by Alban Berg, not too ancient, not too dodecacophonic…

Very well then, now let us think about sustaining our transcendent natures.

What would you say to a potage Germiny, a sorrel soup thickened with egg yolks and cream, and afterwards, some ecrevisses with dill, followed by aiguillettes of duckling with a port wine jelly and the hearts of cos lettuce? Finally, some foie gras of the Three Emperors, perhaps, then finishing on peche flambée. At the risk of shocking you, I might do without petits fours.

As for the wines, I leave the choice not to God but to his Saints, Vincent first. Monks, fathers, abbots who sponsor our vineyards owe for a good part their canonisation to the care they have lavished upon our vineyards.

But it is said that even here in the vines of the Lord, they all have their preferences: some sing the Angelus, and read the gospel, while others consult the Chapter and appeal to Pope Clement. At the height of the exegis, they agree to bow to the Christ child.

Each one speaks in praise of his parish, but to be sure, will look after your bliss.

You will understand that these worries draw me away from more down-to-earth questions. We can still make an appointment.

P.S. I want to make clear that if I invite you, it is because the food is good and the abode in keeping with it (a thousand and one stars in the divine guide).

Claude Terrail, *La Tour d'Argent*

Andre Daguin

While Daguin has never reached the high profile status of contemporaries like Bocuse, Vergé and Guerard, he is nevertheless one of France's best loved and most highly respected chefs. Coming from Gascony, it is hardly surprising that his cooking is laced inextricably with confit, foie gras and Armagnac. At his restaurant in the Hotel de France in Auch, I had the pleasure of meeting 'Le Grande Soup' a horse-trough-sized bowl filled to overflowing with confit of goose, duck and pork. It was overkill in a very big way, but I didn't leave a drop.

Should this arise — but for the moment, there is no hurry — I would like to have on hand a book by Blondin, a sculpture by Abal, a painting by Cavaglieri and hanging in the air, music by Dassin.

Thus surrounded, I would dine gladly on a terrine of foie gras by Marie-Claude Gracia, sweet breads and scallops in the style of Jean-Louis Palladin, a ragout of lambs' tongues made by son Arnaud, before tackling a civet of goose tripes by Coscu, and ortolans cooked by Roger Dufour. Vanel's Pompe au citron and Pierrette Sarrant's Pastis would close proceedings.

Wines from Andre Dubosc, Frederic Laplace and Jean-Michel Cazes would accompany the meal.

Holy water? Perhaps. Armagnac? Certainly, from Tenareze.

So there we have it.

The last act, which is perhaps the first act of another play.

Andre Daguin, *Hotel de France*

Le pastis Gascon 'estirat'
(Gascon apple pie made with stretched pastry)

The recipe is simple, but it is all in the execution, as every air bubble in the dough will result in a big hole once it is stretched.

In order to make a good looking pastis, you will need 500 grams (1 pound) of sifted flour, an egg, a glass of water, a pinch of salt, and a tablespoon of rendered goose fat.

Place the flour, egg, salt and fat in an earthenware bowl. Add the water while kneading. So as not to let air in, flatten it out firmly two or three times. As soon as you have a ball, place it in an oiled salad bowl. Leave in a cool place for a few hours, covered with a tea towel. The tea towel must not touch the dough.

When it is ready, you will need the help of two people. Spread a bed sheet on a large table, sprinkle it with flour and place the ball of dough in the middle.

By pulling the dough gently from all sides at once, you will turn it into a huge thin sheet of dough that will cover the entire surface of the table. Cut out six to eight large circles and let them dry for about an hour.

Before stretching the dough, slice three good-sized apples as thinly as possible and marinate them in Armagnac.

Now comes the time to rise your pastis.

Arrange a layer of dough on an oiled oven pan, then sprinkle with a few drops of orange-blossom water, Armagnac, goose fat and castor sugar and cover with another layer of dough. Oil slightly, then arrange slices of apples. Cover with another layer and sprinkle with sugar, goose fat, Armagnac, and orange-blossom water again. Do this twice.

Sprinkle the last layer copiously and crumple it a little. You can add leftover bits of dough so it looks more crumpled.

Cook for 25 minutes in a 200°C (400°F) oven. Serve warm or cold, but not reheated.

Arrigo Cipriani

Like Venice's Harry's Bar itself, Arrigo Cipriani is very stylish, very Italian, and very much at home with any company. As a boy hanging around his father's world-famous restaurant, he rubbed shoulders with the likes of Ernest Hemingway, the Aga Khan, Orson Welles, and countless counts, duchesses and millionaires. Obviously, a little of his polish rubbed off on them.

Venice, January 2nd, 2030

To the Director of Alcatraz,

The undersigned Arrigo Cipriani (called Harry), being sentenced to death by the High Court of Justice of Restaurant Critics, before his execution, which is going to be held at sunrise on the day of 11 January 2030, would like to order for his supper something light, because the undersigned would hate to have a headache early the next day.

The undersigned humbly begs to be allowed to be served the following.

A Bellini cocktail to start, properly made by Claudio the bartender at Harry's Bar in Venice.

At the same time, he would like to have one chicken sandwich made by Evaristo Cassol, one of the chefs of the said Harry's Bar.

And then.

First, a few slices of smoked salmon sent over from his favourite restaurant in London, Wilton's, formerly owned by Mr Marks, whom the undersigned hopes to meet again in a Higher Place.

Second, spinach ravioli with a sprinkle of white truffles from the hills of Alba, cooked by his chef Paolo Scandella from Venice.

Third, a small portion of John Dory with artichokes cooked by his chef Paolo Rossi, also from Venice.

Fourth, roast duckling with blueberries cooked by his chef Nicola Cicchini who, the undersigned is sure, will finally make it on that night, exactly the way he wants it.

Dessert, two crêpes à la crème properly made by his pastry chef, Giuseppe Apezzeto.

And to finish, a very small slice of chocolate cake made by his chef and friend, Tullio Fabris.

With the first course, the undersigned would like to drink one glass of Taittinger Comte de Champagne vintage 2022.

With the second and third courses, Tocai Livio Felluga 2029.

With the fourth, a whole bottle of Barbaresco Gaja 2022.

With the fifth, a small glass of 1932 Port wine.

With the dessert, a half bottle of Chateau d'Y Quem 2000.

The undersigned also humbly asks the honourable director of this beautiful jail to allow his lawyer, Mr Marshall Bernstein, to make an application which the undersigned hopes will have more success than his desperate defence, in order to allow Mr Lucio Zanon, manager for the undersigned, to supervise the service during the simple dinner that is the object of this petition.

The undersigned has also a last wish. He would like to leave to Mr Terry Durack, the recipe of the chocolate cake, hoping that by selling it, he will become very rich and famous.

Very respectfully,

Arrigo Cipriani, *Harry's Bar*

Torta di Cioccolato from Harry's Bar

The recipe Arrigo Cipriani 'left' me is the same one he gave the world in his book, *The Harry's Bar Cookbook*. So I guess it won't make me rich after all. Just make me feel that way.

Pan di Spagna al Cioccolato (Chocolate Sponge Cake)

    6 large eggs, separated
    ¾ cup sugar (165 grams)
    1 teaspoon vanilla extract
    1 cup plus two tablespoons flour (155 grams)
    6 tablespoons unsweetened cocoa powder (about 20 grams)
    1 tablespoon instant espresso powder (optional)

Filling
    1 cup (250 ml or 8 fluid ounces) heavy cream
    250 grams (8 ounces) bittersweet chocolate, cut into bits
    2 egg whites at room temperature
    50 grams (2 ounces) sugar

To assemble the cake
    1 tablespoon unsweetened cocoa powder
    250 ml (8 fluid ounces) lukewarm water
    2 tablespoons jam (jelly), any kind

Heat the oven to 180°C (350°F).

Butter and flour a 23-cm (9-in) cake or springform pan.

Separate the eggs. Beat the yolks with the sugar until the mixture is very thick and pale yellow. Beat in the vanilla.

Beat the whites until they are stiff but not dry. Using a rubber spatula, fold one-third of the whites gently but thoroughly into the yolk mixture. Then fold in the remaining whites.

Combine the flour, cocoa, and espresso powder if you are using it. Sift the flour mixture into the egg mixture, one-third at a time, and rapidly, but gently, incorporate it.

Do not beat the batter; cut straight to the bottom of the bowl with the spatula and lift the batter up and over the flour. When the flour is incorporated, scrape the batter into the prepared pan and bake until the cake is done — when a toothpick inserted in the centre comes out dry — about 30 to 35 minutes.

Let the cake cool briefly in the pan. Then remove it from the pan and let it cool completely. Using a serrated knife with a long blade, slice it horizontally into four layers. Wrap the layers in plastic wrap until you are ready to use them.

To make the filling, bring the cream to the boil in a small saucepan over a medium heat. Add the chocolate pieces, then reduce heat to low and continue to cook, stirring frequently, until the chocolate has melted and the mixture is smooth and creamy. Remove from the heat and let cool.

Beat the egg whites in a small bowl until frothy. Gradually beat in the sugar and continue to beat to make a stiff meringue. When the chocolate mixture has cooled, fold in the meringue and refrigerate. Chill the filling for at least four hours. It can be made up to 24 hours in advance.

To assemble the cake, stir the cocoa powder into the lukewarm water. Invert the top layer of the cake onto a serving dish and brush it lightly with the cocoa water. Spread one-quarter of the filling over the cake and top it with another layer of cake.

Using a board or the bottom of the cake pan, gently press down on the cake. Brush the cake with cocoa water and spread on another quarter of the filling. Add another layer and repeat the procedure. Put on the final layer of the cake, press it down and spread the jam (jelly) over it.

The remaining filling will be used to glaze the cake. Hold it over the heat or immerse the bowl in hot water and whisk constantly until the filling becomes just liquid enough to pour over the cake. If it liquefies too much, chill it until it thickens a bit. Pour over the cake and spread it evenly across the tops and sides.

Refrigerate the cake until one hour before serving.

Serves 10.

Fred Ferretti

Better known as the 'Gourmet at Large' from his long-running column in *American Gourmet*, Fred Ferretti writes about food like Marco Pierre White, Michel Guerard and Daniel Bouley cook — with flair, wit, knowledge and great appetite. So addicted to good food is he that he made a point of marrying a particularly gifted Chinese cook.

What I would wish for my last supper would require, I expect, a formidable exercise in logistics, but that should be part of one's final wish, should it not?

I would begin with roasted suckling pig as it is cooked and served in the Shangri-La Hotel in Hong Kong. It has never been done better by anyone on earth. With it, I would drink a Lenz Vineyard Gewurtztraminer, soft and full of perfume.

My next course would be a terrine of chicken, but a glorious one, as invented by my wife, Eileen Yin-Fei Lo, surely the finest Chinese chef in creation. She bones a chicken, stuffs it with glutinous rice, chicken meat, water chestnuts and bamboo shoots, and roasts it. It is then sliced across and served. Magnificent! With it I would drink an Arneis, preferably one bottled by Bruno Ceretto in the Piedmont.

I would continue with this wine through my third course, a risotto utterly covered with slivers of white truffles. And it would be cooked by Luigi Caputo of Ristorante Balbo in Turin, Italy, one of the world's great cooks.

I would continue with the same wine through my next course, a perfectly done Dover sole on the bone, sautéd in butter, and touched with a bit of garlic and parsley, as they make it in Wilton's, that most Edwardian of London restaurants.

My next course would be a combination plate by Michel Guerard, who without question is France's greatest cook — never mind these upstarts who pop up annually. He would make a confit of duck as I have had it in his restaurant, and accompany it with a whole black truffle, wrapped in a thin layer of chicken and roasted, then sliced. Marvellous! With this, I would drink many glasses of a Chateau Talbot 1982.

One needs vegetables, even at a last supper, so I would have a portion of the best: snow pea shoots, sautéd with garlic in peanut oil, as done by my wife, who, when she is not cooking for my last supper is the author of *New Cantonese Cooking* and teaches Chinese cuisine.

Dessert must be a tarte Tatin, not those variations that seem to be happening about us, but as it was first concocted near the forests of the Loire, mistake or not. With it, there is nothing better than a Muscat Beaumes de Venise.

And I would have coffee, of course, and with it a wonderful Armagnac, perhaps another glass of that Chateau De Laubade, 1886, which still has its fire after one hundred years. One should finish one's last supper with a bit of fire, no?

Fred Ferretti

Bruno Loubet

When the London *Good Food Guide* voted Loubet Young Chef of the Year in 1985, I doubt if even they realised the impact he was to have on London cooking. From Four Seasons Inn on the Park, to Bistro Bruno in Soho and finally L'Odeon in Regent Street, his relaxed, French flavours have won over an entire city.

In the summer of 1984, my wife's grandparents invited us to Alain Chapel (the god of Mionnay) near Lyon in France. The meal, service and atmosphere was a feast.

My first course had the most exciting and pleasant flavours and texture I had ever tasted: mille feuilles de crêtes et rognons de coq, ecrevisses pattes rouges aux mousserons et jus de cerfeuil. (A mille feuille of cock's combs, cock's kidneys, freshwater crayfish and shellfish with mushrooms and chervil sauce.)

The dish was such a revelation to me that today, nearly seven years afterwards, I can still remember every detail of its conception and flavours.

The dish marked my taste and professional life so much that I would choose it as my last supper. And if God does not allow me into Paradise, it would not matter so much any more, because I know that I have had a bit of it in this world.

Bruno Loubet, *L'Odeon*

Raymond Blanc

Even before it opened in 1984, Blanc's Le Manoir aux Quat' Saisons was awarded two Michelin stars. Two years later, it was voted the best restaurant in Britain by *Gault-Millau* and the *Good Food Guide*. Ironically, when I last visited Le Manoir, shortly after he wrote this piece, Blanc had just been whisked off to hospital with a serious stroke. Fortunately, however, his last supper looks like being a fair way off yet.

At first the thought amused me because of its oddity. Then it shook and depressed me. At the age of forty-one, it dawned on me that immortality is not real any more and that I must prepare myself: make a will, take a couple of days off, invest time in loving, be kinder, admire flowers and butterflies, look kindly upon mankind...

I made an uneasy peace with the thought, for it is not often one is given the opportunity to contemplate, or ponder one's death.

This last supper feels too much like the last cigarette, the very last intake of air, grasping the last colours, scents, animation, feelings, the thoughts invaded me, it swallowed me.

Morally, could I grant my little belly this last earthly pleasure? Why should one assume a chef's last wish would be a sensuous, sumptuous supper before departing? Maybe I would rather invite some professional shriekers to pour tears over me, giving me self-importance; maybe to have beside me just the loved one to hold my hand, or maybe invite comedians so we could laugh my way through it.

Or, simply, I would want to die peacefully, quietly, privately.

Let's put a bit of order before deciding. First, is it possible? Could this last supper take place? For it to happen, I would need to be a healthy man, then I would have to sense my death and time it perfectly. I would need to set a date, send the invitations to the friends that I would want around me, then I would have to become even more accurate: I would have to die well after the supper!

So many obstacles, I do not know if it possible. But assuming it were, then I would ensure that it was the most formidable and lengthy dinner ever. Some extraordinary Babette's Feast! Should I be cooking? Will I have the strength? Of course.

First, I will make my peace with the Good Lord.

'Good Lord, you have created a bounty of beautiful food, be it from the sea and the earth, and you have also created me and given me my own creativity to transform these noble, pure ingredients into the most delicious and appealing works of art. You allowed these dishes to be the catalyst to spark joy and friendship among those present around the table.

'You have yourself broken the bread and given it to the crowd, as an act of love, an act of giving, and if you grant me this last day, dear Lord, be my guest, look upon us, it will not be a sin, but a last communion with the living before departing. We will eat your flesh and drink your blood, with the friend close to me, and I rejoice myself to be soon in that perfect, weightless world; unless you have decided otherwise, I will leave this weary body behind. I sincerely hope that you approve of the companion, the menu and the choice of wines — the tableware is a little bit ostentatious, but I hope you will forgive me.'

So I will eat this last supper among the good friends and loved ones, among the things that are dear to me, summer, plenty of light…no darkness. We will talk about life after death, then take a strong espresso accompanied by a very old Armagnac with just enough liveliness. Then, sipping that elixir, I will let myself go. In that blissful moment, death will then take me.

Raymond Blanc
Le Manoir aux Quat' Saisons

Margrit and Robert Mondavi

Robert Mondavi is the very soul and spirit of California's Napa Valley. His cabernets, Fumé Blancs, and the remarkable Opus One, made in cooperation with Mouton Rothschild have helped to redefine American wine styles. Passionate about all aspects of the arts, the Mondavis have made their winery home to some of the world's finest painting and sculpture, gound-breaking music concerts, and one of America's most prestigious cooking schools.

Since calories and other nonsense would not be a problem for this feast, we selected the following menu. After such a meal, we don't really care where we go.

Margrit and Robert Mondavi,
Robert Mondavi Winery

Fresh oysters in the half shell
1964 Dom Perignon in magnum
A good bucket of the best caviar
1966 Champagne, Krug Collection
Alain Ducasse's truffe en croute
Domaine de la Romanée
Conti Montrachet 1971
Jean Pierre Vigato's crunchy salmon with skin on one side
Louis Latour Corton Charlemagne 1971
Caribou steak prepared by Margrit Biever Mondavi
Robert Mondavi Cabernet Sauvignon reserve 1987
A soft runny Monterey Jack and a ripe Taleggio
1945 Chateau Mouton Rothschild and a 1949 Chateau Mouton Rothschild
An assortment of desserts by Gaston Lenotre especially created for us
1921 Chateau d'Y Quem
Hot roasted pistachios
1864 Malmsey Brandy

Michel Roux

Together with his brother Albert, Michel Roux can take much of the credit for the Great Food revolution that swept through London in the Eighties. For the first time ever, an English restaurant (Le Gavroche) was awarded three stars in the *Guide Michelin*, and it no longer seemed odd to use the words 'good food' and 'England' in the same sentence. When Monsieur Roux arranged to come to my home for an interview over coffee, I spent a week sampling various coffee grinds until I felt sure I had a brew fit for a three-star chef. When he came, he asked for tea.

Given the final decision, it is not easy. It is certainly something to look forward to, however, so here goes.

Boudin noir avec pommes mousseline
Beaujolais Village 1989
Turbotin souffle homardine, julienne de truffe, sauce Champagne
Le Montrachet Marquis de la Guiche 1983
Cotes d'agneau grillés avec haricots verts
Chateau Latour 1961
Fraises et peche blanche nature
Chateau d'Y Quem 1967

Michel Roux, *The Waterside Inn*

Pierre Koffmann

Koffmann's La Tante Claire is one of the very few British restaurants to have received the coveted three-star award from the *Guide Michelin*. While he lives in London, his mind spends most of the time in the Gascony of his childhood.

My last meal on earth.

Soupe de poisson
Bouillabaisse
A good bottle of Batard Montrachet
Croustade aux pommes
Chateau d'Y Quem

Pierre Koffmann, *La Tante Claire*

Marc Meneau

I had never eaten cromesquis until Marc Meneau handed me one at his beautiful Burgundian restaurant, L'Esperance, in Vezelay. It was a life-changing experience, as the warm foie gras oozed through the crunchy coating of the croquette. Life-changing experiences are commonplace at L'Esperance, which was awarded its third Michelin star in 1983, the same year Gault et Millau voted Meneau Chef of the Year.

This mixture of precious and simple foods is a synthesis of my life on my native soil. It is to be eaten at a table of twenty to thirty friends, surrounded by plenty of white flowers.

Consommé of lobster
Twelve-year-old Montrachet
Tête de porc aux herbes
Vin de Vezelay
Bresse capon roasted with a kilogram of truffles
Grand Bourgogne de Henri Jayet
Gateau de chocolat amer avec une gelée d'orange
Muscat du Dr Parce

Marc Meneau, *L'Esperance*

Pierre Wynants

As a child, Wynants practically lived in Brussels' famous Comme Chez Soi, something many a food-loving Belgian has wanted to do. While the restaurant had been in the family since 1926, it was only in the early Sixties, when Pierre took over the stoves, that it became a culinary Mecca for food-lovers from all over the world. His food is at once hearty, joyful, refined and assured.

I dream this to be in two half meals, and to have all the foods available and at their height.

Lunch
Zakouski, a selection of smoked salmon, North Sea shrimps, flat oysters and caviar
A little duck liver and goose liver served 'en terrine'
Salad of langoustines and witloof with white truffles
Lobster tart with new season's asparagus
Vanilla icecream
Infusion of lemon and geranium
Six-year-old Dom Perignon
Five- or six-year-old Puligny-Montrachet 'les Pucelles' from Le Flaive or Morey
Wines: all in magnums
Cigar: Ambassadrice de Davidoff
Afternoon
A large bottle of water and a long walk in the forest.

Dinner
Baby eels with garlic, lemon and olive oil
Scallops stuffed with spinach
Roasted woodcock à la Fine Champagne 'Belle Epoque'
Les truffes comme je les aime (truffles the way I like them)
Swiss Vacherin cheese
Caramelised peaches
Gateau au chocolat 'Trinitarios'
Fine mocha coffee with petit fours
Two-year-old Condrieu from Guigal or Perret
Fifteen-year-old Hermitage de grand millesime from Guigal or Jaboulet
Petrus 1961
Chateau d'Yquem 1945
Nierpoort vintage port 1963
Wines: all in magnums
Cigar: Lanceros de Cohiba

Pierre Wynants, *Comme Chez Soi*

**Les truffes comme je les aime
(Truffles the way I like them)**

240 grams (8 ounces) fresh truffles
   (30 to 35 grams each)
70 grams (2½ ounces) butter, plus extra
   for the table
sea salt and freshly ground pepper
60 ml (2 fluid ounces) truffle juice
20 grams (¾ ounce) veal stock
1 loaf French bread

Make sure the truffles are properly cleaned. If not, dip them into lukewarm water and, with the point of a knife, remove any grit.

Cut the whole truffles into four slices, 4 mm thick. If you do this in advance, immediately place the slices on a plate and cover with plastic wrap.

In a big, flat saucepan, melt 50 grams (1½ ounces) of butter over a moderate heat, and sauté the truffle slices for two minutes. By then, the butter should be hazelnut in colour. Add a little salt and pepper, then deglaze with the truffle juice. Cover and cook over a slower heat for three to four minutes. The truffles should still be slightly crunchy.

As soon as they are cooked, remove the lid, add the veal stock and remove from the heat. Then beat the remaining butter into the sauce. Check the seasoning.

Share out the truffles on warm plates and serve with slices of toasted French bread (a good centimetre thick) with unsalted butter and some freshly ground salt.

On the buttered toast, place a slice of truffle with a little sauce and a small turn of the salt mill. Each mouthful is pure delight for the palate.

Roger Vergé

The distinguished-looking Roger Vergé is one of the most beloved of France's three-star chefs. His 'Cuisine of the Sun' as practised at Moulin de Mougins, near Cannes is one of the great attractions of the French Riviera. This letter blows me away every time I read it. Here is the essence of food as one's heritage: a glorious celebration of tastes and smells and sweet, musty reminiscences all wrapped up in one delicious chicken dish.

'The most memorable dish I have ever eaten was a fricassée of grain-fed chicken that my mother sometimes prepared. Although I have tried on numerous occasions, I have never been able to recreate the taste that has stayed so firmly in my mind. If, just before my death, I was offered the chance to have one last "joie de table", I would love to once again live this wonderful memory.

'It was really very simple. The chickens would be chosen, fattened on grain for two weeks before they were to be killed, then prepared in my mother's special way. These chickens, which had fine, white skin were each cut into four, sealed in a little butter, then cooked in a covered saucepan with a large branch of thyme.

'It is important to check that the butter does not darken. When the chicken is almost cooked, you add a lot of parsley, freshly cut from the garden, and some new garlic.

'The dish would be served, accompanied by new season's potatoes the size of hen's eggs, which were washed in milk and roasted. When they were the colour of fresh bread, they were removed from the oven.

'And there you have it, the final dream in a gourmand's life that has always been inspired by the real and the simple.

'For my last drink, I am not so modest. A bottle of Chateau d'Y Quem 1893, the colour of a sunset, would fulfil me completely.'

Roger Vergé,
Moulin de Mougins Mougins

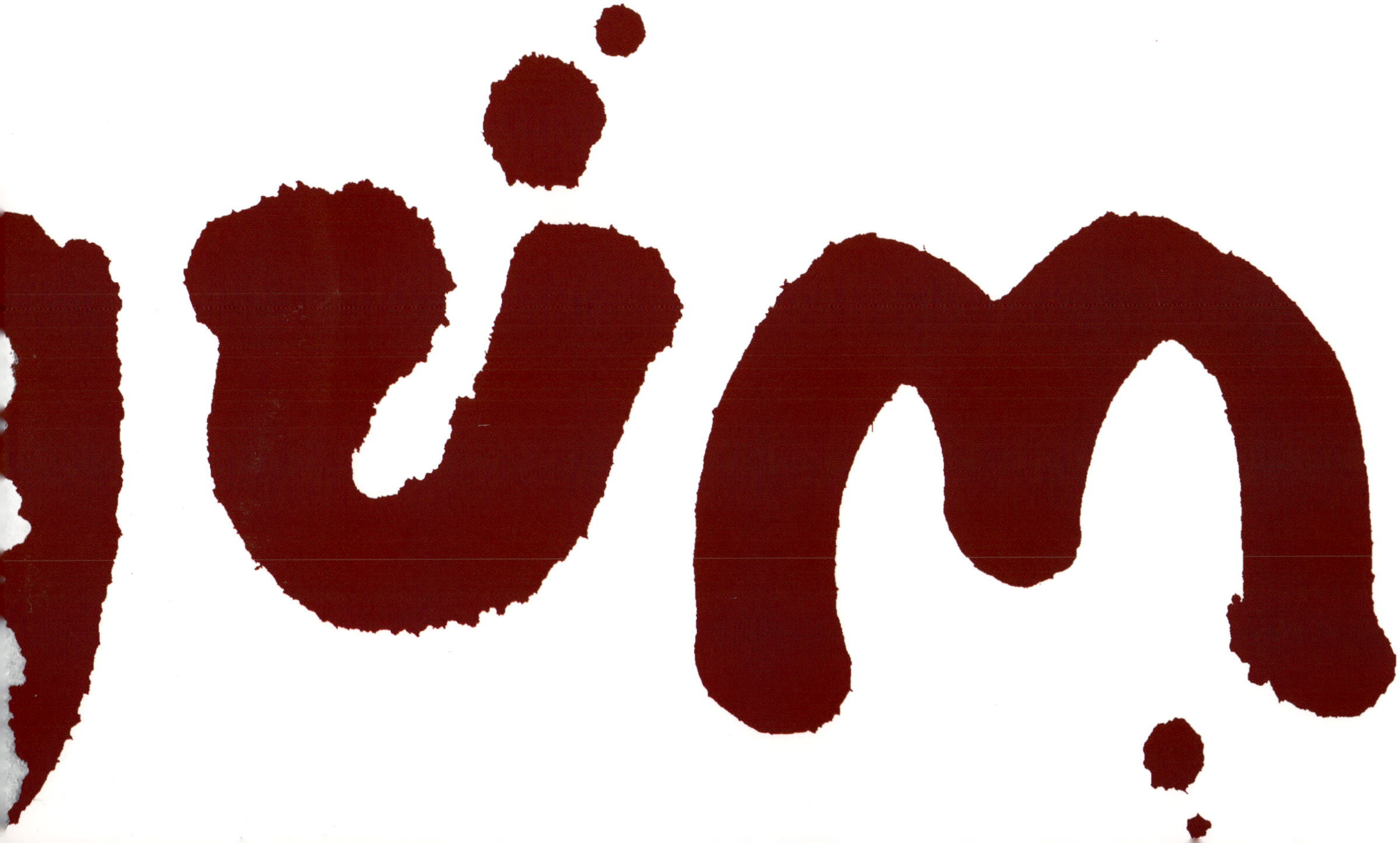

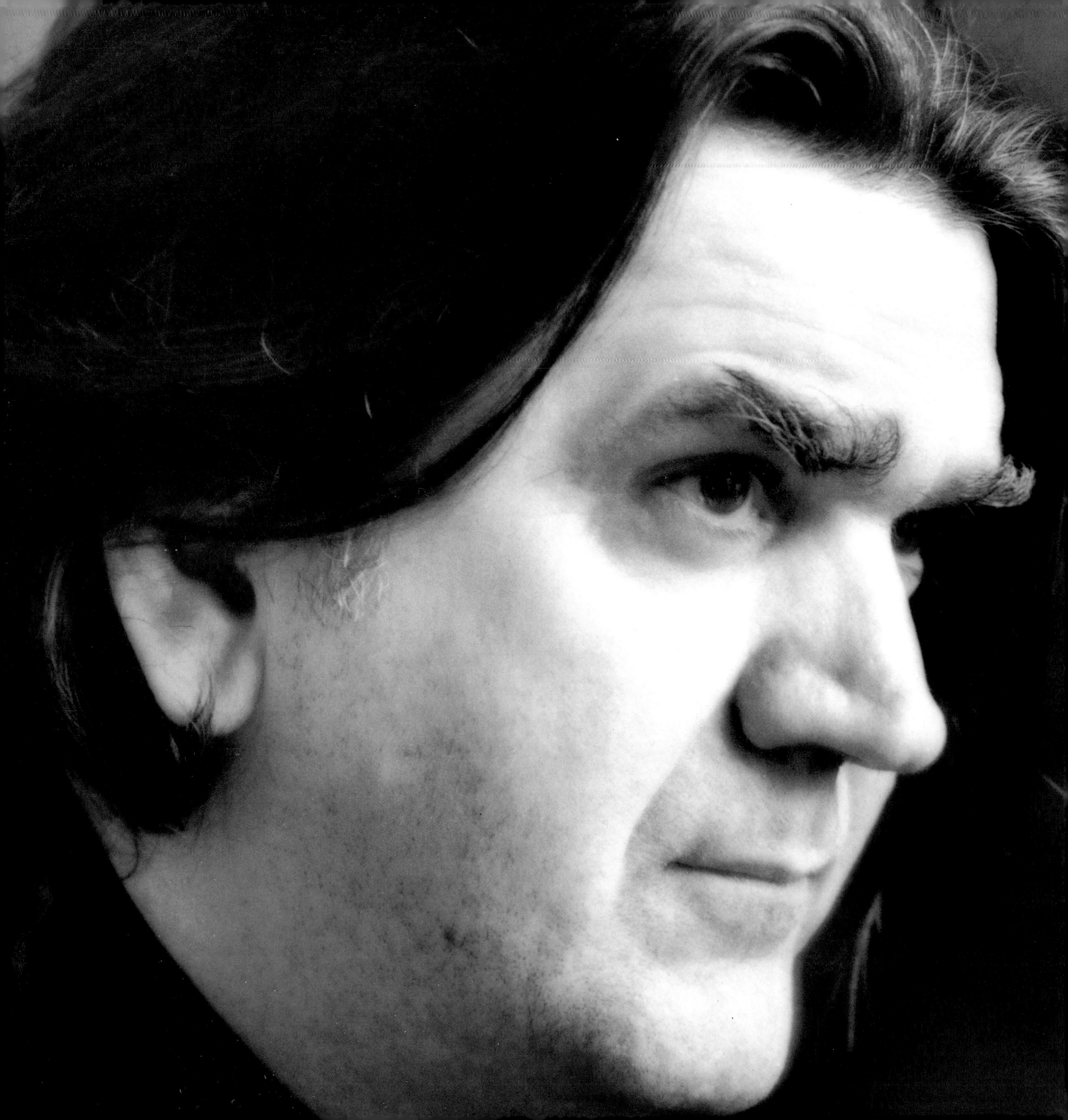

thanks

A hundred years ago when I was writing about food for fun and not for a living, one of my stories managed to make it to the desk of Carolyn Lockhart, then editor of *Vogue Entertaining*, and now editor of *Australian Gourmet Traveller*. Since that fateful day, her encouragement and her enthusiasm have barely waned, and that this book exists at all, has as much to do with her belief in my writing, as my obsession with all things edible.

While many of these stories have been written especially for *Yum*, several have been inspired by pieces originally written for *Australian Gourmet Traveller*, while one (Intestinal Fortitude) first started life in a mildly different form as an article in *Vogue Entertaining*.

Pathetic gratitude also goes to Sue Hines, who as the then publisher at Reed Books, had the knack of making me believe that I could write like Kaufman and cook like Koffmann.

Thanks too to my editor, Theresa Janssen who helped me mind my language, and designer Mary Callahan who plated words and images as elegantly as any three-star chef. And while I'm on the subject of the look of the book, may I take a moment to grovel at the feet of Louise Lister whose photographs so perfectly capture both the sensual nature of food and the foodie nature of sex.

The good people of Reed Books will also forever be in my good books, for their support and faith.

Then there are the chefs and the foodie famous who gave me their time, their recipes, and their thoughts.

My undying gratitude goes to Robert Carrier, Marco Pierre White, Roger Vergé, Michel Guerard, Georges Blanc, Claude Terrail, Jeremiah Tower, Ken Hom, Andre Daguin, Arrigo Cipriani, Fred Ferretti, Bruno Loubet, Raymond Blanc, Margrit and Robert Mondavi, Michel Roux, Pierre Koffman, Marc Meneau, and Pierre Wynants.

And one more.

To Jill Dupleix, my partner in life, love and food, I owe an awful lot more than just this book.

296

bibliog

raphy

Allen, Jana, and Gin, Margaret. *Offal*. Pitman Publishing, London, 1974.

Beard, James. *James Beard's American Cookery*. Little, Brown and Company, Toronto, 1972.

Blanc, Georges. *The Natural Cuisine of Georges Blanc*. Webb & Bower, Devon, 1987.

Bugialli, Guiliano. *The Taste of Italy*. Conran Octopus Limited, London, 1985.

Boni, Ada. *Italian Regional Cooking*. Bonanza Books, New York, 1969.

Campbell, Dolly. *I Hate To Cook*. Mandarin Melbourne, 1991.

Carluccio, Antonio. *A Passion For Mushrooms*. Pavilion Books Limited, London, 1989.

Carrier, Robert. *Feasts of Provence*. Allen & Unwin, London, 1993.

Carrier, Robert. *Taste of Morocco*. Century Hutchinson Limited, Melbourne, 1987.

Chong, Elizabeth. *The First Happiness*. Sun Books, Melbourne, 1984.

Cipriani, Arrigo. *The Harry's Bar Cookbook*. Smith Gryphon Publishers, 1991

Curnonsky. *Traditional Recipes Of The Provinces Of France*. W.H. Allen, London. 1961.

Daguin, Andre. *Nouveau Cuisinier Gascon*. Editions Stock.

David, Elizabeth. *French Provincial Cooking*. Michael Joseph, London 1960.

Scott, David and Inwood, Christian. *A Taste Of Thailand*. Rider & Company, London, 1986.

David, Elizabeth. *Italian Food*. Macdonalds, London, 1954.

Del Conte, Anna. *Gastronomy of Italy*. Bantam Press, London, 1987.

Di Stasio, Rinaldo, Dupleix, Jill and Durack, Terry. *Allegro Al Dente*. William Heinemann, Australia, 1994.

Dupleix, Jill. *New Food*. William Heinemann Australia, 1994.

Freeman, Meera. *The Vietnamese Cookbook*. Penguin Books, Melbourne, 1995.

Ghedini, Francesco. *Northern Italian Cooking*. Gramercy Publishing Company, New York, 1979.

Goh, Simon, Durack, Terry and Dupleix, Jill. *Hot Food Cool Jazz*. William Heinemann, Melbourne, 1993.

Grasso, J.C. *The Best of Southern Italian Cooking*. Woodbury, New York, 1984.

Gray, Rose and Rogers, Ruth. *The River Café Cookbook*. Ebury Press, London, 1995.

Grigson, Jane. *Charcuterie and French Pork Cookery*. Michael Joseph, London, 1967.

Guerard, Michel. *Cuisine Gourmande*. Editions Robert Lafont S.A., Paris, 1978.

Hsiung, Deh-Ta. *Chinese Regional Cooking*. Quarto Publishing, London, 1979.

Hutton, Wendy. *Singapore Food*. Ure Smith, Sydney, 1979.

Mariani, John. *America Eats Out*. William Morrow and Company, New York, 1991.

Mark, Willy. *Chinese Cookery Masterclass*. New Burlington Books, London, 1984.

McGee, Harold. *On Food and Cooking*. Unwin Hyman Limited, London, 1984.

Perkins, David W. *Hong Kong & China Gas Chinese Cookbook*. Hong Kong & China Gas, Hong Kong, 1978.

Rhodes, Gary. *Rhodes Around Britain*. BBC Books, London, 1994.

Robuchon, Joel, and Wells, Patrica. *Simply French*. William Morrow and Company Inc, New York, 1991.

Routhier, Nicole. *The Foods Of Vietnam*. Stewart Tabori & Chang, New York, 1989.

Roux, Albert and Michel. *French Country Cooking*. Sidgwick & Jackson, London, 1989.

Scotto, Elizabeth. *The Encyclopaedia of French Cooking*. Octopus Books London. 1982.

Solomon, Charmaine. *The Complete Asian Cookbook*. Lansdowne Press, Sydney, 1976.

Tsuji, Shizuo. *Japanese Cooking. A Simple Art*. Kodansha International, New York, 1980.

Visser, Margaret. *The Rituals of Dinner*. Grove Weidenfeld, New York, 1991.

White, Marco Pierre. *White Heat*. Pyramid Books, London, 1990.

Willan, Anne. *French Regional Cooking*. Hutchinson, London, 1981.

Wright, Jeni. *The Encyclopaedia of Italian Cooking*. Octopus Books, London, 1981.

Wynants, Robert. *Les Recettes Originales de Pierre Wynants*. Robert Laffont.

Index

agedashi dofu 189
aioli 61
andouillettes 106–7
antipasto 196–9
apple, pie, Gascon 277
    salad, with black pudding 205
    upside-down, tart 223
artichokes, deep-fried 128

bacon, penne all'arrabiata 117
barley, lamb and, soup 21
basil, insalata Caprese 158
    soupe au pistou 90
    tagliatelle with tomato and 160
    Thai chicken and 7
    tomato and, pizza 161
beancurd, pock-marked grandmother's 234
beef, bollito misto 127
    fried hor fun rice noodles with 53
    stuffed cabbage 29
beetroot soup 28
black pudding and glazed apple salad 205
Blanc, Georges 273
    Raymond 284–5
blonde roots soup 17
bocconcini, insalata Caprese 158
bollito misto with salsa verde 127
bortsch 28
broccoli, rigatoni with 93

cabbage, stuffed 29
Caesar salad 222
cake, chocolate sponge 280–1
    miraculous flourless 11
callos a la Madrilena 144
calves liver 6
capsicum, roast, salad 197
carciofi alla Guidea 128
carrot and daikon salad, vinegared 188
cassoulet 84
caviar, tagliolini with lemon and 243
Celtic revival lamb and barley soup 21
cha gio with nuoc cham 113
char kueh teow 118
chawan mushi 187
cheese, fettuccine with Gorgonzola 245
    soufflé 10
chicken, bollito misto 127
    curry laksa 120–1
    liver, crostini 199
    liver, pappardelle with 244
    Moroccan, with tomato, olives and preserved lemon 114
    pho gai soup 78
    Thai, and basil 7
    vaguely Hungarian, soup 16
    white cut 51
chilli, crab, Singapore 100
    curry puffs 119

dipping sauce 113
peanut and, sauce 92
penne all'arrabiata 117
spaghetti with garlic and 62
sweet, sauce 116
chocolate, pudding 153
miraculous flourless cake 11
sauce for icecream 166
sponge cake 280–1
Cipriani, Arrigo 278–81
coconut rice 100
coffee, gelato affogato 267
roast lamb with 266
tirami sù 265
confit for cassoulet 84
cotechino with lentils 178
crab and sweet corn soup 99
crabs 94–8
little spring rolls 113
sand, pasta 101
Singapore chilli 100
crêpes, lemon and sugar 167
crostini di fegato 199
curry, laksa 120–1
Malaysian fish head 172
puffs 119
custard, Japanese savoury 187

Daguin, Andre 276–7
daikon, vinegared carrot and, salad 188
dashi 186
deep-fried tofu 189
dip, spring onion and ginger 51
duck, confit 84
eight treasure 54
dumplings, har gau prawn 253
pot-sticker 221
siu mai 252
vareneki 26

eggs, son-in-law 235
stracciatella 19
eight treasure duck 54

fegato alla Veneziana 6
Ferretti, Fred 282
fettuccine with Gorgonzola 245
fish cutlet with Thai sweet chilli sauce 116
fish, balls, curry laksa 120–1
cake, moon-viewing noodles 228–9
head curry 172
stock, dashi 186
rice congee with white 251
swordfish with lemon and herb sauce 131
fried hor fun rice noodles with beef 53

gado gado 92
garlic, aioli 61
potatoes with rosemary and 62
spaghetti with chilli and 62
Gascon apple pie made with stretched pastry 277
gelato affogato 267
Gorgonzola, fettuccine with 245
Greek salad 207
gremolata 213
grilled pig's trotters 259
Guerard, Michel 272

ham, pea and, soup 151
har gau prawn dumplings 253
harissa 114
holubsty 29
hor fun noodles 118
hot chocolate sauce for icecream 166
hot and sour soup, Sichuan 75

icecream, gelato affogato 267
hot chocolate sauce for 166
Indonesian gado gado 92
insalata Caprese 158
Italian potatoes with garlic and rosemary 62

Japanese savoury custard 187

kidney, pork, scallop and 48
Koffmann, Pierre 288

lamb, roast, with coffee 266
    soup with barley 21
le pastis Gascon 'estirat' 277
leek and potato soup 20
lemon, and sugar crêpes 167
    tagliolini with, and caviar 243
lentils, cotechino with 178
les truffes comme je les aime 291
lettuce bun 50
lion's head meat balls 55
little spring rolls with chilli dipping sauce 113
liver, calves 6
    chicken, pappardelle with 244
    crostini 199
Loubet, Bruno 283

Malaysian fish head curry 172
mascarpone with strawberries 215
mayonnaise, garlic 61
meat balls, lion's head 55
meats, mixed boiled 127
Meneau, Marc 289
miraculous flourless chocolate cake 11
Mondavi, Margrit and Robert 286
moon-viewing noodles 228–9
morels, omelette with 35
Moroccan chicken with tomato, olives and preserved lemon 114
moules à la marinière 5
mushrooms, oil and vinegar, in 197
    polenta with 130
mussels, moules à la marinère 5
    salad 198

Napoletana pizza with tomato and basil 161
noodles 224–7
    char kueh teow 118
    curry laksa 120–1
    fried hor fun rice with beef 53
    moon-viewing 228–9
    pho gai soup 78
nuoc cham sauce 113

offal, callos a la Madrilena 144
    tripe à la mode de Caen 143
    trippa alla Fiorentina 142
old-fashioned oxtail stew 152
omelette with fresh morels 35
osso buco Milanese 213
oxtail stew 152

pappardelle with chicken livers 244
pasta, fettuccine with Gorgonzola 245
    how to make 240–1
    pappardelle with chicken livers 244
    penne all'arrabiata 117
    pumpkin ravioli with mustard fruits 242
    rigatoni with broccoli and pine nuts 93
    sand crab 101
    spaghetti aglio e olio con peperoncini 62
    spaghetti alla carbonara 9
    tagliatelle with tomato and basil 160
    tagliolini with lemon and caviar 243
paste, curry 120–1
pastry, curry puffs 119
pea and ham soup 151
peanut, chilli and, sauce 92
penne all'arrabiata 117
pho ga 78
pie, Gascon apple 277
pig's trotter, bollito misto 127
    grilled 259
pistou, soupe au 90
pizza, tomato and basil 161
pock-marked grandmother's beancurd 234
polenta con funghi 130
pork, andouillettes 106–7
    kidney, scallop and 48
    lion's head meat balls 55
    little spring rolls 113
    pock-marked grandmother's beancurd 234
    pot-sticker dumplings 221
    Sichuan hot and sour soup 75
    siu mai dumplings 251

pot-sticker dumplings 221
potato, Italian, with garlic and rosemary 62
    leek, and, soup 20
    ultimate mashed 41
prawn, char kueh teow 118
    curry laksa 120–1
    har gau dumplings 253
    siu mai dumplings 251
    tom yam goong 79
pudding, lemon and sugar crêpes 167
    sticky chocolate 153
    sticky toffee 137
    tirami sù 265
pumpkin ravioli with mustard fruits 242

quail, san choy bau 50

ravioli, pumpkin 242
rice, coconut 100
    congee with white fish 251
    noodles, fried hor fun, with beef 53
    risotto alla Milanese 214
    risotto with red wine and sausages 179
    suppli 199
rigatoni with broccoli and pine nuts 93
risotto, alla Milanese 214
    red wine and sausages, with 179
    suppli 199
roast, capsicum salad 197
    lamb with coffee 266
root vegetable soup 17
rosemary, potatoes with garlic and 62
Roux, Michel 287

salad, black pudding and glazed apple 205
    Caesar 222
    gado gado 92
    Greek 207
    mussel 198
    Niçoise 206
    roast capsicum 197

    tomato, basil and bocconcini 158
    vinegared carrot and daikon 188
salsa verde 127
san choy bau 50
sand crab pasta 101
sauce, chilli and peanut 92
    chilli dipping 113
    green 127
    harissa 114
    hot chocolate 166
    lemon and herb 131
    nuoc cham 113
    pistou 90
    sweet chilli 116
sausages 175–7
    andouillettes 106–7
    black pudding and glazed apple
        salad 205
    bollito misto 127
    cotechino with lentils 178
    risotto with red wine and 179
scallop and pork kidney 48
Sichuan, hot and sour soup 75
    pock-marked grandmother's
        beancurd 234
Singapore chilli crab with coconut rice 100
siu mai 252
son-in-law eggs 235
soufflé, cheese 10
soup 12–5
    blonde roots 17
    bortsch 28
    Celtic revival lamb and barley 21
    crab and sweet corn 99
    pea and ham 151
    pho ga 78
    pistou 90
    Sichuan hot and sour 75
    stracciatella 19
    tom yam goong 79
    vaguely Hungarian chicken 16

vichyssoise 20
    curry laksa 120–1
spaghetti, aglio e olio con peperoncini 62
    alla carbonara 9
spring, onion and ginger dip 51
    rolls 113
squid, char kueh teow 118
stew, old-fashioned oxtail 152
sticky, chocolate pudding 153
    toffee pudding 137
stock, dashi 186
stracciatella 19
strawberries, mascarpone with 215
suppli 199
sweet, chilli sauce 116
    corn, crab and, soup 99
swordfish with lemon and herb sauce 131

tagliatelle with tomato and basil 160
tagliolini with lemon and caviar 243
tart, upside-down apple 223
tarte tatin 223
tea ceremony 181–5
Terrail, Claude 274–5
Thai chicken and basil 7
tirami sù 265
tofu, deep-fried 189
tom yam goong 79
tomato, and basil pizza 161
    insalata Caprese 158
    tagliatelle with, and basil 160
tongue, bollito misto 127
torta di Cioccolato from Harry's Bar 280–1

tripe, à la mode de Caen 143
    callos a la Madrilena 144
    Florentine-style 142
trippa alla Fiorentina 142
trotters, pig's, grilled 259
truffles, Pierre Wynants 291
tsukumi udon 228–9
tuna, salade Niçoise 206

Ukrainian, bortsch 28
    holubtsy 29
    vareneki 26
ultimate mashed potato 41
upside-down apple tart 223

vaguely Hungarian chicken soup 16
vareneki 26
veal, osso buco Milanese 213
    tongue, bollito misto 127
vegetables, curry puffs 119
    gado gado 92
    rigatoni with broccoli and pine nuts 93
    soupe au pistou 90
Vergé, Roger 292
vichyssoise 20
vinegared carrot and daikon salad 188

white cut chicken 51
wor tip 221
Wynants, Pierre 290–1

yum cha 247–50